1 MONTH OF
FREE
READING

at

www.ForgottenBooks.com

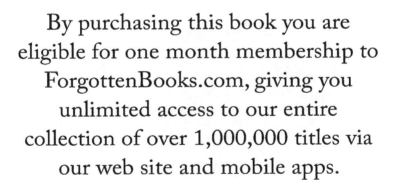

By purchasing this book you are eligible for one month membership to ForgottenBooks.com, giving you unlimited access to our entire collection of over 1,000,000 titles via our web site and mobile apps.

To claim your free month visit:

www.forgottenbooks.com/free149816

ISBN 978-0-484-60550-2
PIBN 10149816

REPORTS OF CASES

ARGUED & DETERMINED

IN THE

3055

SUPREME COURT OF QUEENSLAND

WITH

TABLES OF CASES AND INDEX.

BY

GEORGE SCOTT, M.A. (Oxon.); L. E. GROOM, M.A., LL.M.;

(Barristers-at-Law)

AND

A. DOUGLAS GRAHAM, B.A.,

(Solicitor.)

VOL. II.

(1868-1872.)

BRISBANE:
WATSON, FERGUSON & CO., QUEEN STREET.

——

1900.

TABLE OF CONTENTS.

TABLE OF CASES CITED.

O.

P.

Q.

R.

S.

T.

SUPREME COURT REPORTS.

VOL. II.

In the Estate of PERKINS & HUTCHINSON.

Insolvency—The Insolvency Act of 1864 (28 Vic., No. 25), ss. 3, 24, [IN INSOLVENCY.]
27, 32, 47, 57, 124, Schedule Form C—Debtors' petition—Adjudi-
cation — Jurisdiction — Power of Judge to annul order of
adjudication made by another Judge—Attestation of petitioners'
signature—Statement of affairs.

1868.
17th July,
23rd July,
6th August.

Lutwyche, J.

Where an insolvent has been adjudicated on his own petition, a creditor who has not proved in the estate may petition to have the order of adjudication annulled.

An order of adjudication made by one Judge sitting as a Court of Insolvency may be annulled by any other Judge exercising the same jurisdiction.

A debtor's petition must contain an attestation of the signatures of the petitioners to the petition.

Unless a full, true, and correct statement of the liabilities of the insolvent be filed in accordance with the provisions of the *Insolvency Act* (28 Vic., No. 25) and the rules thereunder, the order of adjudication made on the debtor's petition is liable to be annulled.

PETITION to annul an order of adjudication.

A petition was filed by Henry Box, Son & Co., merchants, to annul the order of adjudication in the estate of Perkins & Hutchinson, and to dismiss the petition upon which the order was made.

In the Estate of
PERKINS &
HUTCHINSON.

Lutwyche, J.

Lilley, Q. C., for the petitioners.

Blake for the insolvents.

Pring, A. G., and *MacDevitt*, for Alexander Raff, Official Assignee.

Blake : There is a preliminary objection : Mr. Lilley cannot be heard. The petitioners have not proved in the estate, and so have no *locus standi.*

Pring, A. G., adopted the argument of Mr. Blake.

Lilley, Q. C. : It is not necessary for a creditor to prove his debt before petitioning to annul an order of adjudication. Any person interested in a bankruptcy may petition : Griffith & Holmes' Bankruptcy Law, Vol. II., p. 800), *Ex parte Bean* (1 De G. M. & G., 486), *Ex parte Bonsor* (2 Rose, 61). A void commission may be superseded even on the petition of a person summoned to attend the commissioners as a witness : *Ex parte Lane, In re Fowler* (Mont. 12). The bankrupt is a creditor who may petition to supersede a commission if assignees do not interfere : *Ex parte Taylor, In re Percival* (2 Mont. & Ayr., 26 ; 4 D. & Ch. 125).

Pring, A. G. In all the cases cited the sequestration has been by a creditor—not by the insolvent. See *Ex parte Greenwood* (33 L. J., Bk., 50).

LUTWYCHE, J. I will not decide the point off-hand, but will give my decision on Thursday next, until which time I shall postpone the sitting. In the meantime, I will consider whether there is any difference between a case of compulsory and voluntary sequestration. C. A. V.

                                                      23rd July, 1868.

LUTWYCHE, J. A preliminary objection was made to the hearing of Mr. Lilley, as counsel for Messrs. Box, Son & Co., on the ground that his clients had no *locus standi*, inasmuch as, as they had not proved under the commission, there was no privity between them and the insolvents. As the point was new, and as several authorities were cited, I took time to look into it, and considered my decision. It will not be disputed by those who raised and supported the objection, that, if there had been an adjudication of insolvency granted upon the petition of a creditor, another creditor might come in and dispute its validity and try to annul it. The authorities cited by Mr. Lilley (especially *Ex parte Bonsor* (2 Rose, 61) are decisive on that point. I was asked to affirm, as an abstract and broad proposition, that under no conceivable state of circumstances could a creditor be allowed to come in and dispute the validity of an adjudication of insolvency when that adjudication had been granted upon the petition of the insolvent himself. No authorities were cited in support of that proposition, but I was asked to look into the matter, upon the construction of an Act of Parliament. I have looked into that section which allows an insolvent to file his own petition and to obtain an adjudication of insolvency, but I can see nothing there which would lead me to suppose there is any difference in principle between an adjudication granted upon the petition of the insolvent himself and a similar adjudication granted upon the petition of a creditor. There being no authorities to guide me, and there being nothing that I can see in the statute inconsistent with the principle, that anyone who is interested might seek to annul the adjudication, I certainly am not bound to say that under no conceivable circumstances can a creditor be heard to annul an adjudication which has been granted upon the petition of an insolvent. It was contended that Messrs. Box, Son & Co. had no privity of interest, but it appears they swore that they were creditors of the insolvent. The law, as it stands at present, might give a creditor rights which I cannot conceive I can deprive him of. A creditor might have an execution at the present moment in the house of the insolvent, and might be prevented from reaping the fruits of his judgment by the circumstance that this adjudication had been improperly attained. What right have I to deprive such a creditor of the remedy he possesses at common law? A creditor might have a bill of sale over a portion or the whole of the insolvent's property, and he might not like to run the hazard of its validity being contested by the Official Assignee. Again, looking at the matter purely from an insolvency point of view with respect to the distribution of assets, a creditor might very fairly suppose that an insolvent had either underrated the value of his property, or he might be unwilling to see it disposed of by the machinery which was placed at the disposal of the Insolvent Court. Many creditors consider that winding up an estate under a deed of composition is a preferable arrangement to resorting to the Court, and I do not see why I should interfere to prevent a creditor taking that course if he thinks proper. For these reasons, in the absence of any authority to contradict me, and seeing no regulation laid down in the statute which would prevent any creditor from applying to annul an adjudication, even when obtained on the petition of the insolvent himself, I must decline to yield to the objection which has been raised. I might add that the

In the Estate of PERKINS & HUTCHINSON.

———

Lutwyche, J.

In the Estate of
PERKINS &
HUTCHINSON.
———
Lutwyche, J.

57th section of the statute seems to contemplate the possibility of a creditor coming in and annulling an adjudication, even when it has been obtained upon the petition of the insolvent.

Lilley, Q. C., thereupon applied on the petition of Messrs. Box, Son & Co., and on the joint and several affidavits of W. D. Box and W. Lyons, that the order of adjudication obtained by Perkins & Hutchinson might be annulled, and that the petition on which it was granted might be dismissed on the following grounds:—That the petition for adjudication was not attested or authenticated, as required by the statute; that it was not dated, and did not comply with the statutory requisites; that the bankrupts had not filed a full, true, and correct statement of their liabilities as required by the rules in pursuance of the Act within the three days prescribed. There was also another ground, to the effect that the duplicate of the original petition had not been filed in the office of the Official Assignee as required by the rules and practice of the Court.

Blake, for the insolvents: The objections raised cannot be made against the adjudication in the present case, as the Court should always look upon objections upon purely technical grounds with great jealousy, as the adjudication was for the benefit of all the creditors. The objection to the want of attestation of the petition is not sustainable after an order has been made upon it; the attestation is clearly supplied by the affidavits of the petitioners annexed to the petition. The objection that no statement of debts had been filed is untenable after adjudication. If the Court is of the opinion that the requisites of the statute have not been complied with, the insolvents might be allowed to amend their petition. The following authorities were cited: Griffith & Holmes' Law and Practice in Bankruptcy, Vol. II. 748, *Ex parte Tanner* (2 D. & Ch. 563), *Ex parte Horsley* (2 Mad. 11), *Insolvency Act of 1864*, s. 27.

Pring, A. G.: If the petition is granted, Box, Son & Co. will obtain the whole property of the insolvents, while the other creditors in the estate will get nothing. Although no formal attestation clause was inserted in the petition on which the adjudication was granted, in strict accordance with the form prescribed by the statute, yet the want has been supplied in another way, and the object of the Act—that the parties signing the petition should be shown to be the parties holding themselves out to be the petitioners—has been carried out. If the Court holds that is not sufficient, it can order the petition to be amended by the insertion of the attestation clause.

LUTWYCHE, J. The statute clearly declares that Form C shall be followed, either substantially or literally. The Court has always looked upon the attestation as essential, and has required the signature of some respectable person to verify the signatures of the petitioners. It is a significant fact that in the affidavits annexed to the petition the insolvents did not swear that their signatures to the petition had ever been attested in the presence of anybody.

Pring, A. G. : The Act is not peremptory that there shall be an attestation clause, or there would have been a penalty imposed in case of neglect. Your Honour has no jurisdiction in the present case, as the order of adjudication having been granted by his Honour the Chief Justice, sitting in Chambers as the Full Court, in its insolvency jurisdiction, it cannot be reversed or set aside except by an appeal to the Full Court in Banco. I refer to the affidavit of F. W. Daly, solicitor, which shews on June 23rd a writ of *fi fa* was lodged at the office of the Sheriff by the present petitioners to levy £369 10s. 9d., which they have recovered against the insolvents by a judgment of the Supreme Court. On June 29th, at noon, the whole of the property of the insolvents was sold at Gympie by the Sheriff's agent, and realised £340 8s. 10d., which the petitioners claimed. On 29th June the insolvents obtained from his Honour the Chief Justice an order of adjudication of insolvency against themselves, and it was registered at 11 15 a.m. on the same day. Even if the legal requirements have not been strictly complied with, yet on equitable grounds alone the adjudication should be upheld, as, if the petition be granted, Box, Son & Co. will swallow up the whole of the assets, leaving other creditors, to the amount of £1,471, without a fraction. The following authorities were cited : *Ex parte Shearman* (Fonb. 32), *Ex parte Johnstone* (4 De G. & S. 204), *Ex parte Bean* (1 De G. M. & G. 486 ; 21 L. J. Bk. 26), *Insolvency Act of 1864*, ss. 3, 14, 27, 35.

Lilley, Q. C. : The case is not in the nature of an appeal ; it is an investigation into an *ex parte* proceeding before the Insolvent Court, which the Chief Justice represented when he made the order. Being an *ex parte* proceeding before that Court, the same Court can examine into the matter, and if the legal requisites to the previous action are wanting, can reverse it. There is an inherent power in the Court which permits it, if it acted without the foundation the law requires, to step back and reverse its decision, and place the parties in the same position they were in before. Under s. 27 the petition must be attested and must be dated, and if it is not in the form prescribed

In the Estate of
PERKINS &
HUTCHINSON.

Lutwyche, J.

by the Act it is a nullity, not simply informal. The following authorities were cited : Griffith & Holmes, Vol. II., 744, 780, *Ex parte Tyrie* (13 W. R. 953), *Ex parte Hirst* (1 Glyn. & J. 76), *In re Pelham & Pelham* (12 L. T. N. S. 642), *Ex parte Cracklow* (Mont. 353), *In re Moore* (5 L. T. N. S. 806), *In re Clarke* (5 L. T. N. S. 403), *Carter v. Dimmock* (4 H. of L. 337), *Insolvency Act of 1864*, s. 47.

Blake, in reply, cited the following authorities : *Allen v. Thompson* (1 H. & N. 15; 25 L. J. Ex. 249; 2 Jur. N. S. 451; 4 W. R. 506; *Sladden v. Sergeant* (1 F. & F. 322), *Nicholson v. Cooper* (27 L.J. Ex. 393), *Insolvency Act of 1864*, ss. 32, 35, 36.

LUTWYCHE, J. I will consider the case; but so many points have been raised, and so many authorities cited, that I cannot promise to give my decision on an early date. I adjourn the sitting.
C. A. V.

August 6th, 1868.

LUTWYCHE, J. The Attorney-General objected to the jurisdiction of the Court as at present constituted, and contended that I, sitting as Judge in Insolvency, could not review an order of adjudication of insolvency made by the Chief Justice, sitting as another Judge under the powers conferred on him by statute. Mr. Lilley, however, contended there was an inherent power in all Courts to review *ex parte* proceedings, and that the decision spoken of in the 3rd section of *The Insolvency Act of 1864*, referred to a decision where both parties had been heard, and upon the construction I must say that it is impossible to come to any other conclusion. At Common Law a Judge in Chambers may review the decision of another Judge, and the familiar instance of a *ca re* is an illustration which suggests itself immediately. So, in Equity, one Judge may be called upon to dissolve an injunction which has been granted on an *ex parte* application made to another Judge. It appears from the 47th section of the *Insolvency Act* that the Legislature contemplated, in the case of a creditor's adjudication order, that that adjudication might be set aside under certain circumstances on application to the Court. Under the 124th section provision is made for expunging or reducing debts which have been admitted on *ex parte* applications of creditors. The very cases cited by the Attorney-General in support of his view and argument— *ex parte Johnstone*, 4 De G. & Sm. 204, and *ex parte Bean*, 1 De G., Mac. & G., 486—are authorities against it. It appears in *ex parte Johnstone* that a Commissioner has power to annul an adjudication for invalidity, even upon equitable grounds, where the formal and legal requisites of the statute have not been complied with. *Ex parte Bean* is an authority to the same effect. I think, therefore, that I, sitting here as Judge in Insolvency, have power to review an order made by the Chief Justice, acting with the same authority, which he then exercised; and I am also of the opinion that the decision spoken of in the 3rd section of the statute, as Mr. Lilley contended, is a decision given by the Judge in Insolvency after hearing both sides from which, and from which alone, there can be an appeal to the Full Court.

Having, therefore, disposed of the question of jurisdiction, I come to the grounds upon which Mr. Lilley contended that the adjudication order ought to be annulled and the petition dismissed. First, upon the ground that there is no attestation of the signatures of the petitioners to the petition, I think that the case cited by the learned counsel—*ex parte Hirst*, 1 Gl. & J. 76—is a clear authority in favour of that part of the argument. The authorities cited by Mr. Blake do not go to the case which is at present before the Court. They are simply instances where there was an attestation, but where it was defective or informal. No case has been cited which showed that where there had been no attestation at all, as in the present instance, the Courts have interfered to uphold the adjudication order. Upon that ground, therefore, and upon the authority of *ex parte Hirst*, the adjudication order ought to be annulled I further think that Mr. Lilley was right when he contended that the want of the statement provided for by the 32nd section of the statute was a sufficient ground for the annulling of the order. That is a matter which occurred subsequently to the adjudication order; and the rules of Court provide most distinctly that within three days after the order has been granted, or within such extended time as the Judge, upon application made to him, upon special grounds, may think fit to appoint, a full, true, and correct statement of the liabilities of the insolvent shall be filed. Commissioner Goulburn, who exercised under the English Act of 1861 precisely the same authority I exercise out here, dismissed the petition of an insolvent upon that ground, stating that the statute was imperative, and that he had no alternative but to dismiss the petition. Commissioner Holroyd extended that to the case where a statement had been filed, but, where important omissions had been made, holding that it was not a full, true, and accurate statement of the debtor's liabilities. Therefore, upon that ground also, it seems to me that the adjudication order ought to be annulled

In the Estate of
PERKINS &
HUTCHINSON.
———
Lutwyche, J.

In the Estate of
PERKINS &
HUTCHINSON.

Lutwyche, J.

and the petition dismissed. I was pressed by the Attorney-General with the case *ex parte Shearman* (Fonb. 32), which is to the effect that a second petition may be taken to be an amended petition of the first, and to take precedence of the petition of another creditor which has been filed in the interval. Supposing that were the case in the present instance, no doubt some weight would be given to it; but such is not the case. The question lies between an execution creditor and the other creditors of the insolvent. As the petition has been presented without the requisites which the statute requires, it must be annulled, and the act of the execution creditor must stand good, and before any second petition can be filed, the right of the execution creditor which has accrued must be acted upon. A good deal was said by the Attorney-General about the hardship of the case, as one creditor would obtain all the available assets of the insolvent. That was well replied to by Mr. Lilley in the course of his argument; but the authorities cited by the Attorney-General are conclusive answers to it. I accordingly annul the order of adjudication made by the Chief Justice, and dismiss the petition of the insolvent. Costs to be allowed out of the estate if any assets are realised.

PATTERSON *v.* AUSTRALIAN STEAM NAVIGATION COMPANY.

Practice—Foreign Company—Service of Writ—Common Law Process Act of 1867 (31 Vic., No. 4), s.s. 14, 20.

[In Chambers.]
1868.
31st July.
12th August.

Cockle, C. J.

A company was incorporated by statute in New South Wales before Separation, and had an office in Brisbane. A writ of summons out of the Supreme Court of Queensland was served on the Secretary in Sydney.

Held that the service was good.

The term "clerk" in s. 14 of 31 Vic. No. 4 means a clerk in the nature of a secretary or principal officer.

SUMMONS, calling on the plaintiff to show cause why a writ of summons issued on 24th June, and the copy of the writ, and the service thereof should not be set aside upon the grounds :—1. That the defendants were not British subjects residing out of the jurisdiction, within the meaning of s. 20 of *The Common Law Process Act of 1867*. 2. That it appeared from the writ of summons the defendants were a foreign Company, carrying on business out of the jurisdiction of the Court.

All the facts appear in the judgment.

Lilley, Q. C., in support of the summons, argued that the Company were British subjects, and incorporated, previous to Separation, by public statute in New South Wales. As that statute was continued in force after Separation by the Orders-in-council creating the colony, the company remained an incorporated company within the colony of Queensland. The company having been treated as a foreign company, and as such served with a writ, they had been brought here wrongfully, and the other side should pay the costs. They were entitled to service within the colony by the ordinary form of writ, and the service in Sydney was a mistake: *Walton* v. *Universal Salvage Co.* (16 M. & W. 438 ; 4 D. & L. 588).

Griffith shewed cause, and contended the service on the Secretary of the Company, in Sydney, was good. As the head office was in that city the Company must be taken to reside there. There was an agency here. *Evans* v. *Dublin and Drogheda Railway Co.* (14 L.J. Ex. 245); *Garton* v. *G. W. Railway Co.* (27 L. J., Q. B., 375).

C. A. V.

12th August, 1868.

COCKLE, C. J. When the matter was argued the summons was treated as somewhat peculiar, but the general question was entered into, and counsel were employed on both sides. I decide upon the broad principle of the case, without any reference to technicality. There is no precedent bearing directly on the point to be derived from the English books, because no such subdivision of jurisdiction has ever taken place in England as that of the division of the colony of New South Wales into the colonies of New South Wales and Queensland; but I find enough in the English cases to enable me to come to a satisfactory conclusion on the point. It was contended on behalf of the defendants that the Queensland Court had jurisdiction in the case, and, there being an office of the Company in Brisbane, that the company might be served in Brisbane. S. 14 of the *Common Law Process Act of 1867*, which is identical with s. 14 of 17 Vic., No. 21, and with 15 and 16 Vic., c. 76, s. 16, was cited, and it was suggested that as a writ of summons should be served upon the clerk or Secretary of the Company, that would extend to the clerk or agent in Brisbane. But I find that s. 14 of 31 Vic., No. 4, is substantially a repetition of 2 Will. IV, c. 39, when the words " clerk " or " secretary " of a corporation occur. The meaning of the word " clerk " in that section has received an authoritative interpretation, and it has been held that it does not mean any clerk in the office of the corporation, but that the words " clerk " or " secretary " must mean a clerk in the nature of a secretary or principal officer. I think, therefore, that service must be on the secretary or on an officer in the nature of a secretary, and I cannot think the agent in Brisbane, or any clerk who happened to be in Brisbane, would be an officer in the nature of the secretary. It has been contended at home that the English Courts have no jurisdiction to try an action against a company that is incorporated in Ireland, but that is not at all analogous to the present case, as the jurisdiction of the Irish and English Courts has always related to different portions of the Imperial territory. In the present case there is a corporation over which, at one time, no other Courts, of course, than those of New South Wales could have any jurisdiction. The effect of dividing New South Wales into two parts was to give a new jurisdiction to the Courts up here, but would not in any other respect, so far as I can understand, affect the legal rights of a corporation which was established under the New South Wales Legislature before Separation. Looking, therefore, at what must have been the practice before Separation, and in conformity with the obvious interpretation of the statute, that the service should be in Sydney (for there was an express recital in the Act that a company, to be termed such and such a company, had been established in Sydney, and that would point out Sydney as the proper place of service) ; and, seeing that service must be either on the secretary, or on an officer in the nature of a secretary, or principal officer of the company, and also·that it would probably unsettle the practice if I were to say that the separation into two parts of the Colony of New South Wales had had an effect upon the service of process, which it would be difficult to determine, and would probably be the cause of a great quantity of litigation, I think it would be safer to hold that the practice has been in no degree affected by the division of the Colony into two parts; and that as it was necessary before Separation that service should be made in Sydney, so it is necessary now. For these reasons I dismiss the summons with costs.

PATTERSON
v.
AUSTRALIAN
STEAM NAVIGA-
TION CO.
———
Cockle, C. J.

WOOD *v.* BEDDEK.

1868.
28th August.

Cockle, C. J.
Lutwyche, J.

Small Debts Court—Appeal—30 Vic., No. 17, s. 15—Recognizance—
Action against Clerk of Petty Sessions.*

S. 15 of 30 Vic., No. 17, does not cast upon the Clerk of Petty Sessions the
duty of paying over forthwith to the successful party on an appeal to the District
Court the amount of debt and costs awarded by the District Court where the
amount has not been received.

APPEAL from the Northern District Court.

In 1867 the plaintiff brought an action in the Court of Petty
Sessions at Rockhampton for the sum of £17 15s. against Frederick
Compton, and recovered a verdict for £4 16s. 8d., with £1 3s. costs.
Compton appealed against it to the Northern District Court, and
entered into a recognizance before the defendant, as Registrar of the
Court of Petty Sessions, in double the amount of the debt and costs,
by which he undertook to abide the event of the appeal, and pay such
debt and costs as the Court should award. The appeal was heard
before the Judge of the Northern District Court, who dismissed it
with £7 6s. 10d. costs, to be paid to the plaintiff. On his applying to
the Registrar of the Court of Petty Sessions to be paid the debt and
costs awarded to him, amounting to £13 6s., the plaintiff did not
obtain the debt and costs. In February, 1868, the plaintiff sued the
defendant for the sum of £13 6s. The defence was never indebted.
The learned Judge gave a verdict for the defendant, holding that s. 15
of 30 Vic., No. 17, did not cast upon the defendant, as Clerk of Petty
Sessions, the duty of paying over to the plaintiff, the successful party
on an appeal from the Court of Petty Sessions to the District Court,
the debt and costs awarded or due, until he had received them.

Griffith, for the appellant.

Handy, for the respondent.

The Court dismissed the appeal with costs.

* See now 31 Vic., No. 29, s. 34.

In the matter of KEANE *and* FOWLES, *Attorneys.*

Solicitor—Agent—Costs—Lien—Particular—General.

A solicitor acting as agent for another solicitor has, as against his client, a lien only on the funds in his hands for his agency charges in the particular matter.

Where a summons is issued by a solicitor calling upon his agent to pay over to him or his attorneys certain moneys, the agent is entitled to set up a general lien.

1868.

26th August.
4th September.

Lutwyche, J.

SUMMONS calling on Keane and Fowles, attorneys of the Supreme Court, to show cause why they should not pay over to John Malbon Thompson, of Ipswich, attorney, or to his attorneys, Roberts and Hart, the sum of £109 3s. 7d., recovered by Keane and Fowles from John Salisbury Thelwell, of London, as agents for John Malbon Thompson, on account of Samuel Grimley, the Official Liquidator of the Ipswich Cotton Company, and why they should not pay the costs of the present application.

Blake, in support of summons.

Lilley, Q. C., contra, to show cause.

The facts sufficiently appear in the judgment.

C. A. V.

4th September, 1868.

LUTWYCHE, J. It appears from the affidavits that Keane and Fowles recovered the money on account of Samuel Grimley, and two guineas more, which Thompson had allowed them in his account. But Keane and Fowles claimed to retain the whole money on the ground that they had a general lien on it for their balance against the attorney. I am of opinion, although there is some conflict of authority on the point, that the decision of the Court of Queen's Bench is right in principle, and should be adhered to. I take it that the law is that the client cannot recover against the agent in an action for money had and received, nor can he, except under one or two circumstances, get the Court to interfere by summary application. He can only get the Court to interfere when the money has come into the agent's hands, not as agent in the ordinary course of business, but accidentally. In the case of *Robbins v. Heath* (11 Q.B., 257–9) the Court did interfere, but, in that case, they distinctly upheld their former decision

In the matter of
KEANE
AND
FOWLES,
Attorneys.

Lutwyche, J.

in *Robbins v. Fennell* (11 Q. B., 248–54; 17 L. J., Q. B., 77; 12 Jur. 157) and in the case of *Cobb v. Becke* (6 Q. B., 930–36; 14 L.J., Q. B., 108; 9 Jur. 439). That was more consistent with sound law than the somewhat conflicting decisions in *White v. Royal Exchange Assurance Company* (1 Bing. 20; 7 Moore, 249; 25 R R. 574), and *Hanley v. Cassan* (11 Jur. Exch., 1088), which was decided on last day of term, when matters are sometimes decided in a hurry. It was reviewed by the Court of Queen's Bench in the case *Robbins v. Fennell*, and that Court dissented from the view of the Court of Exchequer, and upheld their former decision. It being the law, then, that the client cannot recover money received for him by the agent, his remedy must lie against the attorney; and if the attorney had in the present case framed his summons properly, I would have made an order to that effect. If the summons had called upon Keane and Fowles to pay over to Thompson, as attorney for Grimley, the money recovered by them on his account, I should have made an order, because it is quite clear from the case of *Ward v. Hepple* (15 Ves., 297), which was recognised and acted upon by Lord Eldon, in the subsequent case, *Ex parte Steele* (16 Ves., 164). I think it may be taken as clear law that an agent only has a lien on the funds in his hands, for his agency charges in the particular matter in which he was engaged as agent. In the summons, Thompson called on Keane and Fowles to pay the money over to him or to his agents. Keane and Fowles very properly set up their general lien upon the money which they had in their possession as against the attorney; but had Thompson summoned them to pay over the money to him as attorney for Grimley the money they had received on account of Grimley, I feel sure they would not have hesitated for a moment. As it is, I have no alternative but to dismiss the summons with costs.

HARRIS *v.* RUSSELL, *Ex parte* SHERIFF OF QUEENSLAND.

Principal and agent—Money had and received—Sale—Attorney and Client—Stakeholder.

[IN CHAMBERS.]
1868.
30th October.
16th November.
———
Lutwyche, J.

A firm of solicitors, pursuant to instructions from their client, paid certain money, part of the proceeds of an execution into Court, and retained the balance for their costs. By an order of the Court the proceeds of the execution were directed to be re-paid to the sheriff.

Held, that there was no privity between the solicitors and the sheriff, and the former were not liable to repay to him the amount of their costs retained by the direction of their client out of the proceeds of the execution.

APPLICATION before a Judge in Vacation, sitting as a Full Court, to make absolute a rule *nisi.*

A rule *nisi* was issued calling upon Messrs. Roberts and Hart, the attorneys or agents of Frederick Thomas Humphreys, to show cause why the sum of £69 9s. 8d. should not be paid over to the Sheriff, in compliance with an order of the Court.

F. T. Humphreys, one of the Official Assignees of the Insolvency Court of New South Wales, was directed, under an order of the Supreme Court of Queensland, to pay over to the Sheriff of that colony the proceeds of the sale of certain goods wrongfully seized by him in the insolvent estate of Russell. Humphreys sold the goods, and forwarded part of the proceeds, after deducting his own expenses, to Messrs. Roberts and Hart, his attorneys, with instructions for them, after defraying their own costs, to pay the balance into Court. Roberts and Hart accordingly retained £69 7s. 8d. to pay their costs, and paid the balance of the £200 sent to them by Humphreys into Court, but subsequently had it refunded to them, when they paid it to the Sheriff, in compliance with the order of the Court. It was now sought to compel them to pay the balance of the £200.

Blake moved the rule absolute.

Lilley, Q. C., showed cause. Messrs. Roberts and Hart had merely carried out the express instructions of their client. If the client misinstructed them as to how they were to apply the money, he must be proceeded against, for they were not responsible for his acts. If they had not followed their instructions, but had paid the money into the Sheriff's hands, they might have been answerable to their client for misappropriation of the money.

HARRIS
v.
RUSSELL,
Ex parte
SHERIFF OF
QUEENSLAND.

Lutwyche, J.

Blake, in reply : It was the duty of Messrs. Roberts and Hart to have paid the money over in obedience to the order of the Court. C. A. V.

LUTWYCHE, J. In this case, which was heard before me, sitting as a Judge in Vacation, on the 30th October last, the execution creditors obtained an order calling upon Messrs. Roberts and Hart, the attorneys or agents of Frederick Thomas Humphreys, the claimant in the execution, to show cause why they should not pay over to the Sheriff the sum of £69 7s. 8d., part of the proceeds of the goods sold in execution, in compliance with a rule made on 4th September last, which called upon the said F. T. Humphreys to pay the said sum. I have looked into this matter, and consulted the authorities, and find myself compelled to come to the conclusion that this summons must be dismissed with costs. The case of *Stephens v. Badcock* (2 B. & Ad., 354) was quoted in support of the application, but the case of *Bamford v. Shuttleworth* (11 A. & E., 926) is, in my opinion, more to the point. In that case, on a sale of premises by auction, the memorandum of agreement to purchase and sell was signed by the auctioneer as agent for the purchaser, and by the vendor's attorney describing himself as " agent for the said S. S.," the vendor. The purchaser paid his deposit to the attorney, who gave a receipt signed by himself as " agent for S. S." The sale going off by the vendor's default, and the deposit money not being returned, it was held that the purchaser could not bring an action for money had and received against the attorney, for that he was not a stakeholder, but merely the vendor's agent, and payment of the deposit to him was payment to the vendor. It will be found from this case that there was no privity of contract between the defendants and the plaintiff. The defendants received the money from the vendor, and were to account to him. I cannot see any privity of contract here. The money—the proceeds of the goods seized—which is in the hands of Roberts and Hart, is still in the hands of Humphreys, they acting as his agents, and there being, therefore, no privity of contract between them and the plaintiff, consequently, no action for money had and received can be brought. The plaintiff, however, still has his remedy against the Official Assignee, by forwarding a memorial of the order made against him to be enforced in Sydney.

Summons dismissed with costs ; costs of counsel allowed.

HARRIS v. RUSSELL.

Personalty in Queensland—Domicil—Bankruptcy in New South Wales—Execution creditor—Assignee—Mobilia sequuntur personam.

[In Banco,]
1868.
27th August.
4th September.

Cockle, C. J.
Lutwyche, J.

R, who was domiciled in Queensland, had his estate sequestrated in New South Wales. H. obtained a judgment against R. in Queensland, and proceeded to levy execution on R's goods at Toowoomba. The Official Assignee in New South Wales claimed the goods.

Held, that H. was entitled to the goods in priority to the Assignee.

The Courts of this colony alone can deal with the property of a bankrupt domiciled here.

Re Blithman, L. R. 2 Eq. 23, approved.

Interpleader referred to the Full Court by Lutwyche, J.

The facts appear in the judgment.

Lilley, Q. C., for the claimant.

Pring, A. G., for the execution creditors.

The following authorities were cited: *Royal Bank of Scotland v. Cuthbert*, 1 Rose 462; *Re Blithman*, L. R. 2 Eq. 23; 35 L. J. (Ch.) 255; *Selkrig v. Davies*, 2 Rose 97, 291; *Smith v. Buchanan*, 1 East 6.

Lutwyche, J., delivered the judgment of the Court as follows:—

In this case, which was argued before the Full Court on the 27th August, the opinion of the Court was sought as to whether the claimant in the case, F. T. Humphreys, the Official Assignee appointed under an order of the Supreme Court of New South Wales, in the estate of one Russell, was entitled to personal property belonging to Russell, as against the execution creditors. The facts of the case are very short. Russell, who was domiciled in Queensland, and carried on business at Toowoomba, in the earlier part of the present year went to Sydney, and was there arrested by a Sydney creditor. On May 5 his estate was sequestrated by an order of the Supreme Court of New South Wales, and the Official Assignee, appointed under the order of sequestration, took possession of his personal property at Toowoomba. On May 11th, Harris recovered judgment in the Supreme Court of Queensland against Russell, and on May 15th a *fi. fa.* was issued upon that judgment, and was lodged with

B

HARRIS *r.*
RUSSELL.

Cockle, C. J.
Lutwyche, J.

the Sheriff, who, on May 19th, seized Russell's property in Toowoomba. The question for the Court to determine is whether the sequestration of a foreign Court is to prevail against the execution creditors, or whether execution creditors, having used due diligence to recover their debt, are entitled to uphold it as against the Official Assignee, appointed by a foreign tribunal.

The general principle is extremely well laid down in *Wheaton's International Law* 8th edn., p. 147 : " According to the law of most European countries, the proceeding which is commenced in the country of the bankrupt's domicile draws to itself the exclusive right to take and distribute the property. The rule thus established is rested upon the general principle that personal or movable property is, by a legal fiction, considered as situated in the country where the bankrupt has his domicile. But the principles of jurisprudence as adopted in the United States, consider the *lex loci rei sitæ* as prevailing over the *lex domicilii* in respect to creditors, and that the laws of other States cannot be permitted to have an extra territorial operation to the prejudice of the authority, rights, and interest of the State where the property lies." It is quite clear to the Court that the English authorities one and all hold that the right to take and distribute the property of a bankrupt arises in the country where the bankrupt is domiciled, and there only. The authorities cited at the Bar with one exception (to which I shall presently advert) are all collected in *Story's Conflict of Laws* (ss. 407, 408). Upon examination it will be found that in all those cases where the Courts gave an extra-territorial effect to the fiat of a foreign tribunal, the bankrupt was domiciled in the country where the foreign tribunal was ; and the Courts, both of England, Ireland, and Scotland, have therefore held that they will assist the foreign tribunals in distributing the property of the bankrupt when situated in the home jurisdiction. I have searched in vain, and I do not believe that any case can be found where the English Courts have interfered to assist the creditors claiming under a commission of bankruptcy, or what was equivalent to it, in a foreign country, unless the bankrupt was domiciled there ; and it will be found in the great case of *The Royal Bank of Scotland v Cuthbert* (commonly known as *Stein's Case*, reported in the Appendix to 1 Rose, 462) that the contest on both sides was as to the domicile. The point was strongly argued by counsel, and the case was decided on the effect of the domicile. In that case there were two domiciles, and I have referred to this case more particularly because similar cases have arisen, and will arise, no doubt, in these colonies. Lord Bannatyne, in delivering judgment, said: " It is a maxim of universal law that movables follow the person, and, therefore, it is clear that these must be carried either by the sequestration or by the commission, according as the one or other is first issued. Suppose a sequestration were issued against a man not domiciled in Scotland, this cannot receive effect in England. In the same manner, although a commission of bankruptcy was ever so fairly obtained, yet if it be produced here, and we are satisfied that the party is not domiciled in England, but in Scotland, I should hold in that case that we are not bound to give effect to the commission. (1 Rose, p. 483.)" That might be said to be, perhaps, an extra-judicial observation, but there is a clear and decisive authority cited during the argument in this case which shows that is a correct view of the law.   I refer to *In re Blithman* (L. R. 2 Eq. p. 23). There a certain fund in England had been bequeathed by a bankrupt, who died in South Australia, to his widow, and the question was whether the future acquired property, not having fallen in until after the death of the bankrupt, passed under the commission to the Assignees or to the widow of the bankrupt, and executrix under the will. Lord Romilly held that if the bankrupt had an Australian domicile, the fund would go to the Assignees; if not, to the widow and executrix; and the evidence being rather lax and imperfect, he directed an inquiry. According, therefore, to these authorities, the Court has no hesitation at all in holding that the sole and exclusive right to distribute the property of a bankrupt must be vested in the tribunals of the country in which the bankrupt is domiciled. The domicile of Russell in this case was Queensland, and not New South Wales; and therefore the commission against him is inoperative—at least, in this colony. Possibly, the Court of New South Wales may uphold their authority, and deal with the property they may find there as they think proper; but the great inconvenience of such a course is most fully and convincingly pointed out in the great case to which I referred, and is reported in Rose's Reports. These inconveniences have arisen in these colonies; and there are two or three cases present to my mind in which great injustice and inconvenience did arise. But the Court venture to indulge a hope that their judgment in this case may at least awaken inquiry, and cause a single administration of the estate of a bankrupt instead of one, two, or three administrations. The practical result of our decision in this case will have the singular

HARRIS *v.*
RUSSELL.
———
Cockle, C. J.
Lutwyche, J.

HARRIS *v.*
RUSSELL.
———
Cockle, C. J.
Lutwyche, J.

felicity of being in harmony with the decisions of the English Courts and the decisions of the Courts of the United States, because, while we hold that in accordance with English decisions the Courts of this colony alone can deal with the property of a bankrupt domiciled here, we, like the Courts in the United States, protect the rights of our own citizens by refusing to give an extra-territorial effect to sequestration in New South Wales.

Leave to appeal was granted.

* NOTE.—See *Re Davidson's Settlement Trusts*, L.R., 15 Eq., 383.

R. v. PEARSON.

Criminal Law—Venire de novo—Affidavit of juror—New trial refused.

[In Banco.]
1868.
27th November.

Cockle, C. J.
Lutwyche, J.

On an application for a writ of *venire facias de novo*, on the ground of irregularities in connection with the deliberations of the jury on a criminal trial, *held*, that an affidavit by one of the jurymen as to the actions of the jury after their retirement from the Court could not be read upon such an application.

　* *R. v. Murphy*, 7 N. S.W., S. C., R., 24, doubted.

Application to make absolute a rule *nisi* for a writ of *venire facias de novo*, and for a writ of *certiorari*.

George Pearson was arraigned before His Honour Judge Innes and a common jury at Maryborough on the 7th August, 1868, on a charge of feloniously stealing two auriferous nuggets, valued at £64, the property of George Smith, Pearson being a bailee.

The prisoner was found guilty, and sentenced to eighteen months' imprisonment with hard labour in the Brisbane Gaol. On the termination of the case, the jury were locked up in the public Courthouse, and given in charge to the bailiff of the Court. The jury-room was occupied by another jury. Howard, one of the jurymen, had since stated that while the jury were locked up in the Courthouse, and considering their verdict, the police entered the Courthouse with the prisoner Pearson and other prisoners, and remained there during a portion of the time the jury were deliberating. Upon the reopening of the Court, the jury complained to the Judge of the intrusion of the police. While the jury were locked up, the depositions, the notes of the Crown Prosecutor and of the counsel for the prisoner, Roscoe's Criminal Evidence, and other legal works, were in the Court, and the jury had access to and read some of them.

Blake and *Handy*, for the prisoner, cited *R. v. Murphy* (7 N. S. W. R, 24), then under appeal to the Privy Council, *Straker v. Graham* (4 M. & W., 721), *Burgess v. Langley* (1 D. & L., 21), *Harvey v. Hewitt* (8 D. P. C., 598), *R. v. Fowler* (4 B. & Ald., 273), *R. v. Bertrand* (L. R., 1 P. C., 520), *Gould v. Oliver* (2 M. & G., 288), and read affidavits in corroboration of the facts.

R. v. PEARSON.

Cockle, C. J.
Lutwyche, J.

COCKLE, C. J. This application must be refused, on the ground that the evidence is technically insufficient and inadmissible. The presumption to be drawn from the statement that notes and books were lying on the Courthouse table is too faint to induce the Court to grant the rule.

LUTWYCHE, J. It is quite clear from the authorities that the affidavit of a juryman cannot be received as to what passed while the jury were locked up in a private room, and that the statement of a juror to another person of what passed in that private room cannot be accepted. There is nothing, therefore, for the Court to go upon. I consider this case is distinguishable from that of *R. v. Murphy*. I do not see anything in the case to infer a miscarriage of justice. I am not at all prepared to go the length that the Full Court in New South Wales has gone in *R. v. Murphy*, simply because the jury read the reports of the trial, for they read them only during the first three days, and if they had formed any erroneous impression of the evidence. they could have been corrected by the Judge in summing up.

Rule refused.

* This decision was reversed by the Privy Council (L. R., 2 P. C., 535).

McGAVIN *v.* McMASTER.

Trespass—Illegal impounding—Pastoral Leases Act of 1863 (27 Vic. No. 17), ss. 2, 36, 58, 59—Disputed title to land—Possession— Tort-feasor—Conversion.

1868.
1st December.
1869.
16th, 18th March.

Cor. *Cockle, C.J.
Lutwyche, J.*

, The plaintiff and defendant were lessees from the Crown of adjoining runs, and the former placed sheep and cattle on the alleged head of his run. The defendant entered, and impounded and sold them. In an action for trespass and damages, *Cockle,* C.J., directed the jury that possession was sufficient title as against a wrong doer, and left it to the jury to say what was the head of the creek, alleged by the defendant to be the boundary of the plaintiff's run, and the jury found a verdict in the defendant's favour.

Held, on appeal that the direction was right, but that considering the nature of the property and the great difficulty in settling the boundaries there should be a new trial on the question of title to the run, the plaintiff paying the costs of the first action, and that if the plaintiff succeeded he could bring another action for wrongful conversion.

Swinnerton v. Marquis of Stafford, 3 Taunt. 91 followed.

Rule *nisi* for a new trial on the grounds : (1) of misdirection of the Judge in confining the jury to finding what was the head of Gregory's Creek, instead of leaving to them what was the point intended by the plaintiff in his tender, and by telling the jury that possession was sufficient in the defendant as against a wrong-doer ; (2) of improper rejection of evidence ; (3) that the verdict was against the evidence.

The action was tried at Rockhampton, on 17th September, 1868, before His Honour the Chief Justice and a jury, when a verdict was entered for the defendant.

The plaintiff was the lessee of the Red Rock Valley Station Peak Downs, and sued the defendant, the lessee of Mount Eagle, an adjoining station, for trespass and illegal impounding, alleged to have been committed by him, claiming £800 damages. The defendant pleaded justification. The plaintiff rested his case on a license to occupy the Red Rock Valley Station, which he stated included a portion of country which the defendant claimed as part of the Mount Eagle run. The alleged trespasses and impoundings were that the plaintiff, believing he had a right to the country, placed sheep upon it, and erected a yard and hut ; but his sheep and the men in charge of them

McGavin v.
McMaster.

Cor. Cockle, C.J.
Lutwyche, J.

were expelled by the defendant, who, in his turn, placed sheep on the run. The plaintiff retaliated, and placed cattle on the country in dispute; but the defendant seized and impounded them, and subsequently sold them. From the evidence it appeared that the plaintiff had been on the land before defendant, though both had paid rent and assessment on it. The boundary of the plaintiff's run, as described in the license, commenced at a point called the head of Gregory's Creek. The plaintiff contended that the head of the creek was at a point five miles west of the main Drummond Range, and at the confluence of two creeks. The defendant stated the head of the creek was at the foot of the range, and about five miles south-east of point contended for by the plaintiff. Though only licensed to occupy 100 square miles, it was proved that in reality the plaintiff had occupied a far larger extent of country.

1st December, 1868.

Blake (*Lilley*, A. G., and *Griffith* with him) for the plaintiff, moved for a rule *nisi* for a new trial The north-eastern boundary was the head of Gregory's Creek, and the point is what did plaintiff intend. The following authorities were cited: *Goodtitle v. Bailey* (2 Cowp. 597) ; *Waterpark v. Fennell* (7 H. L. C., 650). As to the impounding, an intruder is not justified in impounding for damage feasant: *Harper v. Charlesworth* (4 B. & C., 574, 583). *Coke* on Littleton, 57 b.—"There is no tenancy at sufferance against the King (Ch. Pl., 6 Ed., note 351)." There can be no lawful possession of Crown Lands except under license. An unlicensed person has no right to impound, and to sue in trespass is different. *The Pastoral Leases Act of 1863*, ss. 2, 36 (3 Pring. 142) ; *Graham v. Peat* (1 East. 242). As to the rejection of evidence *Taylor*, p. 1205 was cited. As to the weight of evidence *Humphrey v. Nowland* (15 Moo. P. C. C. 313).

The rule *nisi* was granted: (1) on misdirection in telling the jury that possession was sufficient title in defendant as against a wrong-doer; (2) that the verdict was against the evidence.

16th March, 1869.

Blake (*Griffith* with him) moved the rule absolute.

Pring, Q.C , and *McDevitt*, shewed cause. The plaintiff's claim is under ss. 58 and 59 of 27 Vic. No. 17. In *Harper v. Charlesworth* (*ante*), a parol license from the Crown is sufficient to give a title against a wrong-doer. There should have been a special replication shewing the illegality. *McDonald v. Murray* (5 N.S.W., S.C. R. (L.), 55), ss. 14, 36 of the *Act.*

McGAVIN *v.* McMASTER.

———

Cor. Cockle, C.J. Lutwyche, J.

McDevitt followed. The person in possession was an intruder. The seizure was in September, 1866.

Blake in reply cited *Jones v. Chapman* (2 D. & L. 207) ; *Outram v. Morewood* (3 East. 346 ; 1 Smith, 703-4.) By s. 36 proprietor is occupier of land of whatever tenure. The plaintiff's title is prior occupation. *Swinnerton v. Marquis of Stafford* (3 Taunt. 21). There is no count in trover and no plea.

LUTWYCHE, J. I am of opinion that there ought to be no rule for a new trial on the ground of misdirection. It appears to me that the direction given by the learned Chief Justice was quite correct, viz., that possession was a sufficient title as against a wrong-doer. That was the proposition of law which he laid down, and he left it to the jury to apply it to the facts of the case as proved before them. It has been contended by Mr. Blake, and also by Mr. Griffith that the ruling was too wide, because it ought to have embraced the fact that the defendant was an intruder against the Crown, and that, therefore, he had not lawful possession. But I am of opinion that that defence did not arise upon the record as it stood, and to enable the defendant to avail himself of such a defence, even if it were good in point of law, of which I say nothing, he ought to have replied by confession and avoidance. Upon that state of the record the learned Chief Justice's direction was perfectly good. As to the other ground, that the verdict was against the weight of evidence, the Court feels great difficulty in dealing with it. I understand from my learned colleague that he could not exactly say he was dissatisfied with the verdict of the jury ; but under the peculiar circumstances of the case the Court are inclined to think that the justice of the case would be best met by sending down the record for trial before another jury. We will not, however, send down the record in its present state, but will only allow the first count, and the fifth, if the plaintiff likes, to be sent down with the issues raised upon those counts by the replication, upon the terms that the plaintiff pay the cost of the action. We are induced to do so on account of the nature of the property, and the great difficulty there was in settling the boundaries, a question which ought to have been settled in another way. Looking at the past difficulty there was in determining what really was the head of Gregory's Creek, and also

McGavin *v.*
McMaster.

Cor. Cockle, C.J.
Lutwyche, J.

relying on the circumstance which appeared, on the authority of *Swinnerton v. Marquis of Stafford*, cited above, the Court think that the question of title involved in the case may perhaps be the better for consideration of another jury. At the same time the Court, having eliminated some of the counts, and especially the trover and impounding counts from the present record, it would be well for the parties to the suit to consider in what position they will be relatively placed. The question to the title to the run will be the only question that will be tried before the jury. The question of damages for unlawfully impounding might, and will no doubt, he raised in another action in which the probable defendant. Mr. McMaster, will not be fettered, as Mr. McGavin was in the action then before the Court. The question of bailment will then arise, and very probably he may recover ample damages for unlawful conversion of the cattle. He will in an action of that kind be able to test the strength or weakness of the defendant's title to the run, and unless the latter can shew he had a complete title to the *locus in quo*, he must necessarily fail. It is to be regretted that the matter was not left to be settled by arbitration, as the legislature evidently intended should be. But as that has not been done, the Court think the justice of the case will, under the nature of all the circumstances, be best met by the course we propose to adopt. The rule will, therefore, be made absolute for a new trial on that portion of the record which I have mentioned upon payment of costs by the plaintiff.

    Cockle, C. J., concurred.

Rule absolute for new trial.

WYNDHAM v. CAMERON.

Impounding Act of 1863 (27 Vic., No. 22), s. 40—Jurisdiction of Justices—Question of title to land. *

Where a case is brought before Justices relative to charges for impounding, and such a case involves the question of ownership of land, the Justices have jurisdiction to decide the question of ownership.

1868.
8th December.

Sheppard, D. C. J.

APPEAL from a decision of magistrates at Goondiwindi.

On 13th October, Alex. Wyndham, lessee of Winton Station, brought an action, in the Petty Debts Court, against Hugh Cameron, lessee of Callandoon Station, for illegally impounding certain sheep, the property of the said Alex. Wyndham.

The following decision was given:

1. The Bench is of opinion that the country having been in dispute between the lessees of Winton and Callandoon, the defendant was not justified in impounding the plaintiff's sheep.

2. Evidence has been produced by plaintiff proving him to be the lessee of the country whence the sheep were impounded, by agreement bearing date 1866, subject to further amendment by arbitration.

3. The Bench decides that the defendant make good the sum claimed by plaintiff—namely, £45 10s. 10d.—for impounding charges and damages, and 3s. 6d. costs of Court.

Cameron gave notice of appeal to the Metropolitan District Court.

SHEPPARD, D.C.J. The only evidence before me is that given to the Bench at Goondiwindi. They had, it seems, in hearing the case, declined to receive as evidence certain documents handed in by the defendant, and purporting to give a description of his run, because those documents were not in any way authenticated. I am of opinion, after reading the evidence taken before the Bench, that the decision they made was right, though the reasons they gave in the first and second paragraphs of the order for coming to such decision were wrong. The country from which the sheep were impounded by the appellant may have been in dispute, but that, in itself, was no reason why Cameron (the appellant) was not justified in impounding them. There is, however, the uncontroverted evidence that Wyndham was in possession of the country whence the sheep were impounded. The ground of appeal is that the Goondiwindi Bench had no right to decide the matter, there being an interest in land involved in the question. By *The Impounding Act*, however, when cases are brought before a Court of Petty Sessions relative to impounding charges, and such cases involve, as they do, questions of ownership, the Magistrates have jurisdiction to decide the question of ownership; and it has been so decided in New South Wales. In this case they have so incidentally decided that the sheep, when impounded, were on Winton Station, the property of Wyndham, and were therefore illegally impounded by Cameron. It appears to me, therefore, that the appeal must be dismissed, and that the third paragraph of the order, relative to the return of the charges and damages, should be confirmed. The first two paragraphs of the order are quashed. The appellant must pay the respondent eight guineas costs.

*See *Phillips v. Dowzer* (6 Q.L.J., 210).

MULLIGAN v. BURNETT.

Common Law Process Act of 1867 (31 Vic., No. 4) ss. 48, 67—Capias [IN CHAMBERS.]
ad respondendum—Seal of Commissioner—Irregularity.   1869.
19th, 21st April.

Cockle, C. J.

Where a writ of *ca re* had been issued under the hand of a Commissioner, but without his seal.

Held that the omission was an irregularity only, and not sufficient ground for setting aside the writ.

SUMMONS to set aside a writ of *ca. re*, on the ground that it was only under the signature of the Commissioner who issued it, and not under seal, as required by s. 67 of the *Common Law Process Act of 1867.*

Murphy, for the defendant, in support of the summons.

Macnish, for the plaintiff, showed cause. No irregularity was mentioned in the summons (r. 4). The application is too late. The writ was issued on 16th March. The summons was taken out on 16th April. The money was paid on 16th March, the date of arrest. *Day's C. L. Practice, p. 21; Archbold, p. 777.*

21st April.   C.A.V.

COCKLE, C. J. This is a case in which it is sought to set aside a writ of *ca. re* on the grounds mentioned in the affidavits. Two objections were taken, one that the *capias* had not issued under the seal and signature of the Police Magistrate, and the other that there was some irregularity in the return of the præcipe, or some defect in the proceedings in that certain documents were not returned to the Registry of the Court. Unquestionably the statute provides that a *capias* should issue under the seal as well as the hand of the Commissioner issuing it; and it was contended that the *capias* was bad in consequence of the omission of the seal of the Commissioner. The point turned upon this : Was the omission of the seal, an irregularity, or a nullity ? If it were a nullity, the objection would have been open on the summons; if it were an irregularity, the objection would not have been open, because the nature of the irregularity was not specified in

MULLIGAN v.
BURNETT.

Cockle, C. J.

the summons. The point is a new one, and I have thought proper to consult my brother Lutwyche upon it, and after considering the matter, we have come to the conclusion that, inasmuch as substantially the requirements of the statute have been complied with, this was rather in the nature of an irregularity than a nullity, and we find that, in all respects, the *capias* was regular. There was the certificate required by the statute, and this one omission we both think constituted an irregularity only. Consequently the objection to the summons must be vain on that point. On the other it seems to me there can be no doubt that the non-return of certain documents is a mere irregularity. The summons must be dismissed without costs.

Summons dismissed.

RIDDLE *v.* YOUNG.

Impounding Act of 1863 (27 Vic. No. 22), ss. 36, 47—Trespass—
Damage feasant—Rescue—Appeal—Rehearing.

1869.
15th June.

Sheppard,
D.C.J.

Animals damage feasant can only be distrained while actually trespassing, and should they be distrained after they have ceased to trespass, the owner may rescue them before they reach the pound.

A conviction for rescuing sheep on the way to a pound for damage feasant was quashed, as it was not proved that the person who seized them was the proprietor of the land on which they were alleged to have been trespassing.

Appeal to the District Court to quash a conviction by the Police Magistrate at Goondiwindi, against Riddle on an information charging him with having unlawfully rescued certain sheep which had been impounded.   The facts sufficiently appear in the judgment.

SHEPPARD, D. C. J.   The order made on the information was that the appellant should pay to the respondent the sum of £15 as damages, and should also pay a penalty of £5 for the rescue, and the costs of court   This order being made under the *Impounding Act*, and the appeal lying to a Court of Quarter Sessions, the practice of that Court is followed by the District Court, and the appeal takes the form of a rehearing.   From the evidence which was adduced before me, it appeared that Mr. Young, the respondent, claimed certain country as a portion of his run called Terrawinneba West, and that Mr. Lowe, the owner of the sheep distrained, and the real appellant also claimed the country in question as belonging to his station called Welltown.   Some correspondence had taken place between these parties; it had been intimated by Mr. Young that he should impound the sheep trespassing on his run, and Mr. Lowe had stated if this were done he should rescue them.   No evidence was given on behalf of the respondent of any title to the land in dispute, and it was conceded and proved that, at the time the sheep were distrained, they were in a yard that was then in the actual occupation of Mr. Lowe.   While the sheep were being driven to the pound, by

Mr Young, but before they were impounded, they were rescued by
the appellant, acting for Mr. Lowe. No breach of the peace took
place, the sheep were given up and an information laid for unlawful
rescue.

By the common law, animals, *damage feasant,* at the time of the
distress, can only be distrained while they are actually trespassing;
on their leaving the land the right of the owner of the land to
distrain them is gone, and should they be distrained after they have
ceased to trespass, the owner of the sheep may rescue them before they
reach the pound. *Coke on Littleton* (161 A). The *Impounding Act
of 1863,* does not alter the law in this respect. By s. 47, under which
the order appealed against was made, it is enacted that any person
rescuing any animals lawfully impounded, shall be liable to a penalty
and to pay damages: if therefore the animals be not lawfully seized,
rescuing them is not an offence; the statute merely affirms the
common law. In the present case it is clear that the seizure of the
sheep for the purpose of impounding them was, according to the
evidence given in the District Court, unlawful. Mr. Young was not
proved to be the proprietor of the land on which the sheep were
at the time of the distress; there was no evidence of his being
the lessee of the land, nor was he the occupier of it; the sheep
were, therefore, not trespassing on *his* land. The seizure of the
sheep being unlawful, the owner of them had the right to rescue
them while being driven to the pound. I need hardly say that in
this decision is in no way involved any determination as to the
ownership of the land in dispute. I merely hold that the seizure of
these sheep for the purpose of impounding them was, under the
circumstances, proved unlawful, and the owner of the sheep had
the right to rescue or retake them before they reached the pound,
according to the evidence given in the District Court.

The order of the Police Magistrate must be quashed, and the
appeal allowed with costs.

Appeal allowed.

R. v. WILKIE.

Criminal Law—Embezzlement—Larceny Act of 1865 (29 Vic., No. 6), s. s., 73, 75, 76, 96—Person in service of the Crown.

[In Banco].
1869.
9th, 10th Sept.

Cockle, C. J.
Lutwyche, J.

The word " fraudulently," in s. 75 of 29 Vic., No. 6, is to be applied to the word " embezzle," which precedes it in the section, as well as to the words "apply and dispose of " which follow.

Where a servant of the Crown has received from the Treasury moneys payable to other persons, and there is no evidence that he received them by virtue of his employment, he cannot be convicted of embezzlement of those moneys under s. 75 of the *Larceny Act.*

Crown case reserved by Lutwyche, J.

The prisoner was indicted on an information under s. 75 of the Larceny Act of 1865, charging him with three separate offences of embezzlement and stealing, and a general verdict of guilty was returned. The facts appear in the judgment. It was submitted that the case for the Crown had failed in that the moneys mentioned in the information were the property of the person to whom they were payable, and not of Her Majesty ; that there was no evidence of the prisoner having received the said moneys or having embezzled them; that there was no evidence of the prisoner having received the moneys by virtue of his employment; that there was no refusal by the prisoner to account for the moneys, and that it, in fact, having been shewn that the moneys had been paid over, there was in law no embezzlement and no fraudulent intention on the part of the prisoner. The learned Judge refused to so direct the jury, but reserved the objections for the Full Court.

The prisoner was convicted and sentenced to three years penal servitude.

Blake, Q.C., and *Griffith,* for the prisoner, referred to *R v. Moah* (Dears., 626 ; 25 L. J., M. C., 66). The persons, to whom payments were made, might have received them at the Treasury themselves. The money must be in transit to the employer. *R v. Hockings* (1 Den., 584; 2 Russell, 449-50); *R v. Gill* (Dears., 289); *R v. Smith* (R. &

c

R v. WILKIE.

Cockle, C. J.
Lutwyche, J.

R., 516). The receipt from the bank is receipt from the Crown. *R v. Gorbutt* (Dears & B., 166); *R v. Hodgson* (3. C. & P., 422); *R v. Evan Owen Jones* (7 C. & P., 833); *R v. Williams* (7 C. & P., 338.

Pring, Q. C., for the Crown. Section 75, refers as much to money coming from the Treasury as to money going from the Treasury entrusted to him by virtue of his employment.

LUTWYCHE, J. I have now no hesitation in coming to the conclusion that the conviction was erroneous. I certainly thought, at the trial, that the words of s. 73 of the *Larceny Act*, and those of s 75 so far as related to the offence of embezzlement, being different in phraseology, the Legislature might have intended to apply a more restricted meaning than was formerly applied to the word embezzlement. I am sorry that I had no opportunity at the trial of fortifying my judgment by a reference to any of those cases just cited, for I was only referred to *R v. Moah*. I certainly think now that the word "embezzle" means fraudulent and felonious embezzlement. I am more lead to that conclusion by a more careful consideration of the terms of s. 75. I take it, therefore, that the Legislature meant to apply the word " fraudulent " to the word embezzle, as well as to the words "apply or dispose of ;" and the context seems to strengthen that conclusion. Another clause of the Statute (s. 96) has been pointed out to me by the Chief Justice—that as to to the receiving of stolen goods. The words are :

" Whosoever shall receive any chattel, money, valuable security or other property whatsoever, the stealing, taking, extorting, obtaining, embezzling or otherwise disposing whereof shall amount to a felony either at common law or by virtue of this Act, knowing the same to have been feloniously taken, stolen, ... shall be guilty of felony, and may be indicted and convicted as an accessory after the fact or for a substantive felony, and in the latter case, whether the principal felon shall or shall not have been previously convicted or shall or shall not be answerable to justice, and every such receiver howsoever convicted shall be liable, at the discretion of the Court, to be kept in penal servitude for any term not exceeding fourteen years, etc."

It cannot be intended that a simple receipt of any property, which has been stolen, will make a man liable to be indicted as a receiver, for, if so, a constable who takes stolen goods into his possession may be indicted under s. 96. We must construe enactments according to the meaning of terms which have obtained in the law a certain definite meaning; and I think I have been wrong in the necessarily hasty view I took on the occasion of the trial. I should have been glad to have received more assistance than I did; but, of course, a judge has to do the best he can at the time. I was not freed from responsibility, if I did not get the amount of assistance which I might fairly expect from the Bar. In the *Larceny Act* a distinction between embezzlement and larceny is carefully drawn. There is a distinct section (s.75) with reference to the offence of larceny by persons in the Queensland Civil Service and the Police, and another clause which relates to embezzlement, and to a fraudulent application or distribution of money; and perhaps if the words "fraudulent application" had been followed in the information in this case, the evidence might have supported it. But there would still have remained the question of fraud, which I was asked to put to the jury, and thought it unnecessary to do so. I told the jury it was quite sufficient, if they thought there had been a wilful misappropriation of public money by the prisoner, and declined to put that question to them. The main question in this case turned upon that of embezzlement, and I certainly think there has been no evidence of embezzlement, in the meaning of that term that has been laid down, to go to the jury. The prisoner received money from the Treasury, representing the Queen. He did not, as was the case with the prisoner, whom I tried at Ipswich in April last, intercept money on its way to the Treasury; but he received it from the Treasury, and, therefore, if other facts would have supported the charge, he might have been found guilty of larceny, if my attention had been called to the fact that the evidence would support such charge. Had my attention been so called, I might then have directed the jury to find the prisoner guilty of larceny, not embezzlement. I cannot complain that I was not told the offence, if anything, amounted to larceny. I ought to have seen that for myself, but I did not. The jury having found a general verdict of guilty, the conviction must be quashed according to the authority of *R v. Gorbutt (supra)*, even if the evidence would have supported a charge of larceny. Under all the circumstances, I am clearly of opinion that the conviction was erroneous, and ought to be quashed.

COCKLE, C. J. I concur.

Conviction quashed.

WING WAH v. AUSTRALASIAN STEAM NAVIGATION COMPANY.

1868.
28th November.
1869.
19th, 20th Mar.,
10th, 16th Sept.

Cockle, C. J.
Lutwyche, J.

Contract—Shipment of goods— Gross and wilful default—Negligence— Stranding of vessel—Deviation—Damage.—Breach of Harbour Regulations.

Goods were shipped from Sydney to Rockhampton in one of the defendant's steamers. The contract note provided that the defendants were to be liable only for gross and wilful default. After being berthed at the Company's wharf, the steamer proceeded to another wharf before discharging the goods, and on her return to the first wharf, deviated from the usual course, stranded, swung round, and was exposed to the action of the tide. The captain was on shore at the time, but he gave directions to the chief officer, and a pilot was subsequently obtained, as required by the Harbour regulations. Next morning it was discovered that the goods were damaged by water, which had leaked into the hold through the straining of a bolt. The plaintiff obtained a verdict for damages.

Held, on a motion, pursuant to leave, that there was evidence to go to the jury, of gross and wilful default on the part of the defendants' servants, and a non-suit was refused.

Rule *nisi* for a non-suit or a new trial in an action tried before Cockle, C. J., and a jury, at Rockhampton, on 16th September, 1868, when a verdict was given for the plaintiff for £277 4s., on the grounds: (1) That the verdict was against the evidence and the law: (2) Misdirection: (3) Non-joinder of the necessary party: (4) No gross and wilful default.

The plaintiff, a merchant in Rockhampton, sued the defendants, as carriers of passengers and goods by water, for injury sustained by him in consequence of certain goods carried by defendants from Sydney to Rockhampton, having been received by the plaintiff in a damaged state. The declaration contained five counts. The first on the contract; the second on the loss of the goods; the third in tort for damage; the fourth for negligent stowage; the fifth that the vessel was not fit for the conveyance of such goods in safety and security. The pleas were: (1) That the defendants did not promise as alleged; (2) Not guilty; (3) That the goods were delivered, and defendants were not liable under the contract, as the alleged loss was by reason of an accident, and by peril and danger of the river; (4) That they were not negligent; (5) That proper care was used in shipping and stowage; (6) That the vessel was staunch and tight, and fit for safely and securely carrying the goods.

WING WAH v.
AUSTRALIAN
STEAM NAVIGA-
TION COY.

Cockle, C. J.
Lutwyche, J.

From the evidence it appeared that in May last, Sam Ke On, the plaintiff's Sydney agent—or, as the defendants alleged, his partner—shipped 80 bags of rice, 5 tons of flour, 78 bags of potatoes, and 22 bags of onions, on board the steamship *Saxonia*, bound for Rockhampton. The goods were consigned to the plaintiff, and were to be sold by him, Sam Ke On sharing the profit and loss of the transaction. In the contract, the defendants were to be liable only for gross and wilful default. The vessel arrived at Rockhampton on March 23rd, and was safely berthed at the defendants' wharf at noon of that day. Shortly afterwards she proceeded to the Government wharf for the purpose of discharging a large steam engine, and on her return to the Company's wharf she grounded, through not being midway in the stream. The captain was not on board at the time, but on the river bank, and when he perceived what had taken place, he directed the chief officer, then in command of the steamer, to run out a kedge for the purpose of swinging her round. That did not succeed, and she lay there some little time, until a pilot was sent on board. The vessel was, by the pilot's direction, placed upon a mud bank, near the middle of the Fitzroy. Her stern only was on the ground then. About seven o'clock the same day the vessel was floated, and at ten o'clock at night was safely removed alongside the defendants' wharf. Immediately after she grounded, and on several subsequent occasions, the pumps were sounded, but no water was found in the hold. The next morning about 5.30, when the pumps were sounded, water was found there, and on examination it was discovered that a rivet had been started from a plate affixed to the keel plate, in the fore part of the vessel. The plaintiff's goods were stowed in the fore hold, and the entry of the water caused the damage complained of. The goods were valued at £302 9s., and only a portion of them, valued at £50, was uninjured. A verdict was returned for £277 4s. In the course of the trial, the defendants' counsel moved for a non-suit, on the ground of the non-joinder of plaintiff's partner, Sam Ke On, in the action. The application was refused, but leave to move generally was reserved.

Blake and *Griffith*, for the plaintiff, showed cause.

Lilley and *McDevitt* for the defendants.

WING WAH *v.*
AUSTRALIAN
STEAM NAVIGA-
TION COY.

Cockle, C. J.
Lutwyche, J.

Blake argued that as to the non-joinder plaintiff was a consignee *Coggs v. Bernard* (1 Smith, L. C., 219); Lindley on Partnership, 390; *Cothay v. Fennell* (10 B. & C., 71) ; *Skinner v. Tott* (4 B. & Ald. 437). There was no evidence of gross and wilful neglect. *Corr v. Lanca-shire and Yorkshire Railway Co* (7 Ex., 713) ; *Skinner v. L B. & S. Coast Railway* (5 Ex., 787). The mere fact of an accident was *primâ facie* evidence of negligence. *Grill v. General Iron Screw Collier Co.* (L. R. 2., C. P., 600) ; *Martin v. Great Indian Peninsular Railway Co.* (L. R. 3., Ex. 9.) ; *Davis v. Garrett* (6 Bing., 716) were cited on the meaning of gross negligence.

Griffith followed. The proper person to sue is the consignee. *Wilson v. Brett* (11 M. & W , 113) ; *Doorman v. Jenkins* (2 A. & E , 256, 260.)

Lilley, A. G. So far as the matter lies in contract the consignee may sue. There was no evidence of gross and wilful default. It must be shown that with knowledge the captain acted against his better judgment. The neglect must be wilful. *Colton v. Wood* (29 L. J., C. P. 332). When the circumstances are consistent with the presence or absence of negligence, there must be proof of well defined negligence. The circumstances are consistent with no negligence. *Hammack v. White* (31 L. J., C. P., 329).

COCKLE, C. J. I have consulted for some time with my learned colleague, not because the Court has any doubt as to what their sub-stantial decision should be, but to consider whether or not we shall say there was no evidence to go to a jury. Although it almost requires a microscope to discover what evidence there was to go to a jury, yet the Court are unable to say absolutely that there was no evidence; and although, I confess, I have grave doubts myself whether there is any or not, yet I cannot take the responsibility of saying there was none. The Court has carefully considered the points that have been urged by counsel upon either side, and the cases they have cited. One case, *Grill v. General Iron Screw Co.* (L. R. 1., C. P., 600), was delivered by Mr. Justice Willes, upon which great stress was laid, appears to the Court to be certainly distinguishable from the present. In the first place there was a replication that the loss arose from the gross negligence of the defendants, and, in general, the rule is that the substance of the issue need only be proved. I find that as a less degree of negligence than that called gross negligence would suffice to render the defendants liable, the affirmative gross might be rejected as useless. If a person unnecessarily put in matter of description he would be bound according to the old rule to prove it. In the present case it must be remembered that the phrase, " gross and wilful default " did not occur merely on the issue, but it also appeared on the contract itself. Had there only been counts in tort, I should have had no difficulty in saying there was no evidence to go to the jury, but there were contract counts also, and therefore, although I still have very grave doubts, yet I hesitate to say that there was no evidence of a " gross and wilful default." At the same time, it is perfectly clear that there was no evidence that the jury were justified in acting upon. All would suffer by any injury to the commercial interest ; and all would suffer if these contracts were not fairly interpreted by the Courts, and acted upon by juries. It was quite optional with the plaintiff whether or not he should send the particular goods injured in the vessel named in the action, and, at all events, if he accepted the services of the defendants, he was bound by the terms in which he agreed to accept them. He agreed not to sue except for their " gross and wilful default ; " but if such negligence as would satisfy the ground of negligence in an ordinary action would suffice to prove " gross and wilful default," what was the use of the Company putting such a stipulation as that in their contracts. Though I am not prepared to draw the line between one kind of negligence and another, yet, unless there is some great distinction between negligence simple and gross and wilful default, it would be utterly useless for public companies to seek to protect themselves by such a stipulation, and consequently they must either cease to exist or be obliged to inflict more onerous terms on the public in a pecuniary way. I think the verdict is one which can hardly be satisfactory to the Court, and consequently there must be a new trial.

LUTWYCHE, J. I wish to say a few words about the non-suit point. I confess that during the progress of the argument my opinion fluctuated considerably, and I have not come to the conclusion that the rule as to the non-suit could not be made absolute without very considerable doubt ; and very considerable doubt even now affects me. Assuming that there was a wilful default on the part of the chief officer in bringing the *Saxonia* too near to the bank, and so stranding her, the question arises—was the breaking of the bolt which lead to the leakage subsequently the necessary consequence of the stranding ? Then I confess my mind is not free from doubt. It might have occurred in two or three other ways, some of which have been

WING WAH v.
AUSTRALIAN
STEAM NAVIGA-
TION COY.

Cockle, C. J.
Lutwyche, J.

WING WAH *v.*
AUSTRALIAN
STEAM NAVIGA-
TION COY.

Cockle, C.J.
Lutwyche, J.

suggested; and I might suggest another—that while the boat was moored at the wharf the action of the tide might have forced her against the piers, and so the bolt might have been broken. But that argument has somewhat been removed by the suggestion of the Chief Justice, that, when once a sufficient cause for the breakage of the bolt was shown to exist, perhaps it might be going too far to say there was no evidence to go to the jury of the loss through wilful default. I concur in thinking that that part of the rule which relates to the non-suit ought not to be made absolute.

The new trial was heard before Lutwyche, J., and a jury, at Brisbane, on 23-27th August, when a verdict was given for the plaintiff for £219.

On 10th September, pursuant to leave, counsel moved to set aside the verdict, and to have a non-suit entered, and cited *Giblin v. McMullen* (L. R. 2 P. C., 317).

On 16th September, a rule *nisi* for non-suit was argued.

Blake showed cause, and cited *Czech v. General Steam Navigation Co.* (L. R., 3 C. P., 14); *Lloyd v. Iron Screw Colliery Co.*, (3 H. & C., 284); *Beale v. South Devon Railway Co.* (*Ib.*, 337); *Scott v. London Catherine Docks Co.* (*Ib.*, 366); *Austin v. Manchester Railway Co.* (10 C. B., 474); *Phillips v. Clark* (2 C.B. (N.S.), 156.)

Pring, Q. C.: The defendants had by their contract ticket protected themselves from liability. Nothing like gross or wilful negligence had been shown against them.

COCKLE, C. J. The law in this case has been discussed before, but on a very different state of facts, because there has certainly been one new fact, one new piece of evidence, introduced at the late trial, namely, the letter of Mr. Phillips, secretary to the Company, in which he attributed the starting of the bolt to the vessel having grounded on a rock, or other hard substance, which started one of the rivets, and caused the water to flow in. Of course various interpretations might be put on that letter. The jury may have regarded it as attributing the starting of the rivet to the grounding of the steamer on the rock, or other hard substance in the river. If, however, the letter was written under a mistake as to the facts, or if it had been liable to have had a meaning given to it less prejudicial to the defendants, they might have explained it, as other omissions were explained. Certainly it was by no means an unimportant addition to the evidence which came before the Court formerly. Had gross and wilful evidence on the part of the Company been proved? If not, they were certainly

entitled to have this rule made absolute. When companies choose to WING WAH *v.*
protect themselves by conditions, however hard, the proper way, STEAM NAVIGA-
whenever practicable, is for those who would otherwise have TION COY. ·
employed them, not to employ them.   Once a contract is entered into,
the parties to it are bound by its terms.   It is not necessary to
review the whole of the evidence.   In the first place there was a
breach of the Port and Harbour Regulations. Unless the accident was
clearly attributable to that breach, such breach might entail a penalty
on the company, or their officers, but would afford a ground for an
adverse verdict on the part of the jury.   It is necessary to see how
the accident was attributable to this breach of the Port and Harbour
Regulations in not carrying a pilot. If the regulations only said that
a pilot should be employed, I do not think there would be the slightest
evidence of negligence, because the regulation might then be considered merely a fiscal one, imposed for the purpose of ensuring
employment to the pilots.   The regulations said, however, there must
be a pilot or a person holding a certificate of exemption on board.
To some extent, therefore, we must regard the regulations as pointing
out a certain peril, and as providing, in order to guard against it,
that there should be a pilot on board, or a person with whose payment the Company would not be saddled, a qualified officer of their
own.   Taking the facts of the case, was there gross and wilful
default?   Of course, we are obliged to discuss to some extent the
conduct of the chief officer of the *Saxonia*.   Any man may fall into
a blunder, and nothing that falls from the Court will be prejudicial
to his prospects.   Was he competent or incompetent?   If
incompetent, I cannot regard as anything but an act of gross
default on the part of the Company to leave a vessel containing
property of the person under such circumstances. If competent,
the act of leaving the property of others in the hands of incompetent servants was gross default, and as it was done knowingly, the captain having left the vessel, it would also be wilful
default.   Supposing the accident was traceable to that default, I
think it arose from gross and wilful negligence.   Was the officer
competent?   Assuming he was competent, he must have known the
usual course of safety from wharf to wharf.   One witness said he
had never seen a vessel going so far inside the line of wharves before.
If the officer was competent, he knew the usual course, and there
is evidence that he deviated from it.   If there had been any extraordinary circumstance, such as another vessel coming up, and he had

WING WAH *v.*
AUSTRALIAN
STEAM NAVIGA-
TION COY.

Cockle, C.J.
Lutwyche, J.

injudiciously taken that course in order to get out of the way, it is possible the Company may have been protected under the clause of their contract—which shelters them from anything but gross and wilful default. But here there were no extraordinary circumstances, so far as I can see. The circumstances were of an ordinary kind, and he deviated from the usual course. It was an act of his own mind, and so far was wilful. And, moreover, seeing that the circumstances were of an ordinary kind and that it was a deviation from the usual ordinary course, it might well be left to a jury whether there had not been gross default. I cannot pretend to give a definition of what the judges in England have not defined, gross negligence ; but for the purposes of this case, I think it sufficient and safe to say that the test in this instance is : Under ordinary circumstances was the usual course pursued ? If it was not, I think there would be what falls within the meaning of gross negligence, or rather gross default. Assuming that there was evidence to go to a jury of gross default, and of wilful default, on the part of the Company, is the damage sufficiently traced to that gross and wilful default ? We could not make this rule absolute without saying there was no reasonable evidence that the straining, which started the bolt, occurred in the river and not at the wharf. If it did not occur in the river, another class of considerations would have to come before us. Was there any negligence whatever at the wharf, and, if there was, was it wilful and gross ? If there is any evidence that the straining which started the bolt took place in the bed of the river, it was unnecessary to enter into the question whether there was negligence at the wharf, and if so, whether that negligence was gross. One can hardly say there is no evidence that the straining took place in the bed of the river. In the first place, the suggestion that it took place at the wharf did not arise out of the plaintiff's evidence, but out of the defendants'. In the next place, there are circumstances on which the jury may have relied, tending to shew that the facts were consistent with the theory that the straining took place in the bed of the river. It is possible that the influx of water may, to some extent, have been prevented by the bed of silt on which the starboard side of the vessel was lying while in the river. Or, again, the bolt may not have been displaced till some pressure of the water was exerted on it. It is difficult to say that a non-suit should have been entered, in the face of evidence of the vessel having grounded, swung round, and been exposed to the action of the water for some considerable period. It is not to be forgotten that the difference between the high and low water was six feet, and according to the plaintiff there was then ten feet at low water at the wharf. Remembering that, and that the vessel was found full of water at 6 o'clock the next morning, and that it was high water at 12 p.m., it had been urged for the plaintiffs that the starting of the bolt could not arise from the vessel grounding at the wharf. But all these circumstances have been before the jury, and we cannot set aside the verdict on the ground that there was no evidence that the straining did not take place in the bed of the river. Even supposing it had been satisfactorily proved that the straining took place at the wharf, there would be a rather singular defence to an action of negligence. The defendants would in effect say, "We are not guilty of gross negligence in the river, because the damage arose from our slight negligence at the wharf." The defendants could not say that there was no negligence at the wharf, because the bolt having been sprung from the effect of some force applied; if there had been no such negligence at the wharf, or deviation from the ordinary course of procedure, the question arose, how was it no bolt had sprung there before? This is a case of reasonable evidence, or no reasonable evidence, and we cannot say there was no reasonable evidence. I am of opinion that the rule should be discharged with costs.

LUTWYCHE, J. I am of the same opinion. I think there was abundant evidence to go to the jury of gross and wilful default on the part of the Company.

Rule discharged.

WING WAH *v.* AUSTRALIAN STEAM NAVIGATION COY.

Cockle, C.J.
Lutwyche, J.

PALMER v. SUTHERLAND.

[In Banco.]
1869.
10th, 28th May,
4th June,
22nd September.

Cockle, C. J.
Lutwyche, J.

Debtor and Creditor—Appropriation of payments—Banking practice.

A creditor has a right to appropriate if the payer omit to do so, and there is no ascertained limit to the time during which the receiver may make the appropriation.

Except with regard to a banking account, the law does not interfere with the appropriation, unless in cases where third parties or their rights are affected by the transactions between the debtor and creditor, as for instance in the cases of death, bankruptcy or change of parties.

Rule *nisi* to increase by £4 6s. 3d. a verdict given in an action for illegal distress, in which the plaintiff recovered a verdict of five shillings on the first count, and for thirty shillings on the fifth count.

The plaintiff had distrained on the defendant for £73 16s. 6d., of which £32 14s. was the amount of a promissory note admitted to have been given in payment of rent, except as regards a sum of £4 6s. 3d., which was the balance on a former note for £30, all of which was paid except the £4 6s. 3d. which was all that was due thereon, the consideration for the £30 being rent for £20 secured by a previous promissory note for £20, and £10 for a land order, the purchase of which was made at the time the £30 promissory note was given. There was no evidence of any appropriation by either party at the time the several payments were made on account of the £30 note.

Blake, Q.C., and *Bramston* for the defendant contended that the inclusion of the amount shewed appropriation. Where there are different transactions the party paying can appropriate at the time of payment, but he is restricted to the time of payment, otherwise the right accrues to the creditor who can appropriate up to action brought. (The authorities cited are reviewed in the judgment).

Pring, Q. C., for the plaintiff, shewed cause. The cases cited are not applicable. There was a mixed account and a general account. *Bodenham v. Purchas* (2 B. and Ald. 39.)

C.A.V.

22nd September, 1869.

COCKLE, C. J. delivered the judgment of the Court as follows:—

In this case there was a verdict for the plaintiff. A rule *nisi* to increase the verdict by £4 6s. 3d. was argued in Easter term last, and has entailed upon us an amount of research quite disproportionate to the importance of the amount in question, though not, perhaps, to that of the principle involved. The question was—whether the defendant, a creditor of the plaintiff, was entitled to appropriate a payment made to him by the plaintiff, his debtor? And the conclusion to which we have come is that there is nothing to take this case out of the operation of the general rule that the receiver has a right to appropriate if the payer omit to do so, and that there is no ascertained limit to the time during which the receiver may make the appropriation. [See *Goddard v. Cox*—mentioning *Bloss v. Cutting*, (2 Stra., 1194); *Hawkshaw v. Rawlings*, (1 Stra., 24).] In *Newmarch v. Clay*, (14 East, 239), there was evidence of appropriation. In *Peters v. Anderson* (5 Taunt. 596, 602), the above or a like rule was recognised. In *Clayton's Case* (1 Mer., 606), there was a third party interested, and the appropriation was concurred in by the debtor and creditor. *Bosanquet v. Wray* (6 Taunt. 596), exemplifies the creditor's right. *Bodenham v. Purchas* (2 B. & Ald , 39), was a case of banking account; there was evidence of appropriation, and even of payment, according to Holroyd, J. In *Brooke v. Enderby* (2 Bro. & Bing , 65), there was an unknown dormant partner, dissolution, bankruptcy of the continuing partner, and an account in the nature of a banking account. In *Sterndale v. Hankinson* (1 Sim., 393), there was evidence of appropriation; a widow with assets had an account rendered to her, debiting her. In *Simson v. Ingham* (2 B. & C., 65), the creditor's right to elect was upheld. *Field v. Carr* (5 Bing., 13), was a case of a banker's account; there was a third party interested, and a three years' interval. *Storeld v. Eade* (4 Bing., 154), shews that any presumption is *primâ facie* only. In *Shaw v. Picton* (3 B. & C., 715), there were third parties interested. In *Williams v. Griffith* (5 M. & W., 300), the creditor applied payments so as to avoid the operation of the Statute of Limitations. *Mills v. Fowkes* (5 Bing., N. C., 455), is to the same effect as *Williams v. Griffith*. In *Philpott v. Jones* (2 Ad. & Ell., 41) the creditor applied the payment to a debt for spirits supplied in small quantities. In *Nash v. Hodgson* (6 De G. M. & G., 474), there was no evidence of appropriation by the debtor, and it was a creditor's

PALMER v.
SUTHERLAND.

Cockle, C.J.
Lutwyche, J.

suit for administration. In *Re Medew's Trust* (26 Beav., 592), there was a banking account, and the construction of a covenant was involved. In *Beale v. Caddick* (2 H. & N., 326), there was a banking account, and evidence of appropriation. It seems to us. therefore, that with the possible exception of banking accounts, the law does not interfere with the appropriation, unless in cases of death or bankruptcy of the parties, or of change of parties, or, in short, except in the cases in which third parties or their rights are affected by the transactions between the debtor and creditor. In such cases the law will interfere in the appropriation. The present is not the case of a banking account, neither will the rights of third parties be affected by the manner in which the appropriation is made, as between the parties to this action; the creditor (the defendant in this suit) does not appear to have made any appropriation inconsistent with that he wished to have made at the trial, and we know of no rule rendering it obligatory on him to apply the sum in question to the earliest debt. What we have said has, of course, no reference to those cases in which an appropriation binding as between debtor and creditor may be inferred from the transactions between them. In such cases the law does not interfere with the creditor's right of appropriation, though, the right once exercised, it may restrain him from capriciously receding from the appropriation. The rule will be discharged.

Rule discharged.

R. v. ARCHIBALD.

Crown case reserved—Voluntary confession—Evidence—Offer of pardon—Caution.

1869.
7th December.

Cockle, C. J.
Lutwyche, J.

A. who had been arrested as an accessory before the fact to a murder was informed by the lock-up keeper that there was a reward offered and a free pardon, to any one but the murderer, to any person giving information which would lead to the apprehension of the murderer. A. said he had intended to tell the Police Inspector what he knew on his arrest, and the lock-up keeper replied that he should have done so, as it would have been better for himself. A. then, at his own request, saw the Police Inspector, and said he wished to make a statement. The inspector then took A. before a magistrate, and both the inspector and the magistrate warned A. that any statement made by him might be given in evidence against him. A. then made a statement, and when the same was about half completed the magistrate told him that the evidence was not being received as Queen's Evidence. A. completed the statement.

Held that the statement was not induced by the offer of reward or pardon, and being voluntary was rightly admitted against the prisoner.*

R. v. Rosier (Phillips Ev., 414), approved.

R. v. Blackburn (6 Cox C. C., 333) distinguished.

CROWN CASE reserved by Mr. Justice Lutwyche, on the trial of Alexander Archibald at the Rockhampton Circuit Court, in October last, for being an accessory before the fact to the murder of Patrick Halligan, by George Palmer and John Williams.

Pring, A. G., and *Griffith*, for the Crown.

Blake, Q. C., for the prisoner.

The case stated was as follows:—" In the course of the trial, the Attorney-General tendered, on behalf of the Crown, a statement made by the prisoner in the presence of a magistrate of the territory, which statement was taken down in writing in the presence of the magistrate and the prisoner, and was afterwards read over to the prisoner and signed by him. An objection was raised to the admissibility of this document, on the ground that it was made after a promise had been given to the prisoner, and while he was under arrest, but I over-ruled the objection, and allowed the statement to go to a jury, reserving, at the request of the prisoner's advocate, for the opinion of the Supreme Court, this question of law : Was the statement properly received in evidence or not ? On the night of the

*See 58 Vic., No. 2, s. 10.

R. v. ARCHIBALD. 12th May last, at a public meeting of the inhabitants of Rockhampton,

Cockle, C.J.
Lutwyche, J

held at the Union Hotel Theatre, the Police Magistrate of Rockhampton received a telegram purporting to have been despatched by
the Colonial Secretary, in which a reward of £300 was offered for
any information that would lead to the apprehension or conviction of
the murderer or murderers of Patrick Halligan, and a free pardon to
the accomplice not actually the murderer. It did not appear that the
prisoner, who was arrested the same night about 9 p.m., at the Lean
Creek Hotel, three miles from Rockhampton, was at the meeting;
but, after his arrest, and while he was in the lock-up, be was told by
the lock-up keeper that there was a reward offered and a free pardon
to any person not actually the murderer. The prisoner said that he
had a mind to tell Mr. Elliott (Sub-Inspector of Police) when he was
arrested, and the lock-up keeper replied that he should have done so,
as it would have been better for himself. The prisoner then said
that he would tell Mr. Elliott all that he knew about it. The prisoner
soon afterwards saw Mr. Elliott and said. "I was coming in to tell
you about it, but I was waiting until the meeting should be over, and
a reward offered, as I wished you to get the reward." The prisoner
next told Mr. Elliott that he wished to make a statement. Mr. Elliott
took the prisoner before Mr. Murray, the Police Magistrate of
Springsure, and Chief Inspector of Police of the Northern District,
and said to the prisoner: "Do you know that he is a magistrate?
Do you wish to make a statement?" The prisoner said that he knew
Mr. Murray, and that he did wish to make a statement. Mr. Elliott
said "whatever you say will be taken down in writing, and given in
evidence against you." The prisoner said "All right," or "Oh! very
well," and Mr. Murray then repeated the caution, saying, "Now
Archibald, be cautious what you say, as it will be taken down in
writing and may be used against you on your trial." The prisoner
said "All right, I understand what I am about." Mr. Murray, in
giving his evidence, deposed that when the statement was about half
completed he told the prisoner to bear in mind that the statement
was not being accepted as Queen's Evidence, and that the judge would
have to decide that question; but the Sergeant of the Police, who
was engaged in reducing the prisoner's statement into writing,
deposed that he did not hear Mr. Murray say anything about Queen's
Evidence, and that it could not have been said without his hearing it.
Nothing was said either by or to the prisoner after he had been

brought before Mr. Murray about a pardon or a reward. The statement which was given in evidence contained admissions tending
strongly to show the guilt of the prisoner, and he was found guilty
and sentenced to death, but remains in Rockhampton gaol pending
the decision of the Supreme Court on the question of law above
stated."

R. v. ARCHIBALD.

Cockle, C.J.
Lutwyche, J

Blake contended that the mere knowledge by the prisoner that
a reward and free pardon had been offered by the Government for
the discovery of any person, who had not actually committed the
murder, would not be sufficient to render his confession inadmissible;
but if it was shewn, in addition, that the knowledge had operated on the
prisoner's mind in making the confession, then it would be rendered
inadmissible: *R. v Boswell* (C. & M. 584, and 3 Russell on Crimes,
373) ; *R. v. Blackburn and others* (6 Cox. 333). In Archibald's
case it was shewn that he had the knowledge, and that it had operated
on his mind, and the caution he had received was immaterial. The
prisoner may have said to himself : " If I don't make this confession
I cannot benefit from it ; I will run the chance of it being used against
me." The caution might not have removed the state of mind under
which Archibald was induced to make the statement. He might not
have believed the caution. He was told of the proclamation, and
immediately expressed the wish to make a confession. He was in the
very position of a person to whom the proclamation was directed, being
cognizant of the crime, but not having committed it. Would anyone
say that the proclamation had not operated very strongly on the
prisoner's mind ?

[LUTWYCHE, J. I have no doubt it would. I hope that in all
future proclamations accessories before the fact will be expressly
excepted from the offer of pardon or reward.]

It was evident that the caution was not sufficient to remove the
impression from the prisoner's mind produced by the proclamation, and
it was reasonable to say that the making of the confession was the
very thing that would have entitled him to the pardon offered. If he
had said one word about his statement being secured as evidence he
must have been discharged, as his case would then be that of *R. v.
Blackburn.* There was, however, no substantial difference between
the two. The question was . " Was the evidence purely voluntary ?"
It was not purely voluntary if there had been anything to influence
the prisoner, such as the proclamation in this case.

D

R. v. ARCHIBALD.   . *Pring, A. G*, for the Crown. The case of *R. v. Boswell* had been
Cockle, C.J.   fully distinguished in the subsequent case of *R. r. Dingley* (1 C. & K.
Lutwyche, J.   637), which was particularly applicable to the present case. In *R. v.
Dingley* a caution had been given, but not in *R. v. Boswell*, and in the
former the confession was held admissible. In Archibald's case he was
twice told that his statement would be used against him, and no promise
whatever was made to him, and the caution was given not by a person
not having authority, but by a justice of the peace. In *Boswell's
Case* the statement was rendered inadmissible on the express ground
that it was made on an inducement held out by an authorised person.
The present case differed entirely from that. Not only was no
inducement held out by an authorised person, but there was evidence
that he was distinctly cautioned by an authorised person, not only once,
but twice, and told there was no hope that his statement would be
secured as Queen's evidence. It would not do to say that the mere
knowledge of a reward having been offered operated to such an extent
on the prisoner's mind that the impression could not have been got
rid of by a twice-repeated caution. The prisoner did not intimate at
the time that he made the statement that the offer of pardon and
reward had operated on his mind with respect to his own position ; but
he told Mr. Elliott that he made the statement in order to enable him,
Elliott, to get the reward. In the case of *R. v. Clewes* (4 C. & P.
221), an absolute inducement had been given, a hope of pardon held
out ; but the hope was destroyed, and the confession held to be
admissible. If the learned counsel for the prisoner was right in
his argument, the mere knowledge of a free pardon having been offered
must, *per se*, be held to operate on a prisoner's mind, notwithstanding
repeated cautioning. In *Blackburn's Case* a caution was given, but a
distinction between that and Archibald's was : that in the former there
had been something more than a simple knowledge of pardon offered
on the part of the prisoner. It was shown that he had apparently a
notion that he would be received as Queen's evidence. There had
been referred to at the trial the cases of *R. v. Rosier* and *R v Lingate*
(Phillips on Evidence, 414). These two cases went to shew that a caution
given subsequently to an offer of reward or pardon was sufficient to
efface such offer. In the case of *R. v. Howes* (3 Russell, 384), the
prisoner, previous to making a statement, was told that it might do him
good ; but it was subsequently held to be admissible against him.
Counsel also referred to *R. v. Berrigan* (3 Russell, 376).

Blake, in reply, contended that Archibald's case was entirely different from any cited by his learned friend. In those cases, out of the three in which an inducement was held out, in two it was held out by constables, and in the third, by a coroner, and it was afterwards negatived by a magistrate, when the Court held that the caution of the latter was sufficient to efface any impression received by the prisoner from what the coroner said. It was not to be supposed that Archibald would necessarily place much reliance on the assertion of Mr. Murray or Mr. Elliott that the confession would be used against him. They were not in a position to say whether or not it would have been used as evidence against the prisoner. The proclamation was issued by the Governor of the Colony through the Government, and Mr. Murray and Mr. Elliott could not interfere.

COCKLE, C. J. *Blackburn's* case certainly goes a very great way. It appears that the prisoner was told, before he would say anything, that his statement would be used against him. That statement was tendered as evidence to the presiding judge, Mr. Justice Talfourd, and rejected by him, after consultation by Mr. Justice Williams, on the ground that it appeared that the prisoner, in making it, had a notion that he would be received as Queen's evidence. We should, of course, give every consideration to cases decided by eminent judges, but we are also bound to exercise judgment of our own in the matter. It must be remembered that, in these mixed cases of law and fact, it is almost impossible to lay down any rule that can be applied with certainty and definitely in all cases. We must, therefore, look in this case to the words used, and to the circumstances of the case, as disclosed in the learned judge's report. The prisoner was indicted as an accessory before the fact to a murder alleged to have been committed by two other persons. He was apprehended, and, when in custody, the lock-up keeper told him that a reward and free pardon had been offered to any person not actually the murderer. We ought not to interpret this offer as being addressed so directly to the prisoner as to lead him to think that it was a special offer to him, for at the time the number of persons who had been engaged in the transaction was uncertain. On being informed of the offer, prisoner said that he had a mind to tell Mr. Elliott when he was arrested, and the lock-up keeper replied that he should have done so, as it would have been better for himself. We may regard the alleged inducement in a double point of view—first, as an inducement arising from the offer of reward and pardon, and second, as an inducement from the

(Right margin notes:) R. *v.* ARCHIBALD

Cockle, C.J.
Lutwyche, J.

R. v. ARCHIBALD.
Cockle, C.J.
Lutwyche, J.

lock-up keeper himself. These words of the lock-up keeper may be interpreted as meaning that it would have been better for the prisoner had he told sooner, or as a merely formal continuation of the conversation, or as an expression of opinion that he was too late in making his statement. On seeing Mr. Elliott, the prisoner's words seemed to be rather an excuse for making his statement so late, and it is possible that the interpretation put by him on the lock-up keeper's words was, that it was too late. If this is to be regarded as an inducement of either kind, I think if the prisoner had then and there told all he had to tell to Mr. Elliott, that his statement ought not to have been admitted in evidence, and my learned brother has already intimated the same opinion. But he did not then and there make a statement to Elliott. Elliott took him at once before a magistrate, and, on his saying that he wished to make a statement, told him that whatever he said would be taken down in writing, and given in evidence against him. The learned counsel for the prisoner seemed to have abandoned the ground that the prisoner confessed on the strength of any inducement held out by the lock-up keeper, but argued on the ground of the inducement of the reward and pardon. I shall examine the matter, therefore, with reference to that ground. I think there can be no doubt that, if the prisoner made this statement under the reasonable belief that in doing so, he was either making it as a witness for the Crown, or doing something preliminary to becoming a witness for the Crown, then, on the strength of the recorded cases and general ground of jurisprudence and public policy, this statement should be excluded; because, if once the notion get abroad that offers by the Government of reward and pardon are to be used as snares for admissions and confessions, they will fail as an inducement for confessions. We must, therefore, look to whether the prisoner had reasonable grounds for believing that he was acting in the capacity of a witness for the Crown. To say that he acted under the influence of hope or fear would not, I think, cause the exclusion of this statement; because most statements made in criminal cases are made under such influences. They were to consider whether Archibald made the statement under a reasonable belief that he did so as a witness, or preparatory to becoming so. There was nothing in the demeanour of Elliott calculated to inspire the prisoner with such a belief. He does not invite him to a confession, but takes him before a magistrate, puts questions to him which do not imply a very inviting demeanour, and tells him that what he

says will be taken down and used as evidence against him. These
words were not consistent with the making an impression that
Archibald was to be treated as a witness. The words used by
Murray were stronger still. He said to Archibald " Be cautious what
you say, as it will be taken down in writing, and may be used against
you at your trial." Witnesses are not generally placed on their
trial, and Archibald's object in making the confession was to avoid
being tried. One would think that these words would have been
sufficient to raise grave doubts in Archibald's mind as to whether,
when making this statement, he did so as a witness. I think,
therefore, we must take it that there is sufficient evidence to
show that any reasonable impression of Archibald that he was to be
taken as a witness must have been effaced from his mind. In the
case of *R. v. Rosier*, the prisoner having been told that it would be
better to confess, asked a magistrate if it would be better, and he
replied that he could not say that it would. The subsequent
confession was admitted. What the magistrate said there amounted
to this " what you say, if you say anything, may endanger you."
In that case the judges were unanimous in holding that the
confession was admissible in evidence, on the ground that the
magistrate's answer was sufficient to efface any impression that the
constable might have raised. The case of *R. v. Lingate* is to the
same effect. For these reasons I am of opinion that Archibald's
statement must be deemed to have been voluntary, that it was
properly admitted in evidence, and consequently that the conviction
must be confirmed.

    LUTWYCHE, J. We have to consider how far the promise of
pardon operated on the mind of Archibald, so as to induce him to make
the statement. In the first place, it is to be observed that it does not
appear he was present at the meeting when the telegram, purporting
to be from the Colonial Secretary, was read, and that he received information of that fact from the lock-up keeper, a person who might have been
telling him, for purposes of his own, an untrue story. If the statement
had been made on such an untrue story it would have, consequently, been
inadmissible. But, as the case stands, we must take it that, though
the promise was made by the Colonial Secretary, the prisoner had no
better knowledge of the fact than that obtained from the lips of a
lock-up keeper, a person in a very inferior position. Then, how far
does this promise operate on the prisoner's mind? When Elliott
goes in and sees him, he says : " I was coming in to tell you about it,

R. v. ARCHIBALD.

Cockle, C. J.
Lutwyche, J.

R. v. ARCHIBALD. but I was waiting until the meeting would be over, and a reward

Cockle, C. J.
Lutwyche, J.

offered, as I wished you to get it." Not a word there about a pardon. So far, therefore, there is no affirmative evidence of the operation of the promise of pardon on the prisoner's mind. Being taken by Mr. Elliott before Mr. Murray, he is at once told by the former: " Whatever you say will be taken down in writing and given in evidence against you." Now, here was a person, in a superior position to the lock-up keeper, who gives him that direct warning, and that warning was repeated by Mr. Murray in still more precise terms, as follows :—"Now, Archibald, be cautious what you say, as it will be taken down in writing, and may be used against you at your trial." That, to my mind, would have been quite sufficient to have effaced any impression, if any such had been created, that he could obtain a pardon from the Crown. But, further, he was distinctly informed before the statement was completed, when it was half completed, that it was not being accepted as Queen's evidence, and that the judge would have to decide that question. There was affirmative testimony that he was so informed, and, although the constable who took down the prisoner's statement says that he did not hear it, and that, if said, he must have heard it, that proves little, for he may not have recollected that the words were used, or may not have gathered their purport. Unless we are to go to the length of saying that, after a reward has been offered by the Crown, no caution, however strong and precise in its terms, would be sufficient to prevent a prisoner's statement being used in evidence against him, I think we must hold that, in this case, the statement was properly received. *Blackburn's* case certainly goes a great way, but, the distinction is that there the judges came to the conclusion that there was affirmative evidence of an impression on the prisoner's mind that he would be received as Queen's evidence. Here there is no such affirmative evidence, but it appears that such an idea was distinctly negatived. I prefer to rest my judgment on *Rosier's* case, which was a decision of a Full Court, and appears to me to be most consistent with true principles. I think the conviction should be affirmed.

Conviction affirmed.

GOLDSMITH v. ROCHE.

Cattle Stealing Prevention Act (17 Vic., No. 3), s. 5—Detention of a horse—Absence of stealing—Limitation—Practice—Supplementing depositions by affidavits.

A prohibition was granted to restrain further proceedings on an order for the restitution of a horse, under s. 3 of 17 Vic., No. 3, no evidence having been adduced that the horse was stolen, or stolen within twelve months of the commencement of the proceedings.

Affidavits are not admissible to supplement the depositions as to what took place before justices.

Quaere, whether s. 3 of 17 Vic., No. 3 is a penal section.

[In Banco].
1869.
17th Dec.
1870.
16th March.

Cockle, C. J.
Lutwyche, J.

MOTION to make absolute a rule *nisi* for a prohibition restraining G. W. Eliott, P.M., H. T. Plews, and J. Wonderley, J.J.P., from further proceeding on an order, dated 19th November, 1869, whereby Frederick William Roche was ordered to deliver up a horse to Edward Goldsmith, who had laid an information under s. 3 of *The Cattle Stealing Prevention Act of 1853.*

On 7th September, 1869, Roche appeared at the Police Court, Dalby, to answer a complaint preferred against him by Goldsmith for the unlawful detention of a horse, alleged to be the property of the latter, when the summons was dismissed. On 16th November Roche was served with another summons, issued on the information of Goldsmith, for the restitution to him by Roche of the same horse, under s. 3 of 17 Vic., No. 3, and alleged that the horse in dispute had been stolen from Highfields, and found in Roche's possession, but did not charge Roche or any other person with the stealing. From the depositions it appeared that the horse in dispute was claimed by Roche and Goldsmith. The latter deposed to having purchased it in 1867 from one Ballard. Roche was not examined; but one Wilkie deposed that he had bred the horse, and sold him to one Robinson, who subsequently delivered the horse to him for Roche, and that Robinson had given up the horse in consequence of being unable to meet a debt due by him to Roche. There was no evidence that the horse had been stolen at any time, though there was evidence of a belief that it had been stolen.

The grounds for the rule *nisi* were:—(1) That it appeared by the evidence that the defendant set up a *bona fide* claim of title·

GOLDSMITH
v.
ROCHE.

Cockle, C.J.
Lutwyche, J.

(2) That the title to property being in question, the justices had no jurisdiction. (3) That the justices wrongfully refused to hear evidence of a previous adjudication in respect of the same subject matter. (4) That there was no evidence of the stealing of the horse, the subject matter of the information. (5) That there was no evidence of the stealing of the horse within twelve months before the date of the information. (6) That there was no evidence of the stealing of the horse within twelve months before the date of the information, or of the commencement of the proceedings, or of the order. (7) That the conviction or order was against the evidence.

When the rule *nisi* was granted, leave was given to file additional affidavits by Mr. Ocock, and other affidavits, provided they be filed four clear weeks before the day of return, including copies of proceedings in both cases.

Affidavits were read, including those of Messrs. Eliott and Wonderley, who denied that any evidence of the previous case heard at Dalby was tendered for Roche.

Griffith moved the rule absolute.

Handy, for the respondent, showed cause.

The following authorities were cited:—*R. v. Dodson* (9 Ad.& Ell. 704); *Ex parte Rusden*; *Ex parte Preston* (Wilkinson's Magistrate, p p. 97, 98); *Ex parte Ivill*, 2 N. S. W. S. C. R. (L.), 92.

COCKLE, C. J. It does not appear on the depositions that there was satisfactory evidence before the justices that the horse was stolen, and stolen within a year of the commencement of the proceedings, and on that ground alone the prohibition must be granted. It may be there was more evidence than appears on the face of the depositions, but it would be dangerous to allow depositions to be supplemented by affidavits of what took place before magistrates. The depositions alone must be our source of knowledge of what took place before the magistrates. With regard to the subject of a claim of right, we are not satisfied that the section under which the information was laid is a penal one. Moreover, satisfied or not, there being nothing in the depositions to show that this claim was tendered, the question raised is utterly immaterial, except so far as regards costs. I think this rule should be made absolute, but without costs.

LUTWYCHE, J. concurred.

Solicitors for Applicant: *Wilson and Bunton.*

Solicitor for Respondent: *Doyle, agent for Hamilton.*

THORN v. HOWIE.

Impounding Act of 1863 (27 Vic., No. 22), s. 52—Complaint dismissed with costs—Appeal—Special case—Mandamus.

[In Banco.]
1870.
16th March.

Cockle, C. J.
Lutwyche, J.

Where a complaint under the *Impounding Act of 1863* is dismissed with costs, no appeal lies to the District Court under s. 52 of that Act.

On an appeal to the District Court the Judge refused to hear the appeal, being of opinion that no appeal lay to his Court. At the request of the appellant's counsel he stated a special case.

Held, by the Full Court, that the appellant had mistaken his remedy, and should have gone by mandamus.

SPECIAL CASE stated by the judge of the Western District Court.

The plaintiff, Henry Thorn, summoned the defendants, W. and J. H. Howie, before the Bench of Magistrates at Condamine for a breach of the *Impounding Act of 1863*. On the 12th October, 1869, the Bench, after hearing the case, found for the defendants, dismissing the plaintiff's complaint, with £5 costs against him. The plaintiff gave notice of appeal before Blakeney, D. C. J., and His Honour, sitting at Condamine, refused to hear the appeal, on the ground that it did not lie, no conviction having been made, or penalty inflicted by the magistrates, and costs only having been awarded by them. At the request of the appellant's counsel, His Honour reserved the following point for the decision of the Supreme Court:—Does s. 52 of the *Impounding Act* give to the plaintiff, Thorn, the right of appeal from a dismissal of his complaint, where costs only have been awarded against him?

Bramston, A. G., for the appellant, submitted that the costs against the plaintiff were recoverable by distress or imprisonment under the Statute, which could not properly be construed to debar him from appeal in such a case.

Griffith, for the respondents, cited *Beswick v. Boffey*, 23 L. J., Ex. 89.

COCKLE, C. J. The Court has no jurisdiction. Our judgment must be final. We can only affirm, reverse, or amend a decision. As the matter is submitted to us, we can give no judgment which will determine the dispute. There is nothing for us to go on. The appeal is dismissed with costs.

THORN *v.*
HOWIE.

Cockle, C.J.
Lutwyche, J.

LUTWYCHE, J. The appellant has mistaken his remedy. Instead of asking the learned District Court Judge to state the case he has, he should have applied for a *mandamus*.

Appeal dismissed.

[IN EQUITY.]
1870.
25th, 28th, 31st
March.
4th April.

Cockle, C. J.

MISKIN *v.* MEIKLEJOHN.

Mortgage—Bill of Sale—Default—Insolvency—Discharge of Liability—Injunction to restrain sale—Parol evidence admissible to explain written instrument—Evidence on application for interlocutory injunction

On a motion for an injunction to restrain a mortgagee from selling certain mortgaged premises, of which he had taken possession for breach of covenants contained in a mortgage and a bill of sale, extrinsic evidence was tendered to show the nature of the transaction. *Held*, that in the absence of fraud such evidence was not admissible to interpret the deeds, and that by strict interpretation it must be assumed that the advance was made as alleged, and that as the liability of the mortgagors had not been discharged, the motion should be refused.

The nature of the evidence on an application for an interlocutory injunction explained.

Fraill v. Ellis, (22 L. J. Ch. 467) distinguished.

MOTION by plaintiff, as Official Assignee in the Insolvent Estate of Cooper and Jones, of Maryborough, to restrain the defendant, John Meiklejohn, from selling or disposing of certain premises at Maryborough, known as the Union Saw Mills, lately in the possession of the insolvents, comprised in a mortgage and certain effects, over which the insolvents had given a bill of sale, and from receiving any of their book debts.

In the beginning of 1869, Gladwell and Greathead, timber merchants, were indebted to the Australian Joint Stock Bank, for which indebtedness Meiklejohn, a sugar manufacturer, was surety. To secure him against loss, he held security over the premises and effects. Cooper and Jones were then lessees of the mill. Gladwell and Greathead became insolvent, and it was found necessary that the property should be sold; and Cooper and Jones being desirous of purchasing it for £2,350, and not being able to furnish all the necessary cash, waited upon the General Manager of the bank in Sydney, and asked him to give them an advance of £1,800, by discounting a bill with a good name to it.   The defendant's name was mentioned and approved.   Defendant agreed to assist the insolvents (Cooper and Jones), by lending his name, on obtaining security of the property purchased.   On 7th May, the transaction was completed. Defendant made a promissory note for £1,800 in insolvents' favour, which note was endorsed by the latter and by them handed to the manager of the bank at Maryborough, to be discounted next day; they at the same time handing him a cheque for £1,723 to meet Gladwell and Greathead's liability, for which the defendant was surety.   The bill was discounted, and the proceeds, £1,707, were placed to the insolvents' credit, the cheque being placed to their debit. On the same day, two mortgages were executed, between the insolvents of the one part and the defendant of the other.   By the first, the lands on which the mills were erected, were mortgaged by insolvents to the defendant, for the sum of £1,800 and interest; the second was a bill of sale over the mills, stock-in-trade, machinery, timber, etc., to further secure to defendants the sum of £1,800 and interest. Both the mortgage and the bill of sale contained a proviso for redemption, on the money being paid in six months, on or before 7th November, 1869; and, in both it was alleged, that the sum of £1,800 had been advanced by defendant to insolvents.   In both also, there was a covenant for insurance of the premises.   In the mortgage, the insolvents covenanted to keep the premises insured for £600, in the name of the mortgagee (the defendant); in the bill of sale, the insurance was for £1,100, over the premises, stock-in-trade, plant, etc., and was to be effected in the mortgagee's name, in some insurance office approved by him.   The mortgagee was to hold the policy in each case and was to be at liberty, in default of the insolvents insuring, to effect the insurance himself at their charge.   The bill of sale contained the following proviso: "And it is hereby declared and agreed by and between the parties hereto, that, after default shall be made in payment of the said sum of £1,800 and interest, or any part thereof, respectively, contrary to the tenour and effect of the afore-said proviso, or, if default be made by the said mortgagors in performance or observance of any of the covenants, conditions or agreements herein contained, or, if the said mortgagors shall become insolvent, or threaten to take the benefit of any insolvency law, or

call a meeting of their creditors, or make any assignment for benefit
of creditors, or do any other act, matter, or thing which the said
mortgagee may believe prejudicial to his security, it shall be lawful
for the said mortgagee, immediately on the happening of any of the
aforesaid events, or at any time thereafter, to enter into possession
of the premises, plant, etc." The insolvents swear, that not a shilling
of the money ever passed and not a word was ever said about interest.
The note became due on the 10th November and was dishonoured.
The bank manager, however, agreed to renew on bills with defendant's
name, at three and six months. On 12th November, two more promissory notes were made by defendant in insolvents' favour, one at
three months for £300, and one at six months for £1,500, and were
indorsed by insolvents. Cooper at the same time, for the firm, handed
the bank manager a cheque for £1,800, and on the proceeds of the
promissory notes being placed to insolvents' credit, the cheque was
placed to their debit. Possession was taken under the bill of sale on
21st December, and Cooper and Jones were adjudicated insolvent on
5th January, 1870. The policies of insurance on the premises
existing at the date of the mortgage, expired on 14th November and
the insolvents proposed to renew the same, whereof the defendant
had notice, but suggested to them not to do so, but to insure in
another Company. While they were making the necessary arrangements for so doing, the seizure was made. At the date of such
seizure, they were able to meet their engagements. The defendant's
case is, that the bank acted for him, and him alone, and that at the
time of the execution of the securities, the promissory note was
handed by him to the bank manager, who handed him (the defendant)
£1,800, who handed the same to Cooper, who handed the same to the
bank manager to pay Gladwell and Greathead's debt; and that, by
these means, cash was actually advanced to insolvents. The bills
were renewed in November by the bank for him—not for insolvents,
and he never suggested insurance in another Company, as alleged by
the insolvents. He seized because of the breach of insurance,
because of the non-payment of interest, and because the bank
manager told him that insolvents' credit was stopped at the bank It
was also alleged by the defendant, that at the time of the execution
of the deeds, it was agreed that the securities should be handed over
to the bank, and that of this the insolvents had knowledge, but they
denied any such knowledge.

MISKIN v.
MEIKLEJOHN.

Cockle, C.J.

The questions raised were—Whether the bill of sale and mortgage were ever a security for the defendant's contingent liability on the promissory notes; whether, if it was a security for the first promissory note, it remained as a security for the due payment of those made in November; whether, if they remained a security at the time of seizure, there had been such a breach, as entitled defendant to enter; whether, supposing the seizure legal, the plaintiff was not entitled to an injunction preventing the defendant selling, his bills not being due. Questions were also raised, that the true nature of the transaction was not correctly stated in the mortgage and could be shewn by parol evidence; and that the defeasance, not being comprised in the mortgages and registered with them under the *Mercantile Act*, were, in fact, unregistered and were void.

Lilley, Q. C., A G., and *Griffith* for the plaintiff.
Blake, Q C., and *Harding* for the defendant.

COCKLE, C. J.   There is a preliminary point of practice, a consideration of which, however, does not affect my decision in this case. It is, that I think the Court should not grant an injunction, unless on a case apparent on the face of the bill. That being disposed of, the question arises whether the evidence discloses such a case as would, at the hearing, induce the granting of a perpetual injunction   Unless there are reasonable grounds for supposing a perpetual injunction would then be granted, it will be the duty of the Court now to refuse an interlocutory injunction. One point to which the plaintiff's counsel have particularly addressed themselves, was as to the admissibility of the explanatory evidence. Is evidence affecting this contract to be admitted ?   The rules of evidence are the same at law and at equity. In both a double system prevails. At the hearing of suits, or the trial of causes and issues, certain rules of evidence prevail. At the hearing of motions, rules *nisi*, and other interlocutory proceedings, looser rules of evidence prevail, the stricter being relaxed very beneficially to the suitors.

At a final hearing, primary evidence of a written instrument must be given. At an interlocutory hearing, secondary evidence is admissible. But there are certain rules, which, being rules of evidence, are also rules of interpretation, and which it is incumbent on the Judge to apply for himself. The rules of interpretation are not relaxed on the hearing of interlocutory motions, for there can be no relaxation of such rules. These rules must be applied to the present instruments. With regard to the admissibility of the evidence at Equity, great

stress was laid by plaintiff's counsel on the case of *Fraill v. Ellis* (22
L. J. Ch. 467.) But there was nothing there to warrant the Court
in allowing extrinsic evidence to contradict, alter, supplement, or
limit the action of the deeds. The Master of the Rolls, in giving
judgment said :—"On the first point there is conflict and contradiction
of testimony. It is said, that the form of the deed concluded the
question, and that the agreement was to take £150 and a bill of
exchange for £300. But with that I cannot concur, since in
accordance with the cases it is lawful to bring before the Court the
real nature of the transaction." In accordance with what cases?
Why, presumably the cases cited by the party seeking to import
the exceptional sort of evidence into the matter. Those cases were
Beadles v. Burch (10 Sim. 332) ; and *Teed v. Carruthers* (2 Y. & C.
C. C 32). But in the first there was fraud, when, whether at law
or in Equity, extrinsic evidence is admissible. The second case did
not turn on the admissibility of extrinsic evidence to affect the interpretation of a contract, but on the meaning of words used in a
receipt. The case of *Fraill v. Ellis* may, therefore, be distinguished
on the ground of fraud. There is a case at Common Law, clearly
shewing that when that which, if it appeared by parol evidence,
would ·be latent ambiguity, appeared on the face on an instrument as
a patent ambiguity. then the patent ambiguity was capable of being
explained by parol evidence. (*Doe d George Gord v. Needs*, 2 M.
& W. 129). In that case there were two persons of the name of
George Gord, and the question was, to which a bequest had been
made. Strange to say, there were two of that name in the will.
There was a patent ambiguity on the face of the will, and the Court
held parol evidence admissible. That case, therefore, furnished no
exception to the rules regulating the interpretation of written
instruments of extrinsic evidence. With regard to another
point raised by plaintiff's counsel, as to whether the deed was
illegal, whether it was void for non-compliance with a statutory
requisition, the contract itself seems to represent the transaction
as both parties intended it to be. What must the contract
be taken to mean? What it said; that a certain sum of
money was to be paid on a certain day, with interest. Fraud being
out of the question, and looking at the facts by strict interpretation,
it is to be assumed, that the advance of £1,800 was made. How the
money was advanced, is perfectly immaterial. It has been said, that

MISKIN v.
MEIKLEJOHN.

Cockle, C. J.

the true consideration was the giving of a note, that that note had been paid, that it had gone, and with it the mortgage and bill of sale. I have no reason to think, that that was the real nature of the transaction; and it was not the contract. That liability was never discharged. The twenty-second paragraph of the plaintiff's bill negatived the construction that, by the discharge of the promissory note, the securities went :—"The said cheque, given by the said firm of Cooper and Jones, in payment of the said promissory note in the manner aforesaid, was paid out of the proceeds of two several promissory notes bearing date the 12th November, for the respective amounts of £300 and £1,500, payable respectively three and six months after date, made by the defendant in favor of and delivered to the said Cooper and Jones, and by them discounted, and which said promissory notes are still current and outstanding." Then, has there been a breach ? With regard to the insurance, the insolvents' version was contradicted by the defendant. On the subject of default, *Albert v. Grosvenor Insurance Company* (L. R. 3 Q. B. 123), has been cited. The present case does not go as far as that In the present it can hardly be said there was a consideration. But, cases may arise, in which consent would remove default. The injunction must be refused, costs to be costs in the cause.

Motion refused.

Solicitors for plaintiffs : *Roberts and Hart.*
Solicitor for defendant : *Macpherson.*

HAWKES v. CORFIELD.

District Courts Act of 1867 (31 Vict. No. 30), s. s. 47, 48, 49—   [In Banco.]
Joinder of Causes of Action—Jurisdiction—Aquiescence. .   1870.
          27th May.
The plaintiff sued the defendant in a District Court in two actions for wages
and wrongful dismissal, under one agreement. By consent, the actions were   *Cockle, C. J.*
heard together, and judgment given for the plaintiff on both. On an application   *Lutwyche, J.*
for a *prohibition*
Held, that the causes of action were separate and distinct, and the rule
nisi must be refused.

Rule *nisi* calling on Hirst, D. C. J., and John William Hawkes,
plaintiff in the action, to show cause, why a writ of prohibition should
not issue, to restrain them from further proceeding in two judgments obtained by the plaintiff against the defendant, Hawkes, in the
Northern District Court.   In April last, Corfield was summoned at
Bowen in two actions, at the suit of Hawkes, one action being brought
for £154 for wages, and the other for £200 for alleged wrongful
dismissal. Both actions, by consent, were tried together, and were
brought under and founded on an agreement between the parties,
by which Hawkes agreed to manage Clifton Station, Flinders River,
for two years; and Corfield agreed, in consideration of such management, to pay him by way of salary £10 for every 1,000 sheep shorn
annually.   The wages claimed in the first action were alleged to have
accrued under that agreement, and the second action was in respect
of an alleged breach of such agreement.   The jury returned a verdict
for the plaintiff in both actions, in the first for £150, and in the
second for £125.

Griffith, for the defendant, applied for the rule on the ground
of want of jurisdiction in the Court below, there having been only
one cause of action, which could not be split into two.   The point
was not raised at the trial, but want of jurisdiction could not be cured
by acquiescence.   S. S. 47, 48, 49, of *The District Courts Act of 1867*;
Grimbley v. Ackroyd (17 L J. Ex. 157) ; *Wickham v. Lee* (12 Q. B.
521) ; *Briscoe v. Stephens* (2 Bing 213).

The Court refused the rule.   The two causes of action were
distinct and separate, although they arose out of one agreement.

Rule refused.

E

Re SMART, DONKIN & Co.

[IN INSOLVENCY.]
1870.
30th May.
6th June.

Lutwyche, J.

Insolvency Act of 1864 (28 Vic., No. 25), s. s. 24, 33—Petition for adjudication by Member of Partnership Firm—Absence of Partner from Colony—Annulment—Meaning of "Residence."

One of two partners may, during the absence of the other partner, present a petition for the adjudication of the partnership firm.

"Residence" means corporeal presence.

PETITION to annul an adjudication of insolvency.

This was a petition filed by Arthur Frederick Smart, a member of the firm of Smart, Donkin & Co., and certain creditors in the estate, to annul the adjudication of insolvency made against the firm of Smart, Donkin & Co., on the petition of Henry Donkin, the other partner of the firm.

The facts were as follows:—On 22nd April, 1870, Smart and Donkin were carrying on business together as merchants, under the style of Smart, Donkin & Co., and on that day, without the knowledge or consent of Smart, Donkin presented a petition for adjudication of insolvency against the firm, and the firm were adjudged insolvent accordingly.

The petition represented that, on 21st March, 1870, Smart went to the office of the partnership, in Donkin's absence, and without his consent, took into his own custody certain certificates of goods in bond, the property of the partnership, and valued at £1,000; that Smart also took certain promissory notes, partnership property, and had kept them in his possession, Donkin having no control over them; that Smart, since 18th March, had never attended at the office, or in any way assisted Donkin in the management of the business; that he had been applied to by Donkin to return the certificates and promissory notes, but had not done so; that, in consequence, certain partnership promissory notes had been dishonoured; that the petitioner had been informed, and believed, that A. B. Pritchard, lately in the employ of the firm, but dismissed by the petitioner, had offered to sell some of the goods comprised in the certificates at a price considerably under their market value, Pritchard representing that he was acting under authority from Smart, who was in Sydney; that the firm, being unable to meet their engagements, had committed an act of insolvency. The present petitioners (with the exception of A. F. Smart), were creditors of the firm on 22nd April, and were now. On that date, it was alleged, Smart was temporarily absent from the colony. With regard to Smart's absence, it appeared by the affidavits that, on 14th April, he received a telegraphic message from Sydney informing him that his mother, then in Sydney, was dying, and requesting his presence there immediately. He left Brisbane on April 18, taking a return ticket, and intending to return to Brisbane, informing some parties here, that such was his intention. On 21st April he was attacked by a severe disorder of the brain, which confined him to his bed for some time, and from which he had not, on 20th May (the date of filing the affidavit), recovered sufficiently to return to Brisbane, or attend to business. A. B. Pritchard, in his affidavit, denied the statement in Donkin's petition for adjudication, as to his having offered goods comprised in bond certificates at a price considerably under their market value. From another affidavit it appeared that the petitioners claimed to be creditors to a considerably larger extent than the creditors who had yet proved in the estate. To this it was replied that Smart, for some months prior to the adjudication of insolvency, had, by his intemperate habits, injured the credit of the business. The Official Assignee replied that, after careful investigation, he was of opinion, that the estate would not pay 15s. in the £, and that he had disposed of all the stock-in-trade and was now getting in the other assets. The creditors' Assignee replied that on 16th April the firm of Smart, Donkin & Co. had dishonoured a promissory note for £159, and had never paid the same.

Bramston, A. G , and Griffith in support of the petition.

Lilley, Q.C., and Pring, Q.C., shewed cause against it.

The following authorities were cited: *Whithorn v. Thomas*, (Lutwyche 133) ; *Wheaton's International Law* (6th Edition, 394) ; *Udny v. Udny*, L. R. 1. Ap. (Sc.) 442 ; *Nias v. Davis* (4 C. B. 444) ; *Dunstan v. Paterson*, 28 L. J. (C.P.) 97 ; *Kerr v. Haynes*, 29 L. J. (Q.B.) 70 ; *Ex parte Asher* (4 N. S. W. R. 71) ; *Ex parte Bailey*, (5 N. S. W. R. 17) ; *R. v. Brighton* (4 E. & B. 236) ; *Ex parte Mitchell* (14 Ves. 597) ; *Ex parte Hodgkinson* (19 Ves. 291); *Tacole v. Stowe*, 18 L. J. (M.C.) 44 ; *Ex parte Hall* (17 Ves. 862); *Ex parte Bean* (1 De. G. M. & G. 86) ; *Ex parte Bower* (*ib.* 60) ; *Ex parte Johnstone* (4 De. G. & S. 204) ; *Robinson v. Starson*, 6 M. & G. 762; *Massey v. Burton*, 3 Jur. (N.S.) 1130.

Re SMART,
DONKIN & Co.
———
Lutwyche, J.

LUTWYCHE J. This is a petition presented by A. F. Smart, one
of the partners in the firm Thomas Ware Smart and others, to annul
the adjudication of insolvency against the firm, upon the ground that
it was made during the temporary absence of the partner, Smart,
from the colony.   The application is based upon the 33rd section of
The Insolvency Act of 1864.   It was contended that it is not
competent to adjudicate a firm insolvent during the temporary absence
of a partner of the firm, without the consent of the absent partner.
Such was the construction contended for by the Attorney-General.
But it is a well-known rule, in construing an Act of Parliament, that
the Judge must give effect to every word in it.   If the construction
contended for by the Attorney-General was correct, the word partner
would have no meaning whatever.   Sec. 33 reads as follows : "A
petition for adjudication in insolvency against a co-partnership, may
be filed by the majority of such of the partners of such co-partnership,
as are at the time of filing such petition, resident within the colony,
and any partner, or partners, filing such petition, shall file such
statement as above-mentioned and verify the same in like manner, and
shall pay the fees for adjudication, unless the same, or any part
thereof, shall have been remitted by order of a Judge."   Now, it is
clear from the first part of this section, that if there were three
partners in a firm, all present in the colony, it would be competent
for two of them to file a petition in insolvency against the firm,
though without the will or consent of the third partner.   The
question, therefore, is whether it is not also competent for a partner
in a firm of two to file a petition, when he has had no opportunity of
consulting his partner as to the propriety of taking that step.   It
was contended that the partners must be resident.   Mr. Justice
Maule, in *Nias v. Davis,* (4 C. B. 444), in a decision which has
already been quoted in this case, lays down that the word "residence"
has no technical meaning.   It is a word taken from the popular
language of the country, and must be interpreted in connection with
the subject matter of the Act to which it applies.   The object of
this Act, as well as of all bankruptcy statutes, is that, when a firm is
insolvent, the estate should be realised as soon as possible for
the benefit of the general body of creditors.   If the strict interpretation put upon the word by the Attorney-General were carried out,
the result would be, that whenever there were two partners, and one
was absent for a time from the colony, the estate would be wasted.
Execution after execution would be put in, and especially those

creditors residing in another colony would be the greatest sufferers. My opinion, therefore, is that the word "resident" means corporeally present, and I apprehend that this is the sense meant by the Legis- lature, and I will, therefore, dismiss the petition. I would observe, in doing so, that none of the parties presenting the petition will have any cause of complaint. Smart will have no cause of complaint, for it was his act of abstracting from the safe documents and property, worth £1,000, which caused the insolvency of the firm. Moreover, Mr. Smart is still absent from the colony, and has not deposed on affidavit his intention to return. On the other hand, it was said by two deponents that the estate would not pay twenty shillings in the pound, and Mr. Miskin, who was a gentleman well qualified to judge, stated that it would not pay fifteen shillings in the pound. It might be objected that this decision would be empowering a partner in a firm of two partners, if he was displeased in any way and wished to put a stop to the dealings of the firm, to file a petition in insolvency. But the answer to this is obvious. If the other partner could show sufficient cause, this Court could immediately annul the petition of insolvency, and the partner making such statements would be liable for perjury. I can see no injury that will be inflicted on either party by pursuing this course. If the parties wish to take the estate out of insolvency, they can do so, by getting it brought under the arrangements clause. I will, therefore, dismiss the petition without costs, the costs of the official and creditors' assignee to be allowed out of the estate.

Petition dismissed.

Solicitors for petitioners : *Roberts* and *Hart*.

Solicitors for Henry Donkin, the Official Assignee and Creditors' Assignee : *Garrick* and *Lyons*.

In the matter of JOHN LOUDON, DECEASED.

CRIBB'S CLAIM.

[IN BANCO.]
1870.
10th, 11th, 14th,
15th March.
3rd June.
——
Cockle, C. J.
Lutwyche, J.

Will—Administration of Estate—Creditors—Accounts—Appropriation of Payments—Interest—Rests—Counter-claim by Executors—Equity Act of 1867 (31 Vic., No. 18), ss. 113, 114.

In all cases where a debtor and creditor account has been kept between a deceased person and his representatives on the one side, and a creditor claiming against the estate on the other, rests should, in the absence of any special contract, be made at the date of each payment made on account of the estate, and the amount paid in should be appropriated as far as it will go; first, to the discharge of the interest already accrued, if there be interest-bearing items in the account; and secondly, if there be any surplus, towards the extinction of the earliest item in the principal debt, whether it be an interest-bearing item or not.

Executors are entitled, in an administration suit, to set off any counter-claim against a creditor which may have arisen before the date of the Registrar's report.

APPEAL from a decision of the Chief Justice, as Primary Judge in Equity, dismissing a summons to vary, and confirming the Registrar's certificate in the estate.

Griffith for the appellant, Robert Cribb.

Harding for the respondents, the executors of Loudon's will.

The following authorities were cited:—

SS. 113, 114 of *The Equity Act of 1867; Clayton's Case*, 1 Mer. 572, Tudor's L.C. Mer. Law 17, 26; *Mackintosh v. G. W. Railway*, 4 Giff. 683; 11 Jur. (N.S.) 681; *Re Hooper, Bayliss v. Watkins*, 7 L.T. 847, 9 Jur. (N.S.) 570; *Dawkins v. Morton*, 10 W.R. 339; Story S 459 *b.; Re Read, Pierce and Hammond*, 10 L.T. 261.

C. A. V.

3rd June, 1870.

LUTWYCHE, J, delivered the judgment of the Court as follows: This was a motion by way of appeal from a decision of the Chief Justice, which came before the Court last term, and occupied several days. It arose out of a claim made by Robert Cribb against the estate of the late William John Loudon, for £627 7s. 10d. The late Registrar of the Supreme Court, after taking evidence, left behind him memoranda, in the nature of a draft certificate or report, which, at the request of the parties, the Chief Justice treated as a completed document. In this draft certificate or report, the late Registrar laid down the principles on which the accounts should be taken between the parties, and this certificate or report was approved of by the Chief Justice on 19th

July, 1869. The accounts were then referred by the present Registrar to an accountant, whose calculations, verified by affidavit, formed the basis of the certificate given by the present Registrar, on the 26th August, 1869, whereby he certified that nothing was due from the estate to Cribb. On 13th September Mr. Cribb took out a summons to vary the certificate, and on 29th September the Chief Justice confirmed the certificate, and dismissed the summons. From this decision Mr. Cribb appealed, and at the close of elaborate arguments at the Bar, on the hearing of the present motion, it was agreed by counsel on both sides that the Court should be at liberty to deal with the matter as *res integra*, and to decide on all the facts brought before the late Registrar. The members of the Court, in their anxiety to do complete justice between the parties, have accordingly devoted a very large proportion of the time at their disposal for the consideration of deferred judgments to an examination of the evidence taken before the late Registrar, and to the preparation of a series of calculations of their own with the view of testing the accuracy of the calculations which were submitted to the Court on either side during the argument. Having at length formed their own conclusions, the Court, for greater certainty, referred the accounts again to an experienced accountant, after explaining to him personally the principles on which, in their opinion, the accounts should be taken, and pointing out several items in the accounts which they thought required correction. The accountant's certificate, made in pursuance of this reference, corresponds in the final result with the calculation made by the Court. We should rarely be justified, perhaps, having regard to the interests of the general body of the suitors, in undertaking an investigation like that which we have just concluded, as it strictly falls within the duties which devolve upon an officer of the Court; but we are far from regretting the large expenditure of time and labour bestowed upon it, because it enables us to lay down a rule which will be a guide to the officer of the Court in taking accounts in similar cases. We think that the principle for which Mr. Griffith contended is correct, and that in all cases where a debtor and creditor account has been kept between a deceased person and his representatives on the one side, and a creditor claiming against the estate of the deceased on the other, rests should, in the absence of any special contract, be made at the date of each payment made on account of the estate, and that the amount paid in should be appropriated as far as it will go; first to discharge the interest already accrued, if there be interest.

In the matter of
JOHN LOUDON,
Deceased.
CRIBB'S CLAIM.

Cockle, C. J.
Lutwyche, J.

In the matter of
John Loudon,
Deceased.
Cribb's Claim.

Cockle, C. J.
Lutwyche, J.

bearing items in the accounts ; and secondly, if there be any surplus, towards the extinction of the earliest item in the principal debt, whether it be an interest-bearing item or not. We now proceed to apply this rule to the facts of the case. We think that the late Registrar was right in the view which he took of the nature of the contract entered into between Cribb and Loudon on or about March 1st, 1863. It appears to us that Loudon agreed to pay Cribb 12¼ per cent. interest on all advances, but that he did not agree to pay him a commission of 5 per cent. on such advances, nor to pay compound interest. We think that Loudon agreed to pay Cribb a commission of 5 per cent. on all moneys collected by Cribb for Loudon, and 5 per cent. on all sales of land, but that Cribb was not entitled, under the agreement, to receive an additional 5 per cent. as for moneys collected, when he personally received the purchase money, or a portion of the purchase money, for the land sold. But we think that, in the allowance or disallowance of particular items, the late Registrar was not always consistent with himself, and it will be our duty in the course of this judgment to point out some mistakes which he made on both sides of the account, as well as to correct and supply other errors and deficiencies. The series of calculations, based upon different principles, which Mr. Griffith submitted to the Court as part of his argument, we found, with one exception, that marked C, at first sight, adverse to the claim. When obvious errors were corrected, they showed that a larger or smaller balance was due to the estate from Cribb, instead of to Cribb, from the estate. We do not propose, therefore, to examine them in detail, as all the errors which appear in them appear also in the calculation marked C., where, however, after making the necessary deductions for these obvious errors, there still appeared a balance in favour of Cribb   To that balance there was to be added a sum of £15 17s. 11d., the amount of rent overpaid to the executors of Loudon. and interest thereon £1 6s. 7d., as well as £16 18s. 3d. for interest on the 5 per cent. commission for collections, which Cribb might have deducted at the time of their receipt, and which were as much moneys out of his pocket as if they had been advances, and must be regarded as standing in the same category. These sums assist in swelling the aggregate amount of Cribb's claim against the estate, as represented in C , to a grand total of £121 10s. 8d. On the other hand there are various deductions to be made from the items in this account. In the first place, there must be deducted the interest charged on the first item, £20, which was improperly

placed in the interest-bearing column. Next there is an amount of
£39 18s., made up of three different sums of £20 10s., £13 18s., and
£15 10s. charge for commission on advances, but properly disallowed
by the late Registrar. Again, we find a commission—£3—on money
collected from Cookesley, charged twice, commission overcharged
£8 14s. 8d., and an amount of £22 9s. 6d., which must be deducted for
commissions on land sales, charged twice, in the shape of a commission
on moneys collected. The item of £12 14s. for commission on sale
of portion 14, Toombul, which was allowed by the late Registrar, we
think, ought not to be allowed. The sale was never completed, and
£100 was paid by Loudon to be off the bargain, Cribb being an active
and interested agent in procuring the rescission. And we think that
the item of £40, charged for surveying and partially clearing this
portion of land, must go out of the account altogether. The late
Registrar disallowed £20 for the survey, but allowed the charge of
£20 for clearing. We think that he was wrong in the allowance of
this latter charge. We collect from the evidence that the contract
between Cribb and Loudon, in respect to this particular portion of
land, was to the following effect: Loudon was to be charged £110,
without interest, while Cribb was to pay the expenses of surveying
and selling, and after paying Loudon £11 per acre for the land, the
surplus was to be divided equally between them. We do not find a
word about clearing in William Loudon's letter of 19th June, 1865,
and we cannot gather from any other part of the evidence that the
clearing was effected with Mr. Loudon's knowledge or acquiescence.
The general result of all these deductions is shown in the accountant's
certificate, corresponding with our own calculations, as already
observed, and presenting a balance of £46 2s. 10d. in favour of the
estate. There remains only the question of costs. We think Mr.
Cribb had some reason to be dissatisfied with Mr. Bryant's certificate,
inasmuch as he charged him interest on rent which Mr. Cribb never
agreed to pay; but on the other hand he was improperly allowed
£58 12s. 8d. commission on advances. We think that, in future, where
an accountant's services are required by an officer of the Court, it will
be as well to call in the aid of a gentleman who is easily accessible,
and who can receive oral instructions and give oral explanations.
Calculations made by gentlemen located at Rockhampton or Roma
are not likely to advance materially the settlement of a disputed
account. But, returning to the question of the costs of this appeal,
we think that the executors had much greater reason to be dissatisfied

In the matter of
JOHN LOUDON,
Deceased.
CRIBB'S CLAIM.

Cockle, C. J.
Lutwyche, J.

In the matter of
JOHN LOUDON,
Deceased.
CRIBB'S CLAIM.

Cockle, C. J.
Lutwyche, J.

with Mr. Cribb's claim than he had to object to Mr. Bryant's certificate; and as Mr. Cribb has failed in substantiating his claim, we are of opinion, on the authority of *Hatch v. Scarles* (2 Sim. and Giff. 157); and *Geomars v. Haynes*, (24 Beav. 157), that Mr. Cribb must pay the executors their costs of opposing this motion.

One point was made during the argument, which, although not much pressed, we think it right to notice, as our decision will settle the practice for the future. It was urged by Mr. Griffith that the account ought to have stopped at the death of Loudon, and that no counter claim by his executors ought to be allowed. But, as it appears from the language of Lord Justice Turner, in *Thomas v. Griffith* (2 De G. F. and J. 564), that the practice now is to admit all creditors to claim, whose debts have become due before the report, we think the executors are equally entitled to set off any counter claim against the creditor which may have arisen before that period.

Appeal dismissed.

Solicitor for Appellant: *Macpherson.*

Solicitors for Respondents: *Little and Browne.*

TOUGH v. AUSTRALASIAN STEAM NAVIGATION COMPANY.

Carrier—Negligence—Deck Cargo—Contract, construction of.

1870.
18th March.
6th July.

Cockle, C. J.
Lutwyche, J.

The defendants, a shipping company, received a waggon, the property of the plaintiffs, to be carried on one of their steamers as deck cargo, to be safely delivered at a specified place, for freight. While being so carried the waggon was damaged, and deteriorated in value. The receipt contained a stipulation that the defendants should not be liable for any loss or damage from fire, storm, flood, or tempest, or perils or dangers of the seas, rivers, or navigation, and whether in ships, boats, barges, or at wharves, warehouses, or otherwise, nor for damage to or loss of deck cargo, nor for any loss, damage, or breakage whatsoever, under any circumstances, unless such loss, damage, or breakage should arise from or in consequence of the gross and wilful default of the defendants.

Held, that the defendants were not to be held liable for any loss not resulting from their own gross and wilful default, but on the admitted facts (by *demurrer*) the plaintiffs were entitled to succeed.

DEMURRER.

THE plaintiffs, William George and John Tough, sued the defendants for damages sustained to a waggon, while being conveyed by the defendants from Sydney to Cleveland Bay. The declaration contained, *inter alia*, the following count :— " That the plaintiffs sue the defendants for that they delivered to the defendants, and the defendants received from the plaintiffs a certain waggon, the property of the plaintiffs, to be by the defendants safely and securely carried as deck cargo, in a ship of the defendants, from Sydney to Cleveland Bay, and there safely and securely delivered for the plaintiffs for freight payable to the defendants by the plaintiffs, and upon the following terms (amongst others not necessary to be mentioned):— That the defendants should not be liable for any loss or damage from fire, storm, flood, or tempest, or perils or dangers of the seas, rivers, or navigation, and whether in ships, boats, barges, or at wharves, warehouses, or otherwise, nor for damage to or loss of deck cargo, nor for any loss, damage, or breakage whatsoever, under any circumstances, unless such loss, damage, or breakage should arise from or in consequence of the gross and wilful default of the defendants.

The defendants demurred that the declaration was bad in substance, as the defendants were not liable under any circumstances for damages to deck cargo ; that the count disclosed no duty for the breach of which the defendants could in law be held liable under the circumstances therein alleged.

TOUGH *v.*
AUSTRALASIAN
STEAM NAVIGA-
TION COY.

Cockle, C. J.
Lutwyche, J.

Pring, A. G., and *Bramston,* in support of the demurrer.

Griffith for the plaintiffs.

The following cases were cited:—*Peek v. N. Staffordshire Ry. Co.,* 32 L. J. (Q. B.) 241 ; *Coggs v. Bernard,* 1 Smith, L. C. (note), 216 ; *Shaw v. York and North Midland Ry. Co.* 13 Q. B. 347 ; *Carr v. Lancashire and Yorkshire Ry. Co.* (7 Ex. 707); *Phillips v. Clark,* 26 L J. (C. P.) 168 ; *Lloyd v. General Iron Screw Co,* 33 L. J. (Ex.) 269 ; *Grill v. General Iron Screw Co.* L. R. 1 C. P. 600 ; 3 C. P. 476 ; *Martin v. Great Indian Peninsular Ry. Co.,* L. R. 3 Ex. 9 ; *Czech v. General Steam Navigation Co.* L. R. 3 C. P. 14 ; *Ohrloff v. Briscall,* L. R. 1 P. C. 238 ; *Leuw v. Dudgeon,* L. R. 3 C. P. 17, note ; *Wing Wah v. A. S. N. Co. (supra* 36).

C. A. V.

6th July.

COCKLE, C. J., delivered the judgment of the Court. In this case the fourth count of the declaration in substance states a receipt by the defendants of a waggon as deck cargo, to be delivered at Cleveland Bay for the plaintiffs, for freight payable, and upon the terms "that the defendants should not be liable for any loss or damage from fire, storm, flood or tempest, or the perils or dangers of the seas, rivers, or navigation, whether in ships, boats or barges, or at wharves, warehouses, or otherwise; nor for damage to or loss of deck cargo, nor for any loss, damage, or breakage whatsoever under any circumstances, unless such loss, damage, or breakage should arise from or in consequence of the gross and wilful default of the defendants." The declaration then in substance avers that the defendants so negligently carried the waggon that by and through the gross and wilful default of the defendants the waggon was greatly injured and deteriorated in value. To this count the defendants have objected, on the ground that they were not liable under any circumstances for damage to deck cargo, and that the count discloses no duty for the breach of which they can be held liable. Although the question before us is not the same as that before the House of Lords in the case of *Peek v. North Staffordshire Railway Co.,* 10 H. L. C. 473 ; 32 L. J. (Q. B.) 251, which turned upon the construction of an Act of Parliament, still the reasonableness or unreasonableness of a proposed interpretation of the terms may be a test to aid us in determining their proper meaning. Mr. Griffith suggested that possibly a sentence might end with the word " cargo," and so that " nor " might be the commencement of a fresh sentence. But we cannot take that

Tough *v.*
Australasian
Steam Naviga-
tion Coy.

Cockle, C. J.
Lutwyche, J.

view, for it is improbable that in respect of deck cargo the defendants
should be content with the liability cast upon them by such cases as
Lloyd v. General Iron Screw Company, Limited (33 L. J. Ex. 269),
and *Grill v. The General Iron Screw Collier Co., Ltd.* (L R 1 C. P.
600 ; L. R. 3 C. P. 476), while in respect of cargo under hatches,
they should seek to protect themselves by the further provision
regarding wilful default.   And, however difficult the latter case may
render it to distinguish between negligence simple and gross negligence, the framer of the receipt probably thought that there was
some difference between simple negligence and gross and wilful
default.   We think, therefore, that we ought not to consider the
terms of the receipt as consisting of distinct sentences, but that they
are to be construed as one sentence.   Of their proper construction
(and the point for our decision is one of construction, *Carr v. Lanca-
shire and Yorkshire Ry. Co.*, 7 Ex. 707; see also *Shaw v. York and
North Midland Ry. Co.*, 13 Q. B. 347) as one sentence two views
have been presented to us.   Mr. Pring, for the defendants, wishes us
to confine the application of the word " such " to the loss, damage or
breakage last before mentioned, and he argued that the effect of this
would be to confer irresponsibility on the defendants, even though
loss or damage by fire, for instance, or to deck cargo were caused by
their own gross negligence.   We do not say that the defendants
cannot secure this extent of irresponsibility ; but we think, to use the
words of Lord Chief Baron Kelly, in *Grill v. The Screw Collier Co.*,
that if shipowners wish to except losses resulting from the negligence
of themselves or their servants, they must do so by express language,
though they may thereby make the bill of lading (say in the present
case the receipt) repugnant.   And it must be observed that the interpretation contended for by the defendants renders it necessary for
the words " under any circumstances whatsoever," or words to the
like effect to be interpolated, or implied, after the words "deck cargo."
Analogous words were used in *Wilton v. The Royal Atlantic Mail
Steam Navigation Co.*, 30 L. J. (C. P.) 369 ; and are said by Mr.
Justice Willes (see p. 609 of *Grill's case, supra*) to have caused the
doubt.   The effect of adding or implying these words would be
equivalent to saying that, if the defendants, by their gross and wilful
default, caused the destruction of the waggon by fire, such conduct
would not be a breach of their contract or duty to carry safely.   We
think that by adopting the construction of Mr. Griffith, and holding
that the words " such loss, damage, or breakage " refer to any loss or

TOUGH v.
AUSTRALASIAN
STEAM NAVIGA-
TION COY.

Cockle, C. J.
Lutwyche, J.

damage antecedently mentioned, we shall give an interpretation of the whole, which is, to say the least of it, not less reasonable than that contended for on the other side, and which, while rendering it needless to add or imply any words whatever, is equally comformable with the grammatical structure of the sentence. Without entering into the question of how far the burden of proof may be affected by the receipt (as to this, see *Czech v. General Steam Navigation Co.* L. R. 3 C. P 14), and remarking with Mr. Baron Channell, in *Martin v. The Great Indian Peninsular Ry. Co.* (L. R. 3 Ex. 14), that "no question here arises as to what contract can be made between the parties, but only as to what the contract really is," and treating this case as one of pure construction, we think that the meaning of the condition imposed by the defendants is this, that they are not to be held liable for any loss not resulting from their own gross and wilful default, but are to be liable in the other event. But such default is admitted, and we think the plaintiff must have judgment.

Judgment for plaintiff.

In re PORTER, An Articled Clerk.

Solicitor—Articled Clerk—Service out of the Colony.

[In Banco].
1870.
4th June.
11th July.
___
Cockle, C.J.
Lutwyche, J.

A clerk who had served under acticles to a solicitor in Victoria came to Queensland, and after a lapse of years he became articled to a solicitor in Queensland for five years.

An application to allow the period served in Victoria to be taken into consideration was refused.

Application that a period of service as articled clerk to a solicitor out of the colony be allowed as service in the colony.

Lilley, Q.C., for the applicant.

Griffith for the Board.

All the facts of the case appear in the Judgment.

Cockle, C. J., delivered the judgment of the Court as follows:—The facts of this case as stated in the documents before us seem to be sa follow: The applicant was articled on May 26, 1858, and served until April 7, 1861, when he left Geelong for Brisbane. He travelled in Queensland almost up to the time, July 4, 1864, when he entered into an engagement, not under articles, with Mr. Doyle, to whom, on September 16, 1867, he articled himself. Thus it appears that an interval of more than six years elapsed between the cessation of service under the first articles and its commencement under the second. The Board of Examiners has reported to us, and we attach great weight to that report, while recognising the right of the applicant to our independent opinion. The report consists of four paragraphs, whereof the first is subdivided into three, and the second into two sections. The Board thinks that the applicant's position as an articled clerk was shaken (1) by his service unarticled ; (2) by the lapse of time above noticed ; (3) by the fresh articles embracing a term of five years. We are not much influenced by the last ground, because the applicant, anxious to procure admission into the profession, and uncertain as to the availability of the first service, might well be ready to enter into articles for the usual term. And this course might be justified by that taken in *In re Taylor* (4 B. & C. 341). The previous grounds demand more consideration. The applicant seems to have slept on his rights. No communication

In re Porter,
An Articled
Clerk.

Cockle, C. J.
Lutwyche, J.

between him and Mr. Friend appears to have taken place between April, 1861, and, to take the very earliest date, July 4, 1864. Possibly the applicant did not seek such communication until long after. And yet from paragraph 6 of his affidavit, it appears that before he was sure that Mr. Doyle would allow him to finish his term of (articled) clerkship, he had written to Mr. Friend on the subject of the transfer of his articles. It is difficult to think that the applicant could have entered into an engagement with Mr. Doyle without having his former service under articles recalled to his mind. And it is equally difficult to think that, having such service so recalled, he should take no steps to communicate with Mr. Friend, or defer such steps so long that the death of Mr. Friend rendered them useless. One inference would be that he did not contemplate availing himself of that service, and if such inference were erroneous, the applicant would only have himself to blame for it. The facts seem to have been imperfectly laid before us. We should have been glad to know the sources of the information contained in the fourth paragraph of Mr. Speed's affidavit. We are not informed whether Mr Doyle, at the time when the applicant was articled to him, was aware that the applicant intended or desired to avail himself of his former service. If Mr. Doyle was not then aware of such intention or desire, and did not then so far assent as to deprive himself of the right of opposing the application here, we can hardly, considering the lapse of time and the *laches*, give effect to Mr. Doyle's possibly very recent assent without in effect saying that the power of deciding this application is to rest with him. We do not think it necessary to enter upon the other points raised by the report. Still less would we be understood as reflecting in any way upon the applicant. But he has been dilatory. In *ex parte Smith* (1 E. & E. 928; 28 L.J. Q.B. 263), the application was made to the Court, before fresh articles were entered into. That should have been done here. If Mr. Doyle was not aware, when the articles were signed, that the applicant only intended to serve him for some two years, he is awkwardly placed as having no alternative but either to support this application, or to risk the giving of offence to one with whom he is placed in the closest business relations. The application must be refused.

Application refused.

LAPTHORNE v. WILKIE.

Impounding Act of 1863 (27 Vic., No. 22), s.s. 21, 22, 25, 27, 32, 50—
Duty of Poundkeeper—Mistake of predecessor as to description
of a horse—Neglect to rectify—Certiorari—Form of Order of
Magistrates.

1870.
31st May.
13th July.
———
Cockle, C. J.
and
Lutwyche, J.

A bay gelding, the property of L., was impounded by an acting poundkeeper, who entered the horse with the brands as a bay filly. It was advertised for sale as such. The mistake was discovered at the sale by the newly appointed poundkeeper, W., and sold. The necessary advertisements had been published, the entry was not corrected, nor the true description advertised. L. was unaware of the proceedings. W. was fined, ordered to pay forthwith compensation to L., with costs, in default levy and distress, in further default imprisonment. The District Court Judge affirmed the conviction. *Held*, on a special case stated by the District Court Judge, that the matter could only be heard on an application for a writ of *certiorari*.

Held, further, that the order of the magistrates was bad, and the rule for a *certiorari* must be made absolute.

Semble, there was no evidence of neglect on the part of the poundkeeper.

CASE stated by Blakeney, D.C.J., by way of appeal from the District Court at Dalby.

On 14th June, 1869, Arthur John Robinson was acting as poundkeeper at Dalby, under the direction of the Bench pending an election to that office. On that day a certain "bay gelding, branded H off ribs," the property of Thomas Lapthorne, was impounded at Dalby. The description of the said gelding was entered by Robinson in the pound book kept according to the provisions of s. 9 of the *Impounding Act of 1863*, "as a bay filly, H off ribs." Three days afterwards (June 17), A. D. Wilkie was appointed poundkeeper, and took charge of the pound on that day, and received delivery from Robinson of all stock then in the pound, including the bay gelding. On the 19th of June, Wilkie (taking the description of the animal from the pound book and not from examination of the animal) advertised the said gelding in the nearest local newspaper as a "bay filly, H off ribs." The usual certificate was afterwards given by the police officer, according to s. 32 of the said Act, authorising the sale of the said animal. At the time of the sale the mistake of the sex was discovered, and in place of its being withdrawn the sale proceeded, and

F

LAPTHORNE *v.*
WILKIE.

Cockle, C.J.
Lutwyche, J.

the clerk of the Bench (the auctioneer) gave a receipt to the purchaser as for a " bay colt, H off ribs " All this proceeding took place without Lapthorne's knowledge. Lapthorne then summoned Wilkie before the Clerk of Petty Sessions at Dalby under s. 25 of the *Impounding Act*, for that on or about the 26th day of June, Wilkie, as poundkeeper, did neglect to describe a certain bay gelding then impounded at Dalby, the property of the said Lapthorne, branded H off ribs, with illegible brand on near shoulder, like TL conjoined, in the *Government Gazette* of 26th June, 1869, or in the local newspaper, whereby the said gelding was sold out of the said pound without Lapthorne's knowledge, to his damage of £12. Upon this charge Wilkie was found guilty, and was adjudged to pay 1s., together with £7 as compensation to Lapthorne, and also £6 16s. 4d. as Lapthorne's costs, and if the said sums were not paid forthwith, the same were ordered to be levied by distress, and in default of sufficient distress, Wilkie was adjudged to be imprisoned for one week. From this conviction an appeal was brought before me, and seeing no cause to differ from the Court below, I affirmed the said conviction. The Court is referred to ss. 9, 22, 32, 50 of the *Impounding Act*. The opinion of the Court is therefore sought on the following questions of law : (1) Does the *Impounding Act of 1863*, being a penal statute, cast upon the poundkeeper the *onus* of correcting or verifying the previous mistakes or entries of his predecessor? (2) In this case was Wilkie guilty of neglect in omitting to compare the brands, and if he found them wrong to correct the entry in the pound book made by Robinson three days before Wilkie became poundkeeper, and to have the true description advertised in the *Government Gazette* and local newspaper? (3) Was Wilkie guilty of neglect in not withdrawing the colt at the time of the sale when the mistake was discovered? (4) Were these omissions such neglect as would bring Wilkie within the provisions of the said Act? (5) Is the conviction good, the magistrates in one and the same order adjudged the penalty, compensation and costs to be paid forthwith, in default of payment distress, in default of distress imprisonment?

Griffith for appellant.

Pring, Q.C., for respondent.

Ex parte Cockburn, Plunkett 89, 2 *Legge* (N.S.W.), 1012 was cited.

C.A.V.

13th July.

Cockle, C.J.: In strictness we think that we cannot decide such a case as the present, except upon the return to a *certiorari*. Unless other provision is made by statute (as in the instance of cases reserved under *The Criminal Practice Act of 1865*), when a special case is granted, the proper course is to obtain a *certiorari*, which ordinarily issues upon the consent of the other party to remove the order into this Court. *R. v. The Inhabitants of Basingstoke*, 19 L.J. (M.C.), p. 28. That has not been done here, and we can only deal with this matter as if application had been made to us for a *certiorari*. We have considered the case, and the sections of the Act (ss. 9, 21, 22, 25, 27, 32, 50) referred to in the case, or cited in argument. We entertain doubts whether there is any evidence that the appellant was guilty of neglect whereby damage was incurred, or even of any neglect whatever. But it is unnecessary to go into this matter, because the order of Petty Sessions is bad, and might have been quashed by the Court of Appeal, and would, Mr. Pring observed, have been quashed by that Court had the objection implied in the fifth and last question been properly stated to the learned Judge on the hearing of the appeal. Had we finally to decide the matter now, our order would be to reverse the proceedings with costs. But we can do no more than order a *certiorari* to issue, and that the Registrar be at liberty to treat the original case, already in the office, as transmitted with the order, and, on the return of the *certiorari* and with the consent of parties, to draw up an order of reversal. Such consent should be applied for by the appellant, and will scarcely be withheld, for it is not easy to see what result, other than the not unlikely one of saddling himself with costs, could ensue to the respondent from withholding it. The return day will be the first day of next term, by which time it will probably suit the convenience or engagements of the learned District Court Judge to have the return made.

Rule absolute for certiorari.

STEVENSON v. CONNOLLY.*

Hospitals Act of 1847 (11 Vic., No. 59) s. 4—The Medical Act of 1867 (31 Vic., No. 33), s. 10—Treasurer—Detinue—Appeal from Justices—Objection not taken in Court below—Evidence—Land Police Act (III.), 19 Vic., No. 24, s. 10.

A person, who had been treasurer of a hospital, was, upon the complaint of the then treasurer, ordered by Justices to deliver up a book, alleged to be the property of the hospital. On appeal it was objected that there was no evidence that the then treasurer had been registered as required by s. 4 of 11, Vic., No. 59, and that the Justices had no jurisdiction under 19 Vic., No. 24, s. 10.

Held, that as the objections were not taken in the Court below, they must be taken to have been waived, and could not be heard on appeal.

S. 4 of 11 Vic., No. 59 confers no rights, but restricts proceedings.

1870.
th, 8th Sept.

MOTION to make absolute a rule *nisi* for a prohibition to restrain further proceedings on an order made by R. Strathdie and Thomas Major, Justices at Gayndah, upon an information laid by J. R. Stevenson against John Connolly, on the grounds:—(1) That the plaintiff was not registered as treasurer of the Gayndah District Hospital at the time of laying the information, in respect of which the said order or conviction was made, or at any time duly pursuant to *The Hospitals Act* (11 Vic., No. 59). (2) That it was not proved at the hearing before making the order or conviction that the plaintiff was registered as treasurer of the said Hospital pursuant to 11 Vic. No. 59. (3) That there was no evidence of the book being the property of the hospital or the treasurer (plaintiff). (4) Want of jurisdiction on the part of justices, under s. 10 of *Police Act* (19 Vic., No. 24), the book referring to matters over the value of £50.

Connolly had been the treasurer of the Gayndah Hospital, and was sued by his successor for illegally detaining a book and certain papers, the property of the hospital. From the evidence it appeared that the book was entitled the "Hospital Treasurer's Book;" that the defendant had purchased it for five shillings with his own money, and that it had never been paid for by the hospital. The defendant alleged that he had private accounts in the book, and that he wished to keep it for reference in a pending action, but stated the hospital committee or officers could inspect it whenever they chose.

* See Markey v. Murray, 2 Q. L. J., 7.

The defendant was ordered to give up the book on payment by the plaintiff, or on his tender of payment of five shillings.

Pring, Q.C., moved the rule absolute, and cited *Ex parte Hegarty*, 3 S.C.R. (L.) N.S.W., 212; *Ex parte Monson*, 5 S.C.R. (L.) N.S.W., 256; *Ex parte Ivill*, 2 S.C.R. (L.) N.S.W., 91.

Lilley, Q.C., showed cause. There was evidence to support the conviction. Connolly had been treasurer for years, and resigned. How far can the case before magistrates be supplemented?

C. A. V.

8th September, 1870.

COCKLE, C.J. Section 4 of 11 Vic., No. 59, like section 21 of *The Apothecaries Act* (55 Geo. III, c. 194), and s. 32 of *The Medical Act* (21 & 22 Vic., c. 90), and s. 10 of our *Medical Act*, and s. 4 of *The Statute of Frauds* (s. 5 of our consolidated Act) does not confer, but restricts rights of action or other proceedings; but the opposite party may waive his advantage, and has done so. The attention of the magistrates should have been called to the point; we might then have possibly interfered. As it is we decline to give effect to the objection. The first two grounds of this rule therefore fail. Again, there was evidence the book belonged to the hospital, and the third ground fails, as does the fourth. The attention of the justices was not called to the objection, which is the subject of the fourth ground. If the applicant has merits, he has his remedy under the concluding portion of s. 10 of 19 Vic., No. 24. The rule must be discharged with costs to the respondent, Stevenson.

Rule discharged with costs.

STEVENSON
v.
CONNOLLY.

WHITE v. FAIRCLOTH & MOORE.

[In Banco.]
1870.
6th and 14th
September.

*Butcher—Slaughtering cattle without notice of intention—No
evidence of slaughtering within District—Appointment of
Inspector—Licensed Butchers Act (5 Wm. IV. No. 1), s.s. 4, 5.*

Cockle, C. J.
Lutwyche, J.

A butcher was convicted on an information laid by an Inspector under
Sec. 5 of 5 Wm. IV. No. 1, for having slaughtered cattle in the Police District
of Maryborough, without having first given twelve days' notice in writing to the
inspector.

There being no evidence that the cattle were slaughtered in the Wide Bay
District, the conviction was quashed.

Quaere as to the sufficiency of the appointment of inspector.

MOTION to make absolute a rule *nisi* for a prohibition to
restrain further proceedings on an order made by George Faircloth,
Police Magistrate, of Maryborough, on the 24th June.

Blake, Q.C., and *Griffith* for White, to move the order absolute.

Lilley, Q.C., for Moore, to show cause.

The facts were as follows:—John Moore, Inspector of Slaughter-
houses for the Wide Bay District, laid an information against
William White, butcher, in the Police District of Maryborough,
under Section 5 of the *Licensed Butchers' Act* (5 Wm. IV. No 1),
for the slaughtering of twenty-two head of cattle, between the 1st
of January and 17th June, 1870, without giving him the requisite
twelve hours' notice. The Police Magistrate, sitting alone, considered
the charge proved, and inflicted a penalty of £5 for each beast and
£3 7s. 6d. costs, making a total of £113 7s 6d. The rule was
applied for and granted on the following grounds: (1) That the
Bench had no jurisdiction, as the Police District of Maryborough
had not been brought under the provisions of the Act. 5 Wm. IV.
No. 1, inasmuch as no notification had been published in the *Government Gazette* appointing a person called inspector of slaughter-
houses and of cattle intended for slaughter; (2) that assuming the
appointment of the said John Moore to have been a good one, he
was only appointed inspector of slaughter-houses, and the defendant
was not bound to give him notice of cattle intended to be slaughtered;
(3) that there was no evidence that the cattle alleged to have been
slaughtered were for sale, barter, or shipping; (4) that there was

[* Repealed, 62 Vic., No. 23, s. 3.]

no evidence that the cattle had been slaughtered in the Wide Bay *White v. Fair-cloth & Moore.*
District; (5) that the case ought to have been heard by two justices,
which was not done, the Police Magistrate not having the power of Cockle, C. J.
Lutwyche, J.
two justices in this case.

Lilley : In respect of the first and second grounds, the appointment of Moore as Inspector, which was published in the *Government
Gazette* of November 17th, 1869, in the following words—"John
Moore, Sergeant of Police, to be Inspector of Slaughter-houses
within the Police District of Wide Bay," brought the Police District
of Maryborough under the Act.   Section 4 of the Act specified that
such officer shall be called "inspector of slaughter-houses and cattle
intended for slaughter," and the omission of the words "and cattle
intended for slaughter," does not affect his authority in any way,
his duty being explicitly defined by the Act.   There is no evidence of
any defect in the jurisdiction of the Police Magistrate.   The third
ground is unimportant, inasmuch as the Act requires 12 hours' notice
from all persons slaughtering, except persons who slaughtered at
their residences or farms, cattle for their own use (section 7) ; and
there is sufficient evidence to warant the Magistrate in coming to the
conclusion, that the cattle in question were not for private use.   In
regard to the fourth, there is ample evidence of the cattle having been
killed in the Wide Bay District; and on the fifth ground, the Police
Magistrate is empowered under 17 Vic. No. 39, s. 11, to sit alone,
and adjudicate with the same power as two justices.

Blake was not called on in reply.

Lutwyche, J. It is unnecessary for Mr. Blake to reply, the
Court having come to the opinion, that on the fourth ground alone,
the rule must be made absolute.   There is not a scintilla of evidence
to show that the cattle were slaughtered in the Wide Bay District.
There were other grounds upon which the rule might be made
absolute, but it is sufficient at present to grant it on the fourth.

Cockle, C.J.   I agree with what has been said, and I
recommend that in all cases that the words of the Statute be strictly
adhered to.   I am not now called upon to decide the point respecting
Moore's appointment, but I make these remarks in view of not having
to decide it.

Lutwyche, J. We quash the conviction and order the restitution of the money.   No costs will be granted.

Rule absolute.

THE BANK OF QUEENSLAND *v.* BOURNE.

[In Banco.
1870
3rd, 5th, 10th
August.
15th, 20th, 21st,
22nd, 24th Sept.
———
Cockle, C.J.
Lutwyche, J.

Building Contract—Assignment of Debt—Arbitration—Insolvency—
Action of detinue against Corporation—Injunction by Assignee.

B. entered into a contract with the Municipal Corporation of Brisbane to
build a bridge, and it was agreed that all the plant of B. should become the
property of the Corporation until completion. B. assigned his interest to the
Bank for advances to carry on the works. B.'s claim against the Corporation
was submitted to arbitration with the Bank's assent The Bank refused to
advance, B. became insolvent, obtained his discharge, and bought in all book
debts from the Official Assignee. B. started an action to recover the plant from
the Corporation. The Bank applied for an injunction against B. to restrain the
action.

Held, affirming Cockle, C.J., that the application was without precedent,
would lead to no beneficial effect, was premature, and should be refused.

Motion for an injunction to restrain the defendant, John
Bourne, from further prosecuting an action at law against the
Municipal Corporation of Brisbane for detinue, so long as any money
should remain due on the security of an indenture made on the 29th
April, 1865, between the said Bourne and the Bank of Queensland. The suit was instituted by James Cairns, the official liquidator
of the Bank, whose bill of complaint set out that, by articles of
agreement, dated 11th March, 1864, and made between the defendant
and the Municipal Corporation for the erection of the Town Hall in
Brisbane for £19,329. By a further indenture, dated 1st July, 1864,
and made between the same parties, the defendant contracted to erect
a bridge over the Brisbane River for £52,559 8s. In the specification
it was provided that all materials, tackle, implements (except work-
men's tools), brought upon the works should become the property of
the Corporation until the completion of the contract ; also that the
insolvency of the contractor should entitle the Corporation to enter
on the works, take possession of the plant, and eject the contractor,
and all claims on the part of the contractor should cease, but such
insolvency should not effect the security given by him upon the contract for *bonâ fide* advances made to him for carrying on the work.
The bridge was to be erected within twenty-four months from the
date of the contract. In April, 1865, the defendant had nearly completed the erection of the Town Hall, had erected part of the bridge,

had also put up a temporary wooden bridge, and had borrowed £10,200 from the Bank. On the 29th April an agreement was entered into between the manager of the Bank, in order that the defendant might obtain further advances to complete the two contracts. In the said agreement it was stated that in consideration of the amount then owing by the defendant to the Bank, and also of all further advances to be made from time to time, the defendant assigned to the Bank both the articles of agreement referring to the Town Hall and the bridge, and the full force, benefit and effects thereof, and all money due then or thereafter to become due either by virtue or in respect of the said agreements ; and also all moneys afterwards to become due for work and labour done in reference to the said works ; and also all the right, title, and interest both at law or in equity of the defendant to the said articles of agreement and indenture, the whole to be subject to the proviso of an equity of redemption. By the said agreement the defendant constituted the manager of the Bank his lawful attorney to sue for and recover, if he should think it expedient, the moneys assigned, as they become due, and to perform all requisite acts to give complete effect to the assignment. In pursuance of the indenture of 1st July, 1864, and in part performance of such bridge contract, the defendant brought plant upon the works, and the plaintiff claimed that such plant became the property of the Corporation until the completion of the contract. The bridge was not completed within the contract time, and its construction was suspended. Disputes having arisen between the Corporation and the defendant with regard to the bridge contract, and the work done thereunder, the matters were referred to arbitration in September, 1868. In December following the arbitrators made their award, adjudging that there was due from the Corporation to the defendant the sum of £18,372 5s. 2d. ; and, concurrently with the payment of that sum, they directed the defendant to deliver to the Corporation all plant, &c., relating to the bridge works. The plaintiffs previously assented to the arbitration. The defendant Bourne was adjudicated insolvent on 23rd December, 1868, and received his certificate on 29th April, 1869. In July, 1869, the book debts and unrealised assets of the defendant's estate were sold to one Bruce for £100, and the defendant alleged that Bruce had since transferred the same to the defendant. The defendant never exercised his right of redemption, and there was now due to the plaintiffs on security of the agreement of 29th April, 1865, £34,036 15s. 10d., which had been demanded in accordance

BANK OF
QUEENSLAND
v.
BOURNE.

Cockle, C.J.
Lutwyche, J.

with the provisions of the agreement. The debts due by the Corporation to the defendant on both agreements amounted to £25,741 5s. 2d.
The defendant had recently commenced an action of detinue
against the Corporation, claiming a return of the material used in the
construction of the bridge, and then in possession of the Corporation.
It was submitted by the plaintiff Bank that their security would be
prejudiced by such proceedings, and that the bringing of such an
action was a violation of the defendant's contract with the Bank, and
therefore the injunction was asked for. The defendant, in his
affidavit, replied that the suspension of the bridge works was due to
a breach by the plaintiffs of their promise made to him to advance
moneys on the security of the indenture of 29th April, 1865, to enable
him to carry on and complete the said works.

Lilley, *Q.C.*, and *Harding* for the plaintiff.

Blake, *Q C.*, and *Griffith* for the defendant.

The motion was heard by COCKLE, C.J., on 3rd, 5th, 10th August.

Lilley, *Q.C.* : Whatever rights the defendant acquired under the
contracts passed in equity to the Bank. The whole benefit thereunder was assigned as security to the Bank. The defendant could
not derogate from his security (*Kerr* 195.) The assignment carried
with it everything necessary for the realisation of the debt.
In 1865 the debt was unascertained ; in 1868 the amount was ascertained by arbitration. The parties in equity were bound by that
award, which treated the materials as defendant's property. It was
only under the award that the defendant could try to get possession
of them. The plaintiff could not get the £18,000 without the
materials. The assignment of a debt carries with it the mortgaged
estate. In equity the debt is the principal, the estate the accessory
(*Coote on Mortgage* 301). The assignment of the debt carries with it
all the incidents. The result of the arbitration made the plant (1) an
incident, (2) an accessory. The defendant could not possess himself of the accessories till he had redeemed his debt. He was bound
to put the plaintiff in a position to hand over the plant. The
defendant may say the plaintiff is seeking to improve his security.
The plaintiff says the plant is part of his security. The Bank being
entitled to the debt by force of the instruments had become equitable
owners thereof. Whatever was purchased by their advances, or was
brought on the ground under the contract, they became interested in
as equitable owners. The defendant could not, by increasing the
value of his security, deprive the Bank of any right they had before

(*Fisher* 334.) The accretion to plaintiff's security did not invalidate it. As accretions, the materials had come into the equitable ownership of the plaintiff, and must do so, whether they had become accretions by a fraudulent incorporation with plaintiff's debt, by an accidental incorporation, or by an incorporation by contract with the assent of all parties. The plaintiff's security would be impaired if the defendant could possess himself of the materials without first redeeming his debt. The defendant having assigned could not derogate from that contract.

Blake, Q.C.: The defendant did not assign the plant to the Bank, but only what moneys he was to receive under the contracts. In mortgages, a mortgagor is only liable for what he mortgages. In this case the plant, not being included in the terms of the mortgage, was the property of the mortgagor, not the mortgagee Articles, which a mortgagee claims, must be specifically mentioned in the mortgage; they cannot come in under general words, or by implication. *Holroyd v. Marshall*, 7 Jur. (N.S.) 319; L. R. 10 H. L. 191. Things introduced by implication are such as are necessary for the enjoyment of the subject matter of the mortgage, or without which the security would be deteriorated. At the time of defendant's insolvency, the plant not being in the security, passed to the Official Assignee. The legal right to the plant was now vested in the defendant, subject to the payment by the Corporation of the amount awarded. No precedent for the injunction prayed for could be found. It was sought by a third party to restrain the defendant from proceeding with an action of detinue against the Corporation. The regular form of injunction was when a defendant at law on an equitable claim brings a bill to restrain the plaintiff at law from proceeding with his action. If the injunction sought for was granted the defendant in the action at law (the Corporation) would enter up judgment against Bourne in the action at law. They might do that, being strangers to this suit. If they did, Bourne's right being entirely derived from the award, he could not proceed against them again, and his right to the property would be decided against him. The effect of granting the injunction would be remarkable. It would give the property absolutely and for ever to the Corporation. The Bank are strangers to the action between Bourne and the Corporation, and have no right to interfere in it. Their proper course was to wait until the defendant obtained judgment, and then file a bill against him, alleging they were entitled

BANK OF
QUEENSLAND
v.
BOURNE.

Cockle, C.J.
Lutwyche, J.

BANK OF
QUEENSLAND
v.
BOURNE.

Cockle, C.J.
Lutwyche, J

to the benefit of such judgment. That question could be properly
decided in a suit between the present plaintiff and defendant. The
Court will not decide on equitable principles until all the legal rights
of the parties are ascertained. The following authorities were cited:
Barnard v. Wallis (Cr. and Phil. 85); *Playfair v. Birmingham Railway Co.*, 9 L J. (Ch.) 253; *Balls v. Strutt*, 1 Ha., 146. There
should be an interpleader, and the stakeholder made a party.

Lilley, Q.C, in reply: The relation between the parties is that
of mortgagor and mortgagee. If the plaintiff was out of the way
there is no question but that defendant would have a right to sue the
Corporation for the materials. The present suit is to prevent Bourne,
in breach of his contract with the plaintiff, from getting possession of
plaintiff's means of payment until he has paid plaintiff. There are
common equities between plaintiff and the Corporation, and nothing
between the defendant and the Corporation could be settled in this
suit. *Lloyd v. Eagle Co.*, 28 L.J. (Ch.) 389; *Collins v. Lamport* (34
ib, 196). Notice to the Corporation is not disputed.

CCCKLE, C.J.: For the purposes of this motion, I shall assume
that the plaintiff has such an interest in the plant as would, under
some circumstances, entitle him to a suitable injunction. The bill
prays an injunction to restrain proceedings in an action at law,
wherein the present defendant is plaintiff. The common cases upon
such injunctions do not apply here. The plaintiff is not a party in
the action, and the defendant in the action is not a party to this suit.
So far as I know, such a motion has never been made or granted. It
is as if a mortgagee should seek to restrain a mortgagor from suing or
evicting a trespasser, or as if a *quasi* mortgagee of an *interesse
termini* should seek to restrain the *quasi* mortgagor and intended
lessee from entering upon the demised premises, and in either case
without assigning sufficient reason for the application. The injunction
would not restrain the defendant in the action, or compel him to
persist in his defence, or retain the custody of the plant. I have
before me no means of judicially ascertaining, and I decline to con-
jecture, whether any two, and which two, of the parties pretending to
interest in the plant, conceive that they have interests which may be
advantageously combined against the third party, and I have no
judicial knowledge of, or security for, the permanent willingness of
the defendant at law to retain the custody of the plant, and I can
impose no such duty on them. The award recognises the right of the
defendant to the possession of the plant, and at present I can see in

the action nothing more than a step towards obtaining the possession. The defendant has not only a bare title but an interest. If a mortgagee he has his equity of redemption. The motion must be refused. Then as to costs. This seems to be one of those experimental motions which at law are refused with costs. *Smith v. Goldsworthy* (1 Dowl. *Prac. Ca* 288-291.) I shall not go quite so far, but I shall not make the costs costs in the cause. The question of costs will be reserved, but in all probability, unless something should hereafter be done, leading me to believe that the action was not a mere step towards enforcing a just claim, or unless the plaintiff succeeds at a hearing without introducing any substantial amendments into the bill, the defendant will ultimately get his costs.

Motion refused.

The plaintiff appealed, and the matter was heard before COCKLE, C.J , and LUTWYCHE, J., on 20th, 22nd, and 24th September.

Lilley, Q.C.: The debt has been mortgaged to the plaintiffs, and the defendant is now trying to get possession of the materials so as to damage the plaintiffs' security ; the defendant has, by power of attorney, given the plaintiffs the use of his name, and in order to get payment from the Corporation the plaintiffs will have to use Bourne's name ; but he is now suing the Corporation so as to get possession of the plant ; and thus he is violating his contract with the plaintiffs. This is in effect a suit for specific performance. [LUTWYCHE, J.: That is to say, if you prevent a man from breaking his agreement, you compel him to perform it.] *Lumley v. Wagner* (1 De. G. M. & G. 604) shews that restraint of violation is equivalent to specific performance. *Wood v. White* (4 My. & Cr. 460, 483) shews that parties to a contract of sale are the only parties to specific performance. The Corporation being strangers to the agreement need not be a party to the suit. *Tasker v. Small*, 3 My. & Cr. 63 ; 5 L. J. Ch. 321. A mortgagor in possession retains his rights of ownership, if he does not impair the rights of ownership, but it is otherwise if he acts in derogation of the security ; *Collins v. Lamport (supra)*, 34 L. J. (Ch.) 196. The Bank is mortgagee in possession of the debt and materials. It is a derogation of the power of attorney given the plaintiff to sue for the debt. In general the mortgage of a debt carries the security. An injunction has been made to restrain a defendant from receiving: *Stannus v Robinson* (Hayes v. Jones 622). This is not a suit to make Bourne redeem, but to restrain Bourne from receiving. Even if the Corporation is a neces-

BANK OF
QUEENSLAND
v.
BOURNE.

Cockle, C.J.
Lutwyche, J.

sary party, that is no objection to the injunction. *Const v. Harris*
(T. & R. 496, 514); *Evans v. Corentry* (5 De. G. M. & G. 911.)
The mischief need not have commenced. The defendant is insolvent.
It is sufficient that the defendant claimed a right to do the act complained of. Bourne insisted on bringing the action, and that would
prejudice the Bank's security. *Macbeath v. Ravenscroft*, 8 L.J. (Ch.)
208; *Herries v. Griffith* (2 W R 72); *Tipping v. Eckersley*, 2 K.
& J. 264; *Gibson v. Smith* (2 Atk. 182). This is not a suit for
specific performance. A right to specific performance is not a condition precedent to the right to bring an injunction. The object
sought by the Bank would be better gained by an injunction than
by an action for specific performance. *Lumley v. Wagner* (*supra*);
Holmes v. Eastern Railway Co. (3 K & J. 675); *Seawell v. Webster;*
7 W. R. 691; 29 L. J. (Ch.) 71. Where a right has been given
under a contract, there should be no derogation, *Lumley v. Wagner*
(*supra*). The Court will not allow men to make contracts, and then
depart from their agreements, leaving the other parties to seek for
damages. *De Mattos v. Gibson*, 4 De G. & J. 276; *Sevin v. Deslandes*,
30 L.J. (Ch). 457; *The Messageries Imperiales v. Baines*, 11 W. R.
(Ch.), 322; *Heriot v. Nicholas*, 12 W. R. (Ch.) 844. Bourne, when
he assigned the debt to the plaintiffs, gave the right to recover the
debt to the plaintiffs, and he has no right to possess himself of the
materials, because it is inconsistent with the right he previously
gave to the plaintiffs. An agreement to grant a right was implied
by an agreement to do nothing inconsistent with that right. *Newmarsh
v. Brandling* (3 Swan. 99); *Barfield v. Nicholson* (2 Sim. & St. 1);
Webster v. Dillon, 3 Jur. (N.S) 432; *Lane v. Newdigate* (10 Ves.
192); *Earl of Mexborough v. Bower*, 7 Beav. 127, affirmed 2 L.T. 105;
Barfield v. Kelly, 4 Russ. 355; *The Shrewsbury and Chester v. The
Shrewsbury and Birmingham Railway Co.*, 1 Sim. N. R. 410 Bourne
granted the Bank a power of attorney to recover the debt, and to
make it recoverable it was ascertained by an award, which awarded
that certain materials, described to be in Bourne's possession, were to
be delivered up to the Corporation concurrently on their payment of
the money; and the defendant could not, by asserting a right, possess
himself of the materials by proceeding entirely behind the back of
the plaintiffs. By trying to get the materials he was doing that
which was incompatible with the spirit of the agreement. This was
an equitable assignment of the debt, and it was not countermandable
by the assignor, nor could he do anything which would amount to a

right to countermand the assignment; and if the defendant got possession of the materials it would amount to a countermand of the right of the Bank to recover. This was an equitable assignment of the debt, and not recoverable, even indirectly *Fisher, p.* 45; *Smith v. Everett* (4 Bro. Ch. Ca. 64); (29 L. J. Ch. 236); *Row v. Dawson,* 1 Ves. Senr. 331; *Burn v. Carvalho,* 4 Myl. & Cr. 690; *Ex parte Steward,* 3 Mont. D. & De G. 265; *Rayner v. Harford,* 6 W R. 743; *Ex parte South,* 3 Swanst. 392. The Bank wish to prevent Bourne from using his name to their detriment in suing the Corporation for the materials. .The plaintiff is using his name at law, where he has given the plaintiffs, by the power of attorney, the right to use his name in an action at law against the Corporation. And there has been no attempt to revoke the power of attorney. The defendant is attempting to possess himself of the means which the plaintiffs should have, in order to recover the debt, and if he has made the materials incident to the debt, they became the property of the plaintiffs. The plaintiffs do not deny that the defendant has the right to sue at law, but the substantial and equitable right to the possession of the materials is in the plaintiffs. in the suit, and the defendant has no more right to sue for the recovery of the materials than he has to sue for the debt itself. That is the first step towards the mischief, viz., the bringing of the action; and the plaintiffs are not bound to wait until he has gone any further before applying for an injunction to restrain him. The defendant has the right to sue at law, but the substantial and equitable right to the goods is in the plaintiffs, and for those reasons the defendant should be restrained.

Harding followed, and cited *Ackroyd v. Mitchell,* (3 L.T. 236); *Walker v. Jones* (1 L.R., P.C. 50, 61); *Godfrey v. Tucker* (33 Beav. 280). Fry on Specific Performance, p. 329. Fisher on Mortgage, p. 408. *Holroyd v. Marshall,* 7 Jur. (N. S.) 319; 10 H. L. 191; *Barnard v. Wallis* (Cr. & Ph. 85); *Playfair v. Birmingham, Bristol and Thames Junction Railway* (9 L.J. (Ch.) 235). Kerr, p. 19. Lewin on Trusts, p. 730.

Blake, Q.C.: The question in issue is entirely between Bourne and the Corporation, and the former was only doing his duty in bringing the cause to trial. The plaintiffs must show defendant is a trustee for them. If he has independent rights there is no pretence for stopping him, and the defendant must either have a defence or not. *Hilton v. Lord Granville* (Cr. & Ph. 283). If defendant succeed below, then the plaintiffs' title in this Court goes. Lewin, p.

611. In *Herries v. Griffith* (*supra*) it does not appear either that
the tenant was or was not a defendant in the equity suit, or that the
plaintiff in equity had made himself a defendant in the action at law.
Perhaps (and it is consistent with the judgment) plaintiff was a
defendant in the ejectment action, and the case is cited in both
Fisher, at p. 358, and in Kerr, at p. 208, and also in Daniell, at p. 204.
If it could be shewn that the defendant intended in any way to
injure the property, then there might be an injunction to prevent
him from doing so. The plaintiffs were parties to the award, and the
award was a final settlement of all matters between the parties, and
all rights in respect of the insolvency of the defendant became
extinguished in that award. If the Corporation were necessary
parties to the action, the position of the plaintiffs would not be at all
impaired. They would have to look at the injury which would result
to Bourne should the motion be granted; but on the other hand the
plaintiffs might enter an action against Bourne afterwards. The
plaintiffs' only right was that, whenever the Corporation should pay
the money to Bourne, he should have the goods to deliver up according to the award; but what right had the plaintiffs to deprive the
defendant of the use of the materials? But if the Corporation were
successful, then there would be no necessity for the injunction, and
the question of equity did not arise. As to the question of parties,
nothing can be done against the defendant upon the bill of the
plaintiffs as framed, but even assuming, though not admitting, that
anything could be done in the suit it was imperfect without the
Corporation as defendants. *Saville v. Tankred* (1 Ves. Senr. 101);
Peacock v. Penson (11 Beav. 355); *Wood v. White* (4 M. & Cr.
460) ; *Stannus v. Robinson* (Hay & J. 622) ; *Collins v. Lamport* (34
L J. Ch. 196). In a Bill to restrain ejectment the tenant must be a
party *Lawley v. Walden* (3 Swanst. 14 (n.) ; *Poole v. Marsh*
(8 Sim. N.S. 428); *Hodgson v. Forster* (1 B. & C. 110). If, ultimately,
this injunction were dissolved, the plaintiffs would have to begin
again against the Corporation *Stewart v. Great Western Railway
Company* (2 De. G. J and S. 319); Lewin, p. 311. There should
be no injunction unless the parties can be put in the same position.
Sanxter v. Foster (Cr. & Ph.302). Here the Court has no control over
the subject matter of the suit and cannot preserve the property *in
statu quo*. The only right that the plaintiffs can have is to have the
plant ready to give the Corporation, and the right to use the plant is
not now in question. It is necessary in bringing a suit of this sort

to shew that injury had been or would be done, or waste was threatened.   BANK OF
Potts v. Potts (3 L. J. Ch. o.s. 176,).   There is no precedent for such   QUEENSLAND
an application as this, and where there is none, the injunction should   *v.*
be refused; *Monteiro v. Bannister* (ib. 177).   No doubt equity   BOURNE.
would prevent the impairing of a security or violation of a contract;
Campbell v. Allgood (17 Beav. 623).   Plaintiffs claim to be entitled
either under contract or by accretion at law.   No chattel interest in
possession can pass by assignment; *Holroyd v. Marshall* (*supra*);
property specifically named passes.   *Reeve v. Whitmore* (33 L.J. Ch.
63), carries this principle to a license to take possession.   It may be
done by assignment and power to enter and seize the things on the
premises; nothing of either kind has been done here.   Everything he
could have assigned was subject to the Corporation's rights.   If everything is settled by the award nothing could pass on the insolvency.
The plaintiffs should have filed a bill to have the defendant declared a
trustee for them of this plant, and to have a receiver appointed,
which receiver could bring an action for detinue in the name of the
person having the legal right; *Fisher* 336.   As to the effect of the
insolvency on the contract; see *Hudson v. Granger*, 5 B. & Ald. 27;
Brown v. Bateman, L.R. 2 C.P. 272.   The award concludes the
matter, it has determined the contract, and the property may have
passed to the Corporation on the insolvency.   Bourne is a purchaser.
The trust estate will not pass under the insolvency.   There is no fact
stated from which danger can be apprehended.   (LUTWYCHE, J.:
Except insolvency a year and a-half ago.)   After the award, which
was a final judgment between the parties, actual waste is not necessary.   It is an assumption that there has been a breach of contract.
But why?   Here the act itself is not wrong, but in accordance with
the award.   The act is legal in itself and a duty.   *Potts v. Potts*
(3 L.J. Ch. (o.s.) 176).   Equitable waste will not be restrained unless
the same is proved to have been committed or threatened.   In the
cases cited by the counsel on the other side, with reference to actions
for specific performance, the parties were all parties to the contract,
and the principle upon which they were decided was that the rights
of third parties were not affected by the contract between the plaintiff
and defendant.   *Knight v. Bulkeley* (27 L. J. Ch., 592).

Griffith followed, and cited *Scott v. Avery* (5 H. L. C. 811)
Story 1957 (a) : 240 (1) (2) ; *Jennings v. Bond* (2 J. & L. 720).

Lilley, in reply, referred to *Knight v. Bulkeley* (27 L.J. Ch. 592);
Tunstall v. Boothby (10 Sim. 542), *Ex parte Alderson*, 1 Mad. 53.

BANK OF
QUEENSLAND
v.
BOURNE.

Cockle, C. J.
Lutwyche, J.

LUTWYCHE, J.: I am of opinion that this motion must be dismissed. I will assume, for the purposes of this motion, that the plant is an accessory or accretion to the debt, but I cannot see why we should be called upon to restrain the defendant from further prosecuting the action which he has commenced at law for the recovery of the plant, which would appear to have been taken out of his possession by the Corporation. We are asked to restrain Mr. Bourne from prosecuting his action because, it is said, there is danger to the plant. There is no allegation in the bill that the security is in danger, and the only argument upon which the likelihood is founded is upon the past insolvency of Bourne. In *Evans v. Coventry* (5 De G. M. & G. 911), which was relied upon by the learned counsel for the plaintiffs, the money, or a large portion of it, had already been lost through the negligence of the directors who were parties to the suit, and it was sworn that some of them were in poor circumstances; but it might be that Mr. Bourne is a millionaire, and we cannot assume that on account of his past insolvency a year and a-half or two years ago he would at once make away with the property and the trust reposed in him. I found my judgment in this matter upon the principal ground of the judgment given in the Court below. We cannot affect the Corporation; it will not bind them; and if the injunction were to go, it would not in any way tend to preserve the Bank's security. It was said there was a danger, because the defendant in this suit might sell the property to an innocent purchaser. But assuming this injunction were granted, would the plant be any safer? The Corporation might sell the property to an innocent person. But, going further, I have said that I would assume that the plant was an accessory to the debt. Supposing Bourne had sued the Corporation at law for the debt, has any precedent been shown where a Court of Equity has restrained by injunction an assignor from suing for the debt at law? The only case which comes near is *Herries v. Griffiths* (2 W.R., 72); but it is not at all applicable to the circumstances of the present case. The objection was that the co-heirs were not made parties It would clearly appear that the defendant was a party to the action at law. It is enough for me that this motion appears to me to be an experimental motion, and if it were granted it would have no beneficial effect; and that, at least, it is premature. I think that the motion must be refused or dismissed with costs.

COCKLE, C.J.: I am of the same opinion.

Motion dismissed with costs.

Solicitors for plaintiff: *Little & Browne.*
Solicitor for defendant: *W. E. Murphy.*

MACDONALD v. TULLY.

Crown Lands—Occupation without issue of lease—Refusal to grant lease—Acquiescence—Action for damages—Special damage—Demand for lease—Parties—Joinder of—Claims on the Government—Action against Crown for liquidated damage—Nominal defendant—Evidence—Admissions by nominal defendant—Interpretation of statute—" Shall "—The Tenders for Crown Lands Act (24 Vic., No. 12), s. s. 3, 4, 5, 8 *—Claims on Government Act (20 Vic., No. 15), s. 2†—Acts Shortening Act (22 Vic., No. 12), s. 8.‡

[In Banco.}
1869.
9th, 14th Dec.
1870.
10th March.
11th April.
27th May.
13th July,
6th September.

Cockle, C. J.
Lutwyche, J.

A plaintiff who has paid rent to the Crown, and occupied and stocked Crown lands under an accepted tender under *The Tenders for Crown Lands Act* (24 Vic., No. 12) the interest wherein has been transferred to him, and is assumed to have been transferable, although no lease has been granted to him under section 3, is a lessee within the meaning of section 5, and has a right to occupy as against disturbers.

If such lessee acquiesces in the disturbance of his occupation he is not entitled to recover compensation, on account of his own withdrawal from the runs without notice to or knowledge on the part of the Crown.

Particular or special damage arising from the refusal of the Crown to grant a lease must be averred.

The Claims on the Government Act (20 Vic , No. 15) does not confer a right to claim unliquidated damage against the Crown.**

" Nominal defendant " in section 2 of 20 Vic., No. 15, has a statutory and not a colloquial meaning, and accordingly where in an action against the Crown the Chief Crown Lands Commissioner has been appointed a nominal defendant, certified extracts made by him as Chief Crown Lands Commissioner, rendered inadmissible on other grounds, are not admissible by reason of the appointment of such officer as nominal defendant.

Quaere.—Whether, in an action brought by a lessee of the Crown for compensation for refusal to grant a lease of Crown lands to him, such lands having been leased subsequently to third parties, such parties should not be made parties to the action.

Semble—that no claim against the Crown for damages for refusal to grant a lease can be made without a demand or request therefor before petition made.

MOTION to make absolute a rule *nisi* calling on the plaintiff to shew cause why judgment should not be arrested, or why the record should not be amended, or why the verdict should not be set aside and a non-suit entered, or why a new trial should not be granted.

*Repealed.
†See now 29 Vic , No. 23, s.s. 2, 10.
‡See now 31 Vic., No. 6, s. 20.
** But see contra *Macdonald v. Tully*, I Q. L. J. Sup. 27.

The action, which was tried at the Rockhampton Circuit Court, in October, 1869, before Mr. Justice Lutwyche, was brought by the plaintiff, Peter Fitzallan Macdonald, grazier, against the defendant, William Alcock Tully, Chief Commissioner of Crown Lands (nominal defendant for the Crown), to determine a claim of right which the plaintiff had submitted to the Crown, and which had been referred to that Court for trial. In 1858 James Leith Hay tendered for three runs in the Leichhardt district, under the names of Ludwig, Durah, and Kilmore. The tender was made under sections 12 and 13, of Chapter 2, of the Order-in-Council of March 9, 1847, and contained the proposed boundaries Under the same order W. H. Wiseman, then Commissioner of Crown Lands for the Leichhardt district, officially examined the blocks tendered for in 1860, and sent in amended descriptions of the same. In July, 1861, M. E. Burrowes, Deputy Surveyor-General, sent a letter to Hay, stating that the Governor "has been pleased to accept your tender for the run in the Leichhardt district, called Ludwig, subject, however, to the right of hereinafter reserving any portion of the run for any of the purposes stated in section 9, chapter 3, of Order-in-Council of March 9, 1867. You will, therefore, be good enough to pay into the Colonial Treasury the sum of ————, being the amount of premium offered by you. The rent for the next four years will be £12 10s , being computed according to the estimate of the area of the run ————, namely, twenty-five square miles, at 10s. per mile. As soon as the Colonial Treasurer shall have reported the receipt of the premium, a lease for the term of fourteen years, commencing from July 1, 1861, will be prepared and issued to you under the provisions of *The Tenders for Crown Lands Act of 1860* (24 Vic., No. 12), subject to the annexed amended description." Wiseman's amended description followed. Similar letters were on the same day sent to Hay, for Durah and Kilmore. In April, 1861, Hay transferred his interest to the plaintiff, with the sanction of the Government. The plaintiff had regularly paid all rent and charges when due, had fulfilled all the necessary conditions to prevent forfeiture, though without obtaining leases, and continued in undisturbed possession and occupation of the land till about May, 1866, when he received a letter from W. H. Richards and Co., informing him that he was trespassing on their runs, and threatening to impound his sheep. He thereupon removed from the country, and sent in a petition to the Governor, setting forth his claim to have had the leases of the land granted to him, and that the leases

had instead been granted to Richards and Co., and estimating his
probable loss at £20,000.   The petition was presented under *The
Claims on Government Act* (20 Vic., No. 15), and under that Act
was referred to the Supreme Court, which directed the issues raised
to be tried at the Rockhampton Circuit Court.   The action was tried
accordingly, the declaration embodying the petition, and claiming
damages £25,000.   The defendant traversed all the allegations in
the declaration, pleading that the land leased to Richards and Co. did
not include any of the land in Hay's tenders, Wiseman's descriptions,
or Burrowes' acceptances.   During the trial, the counsel for the
defendant moved for a non-suit, on the ground that there was no
evidence to support the allegation in the declaration of plaintiff's
right to a lease of the country in Wiseman's amended descriptions,
inasmuch as, at the time of the notification of the acceptance of Hay's
tender, and for some years after, the survey required by the Orders-
in-Council (under which the country in question was taken up),
previous to the issuing of a formal lease, had not been complied with.
His Honor ruled there was evidence of the allegation, but reserved
the point.   The counsel for the plaintiff tendered as evidence
the lease to Richards and Co. not being forthcoming, a certified copy
from the register book of the Lands Department of an epitome of
that lease.   Its admissibility was objected to by the counsel for the
defendant.   The objection was over-ruled by His Honor, who, however, expressed no opinion on the point.   The jury returned a verdict
for plaintiff; damages £16,926.   The rule *nisi* was obtained calling
on the plaintiff to show cause why the judgment on the verdict
obtained in this cause should not be arrested, or why the record in
this cause should not be amended, or why the verdict obtained in this
cause should not be set aside, and a non-suit entered on the ground
that there was no evidence to support the 11th paragraph of the
declaration averring that the plaintiff was entitled to have had leases
of the said runs granted to him by the Government, because there
was no proof that the runs had been surveyed in conformity with
the Waste Lands Regulations, page 61, paragraph 9, and page 63,
paragraphs 1 and 3, and page 68, paragraph 1; or why a new trial
should not be granted between the parties on the following grounds:
for the erroneous admission of certain certified extracts by the Chief
Crown Lands Commissioner from the Register of leases relating to
the leases of Springsure, Spring Creek, and Miallo, granted to Messrs.
Richards and Co., and of certain certified extracts by Chief Crown

Land Commissioner from the Register of leases relating to the leases Goddstone, Cowley, and Riversleigh, granted to John Brown Watt; of Dooumuuya, granted to Edward Orpen Moriarty; and for misdirection, the Judge having told the jury that there was evidence of such a survey as would satisfy the requirements of the Waste Land Regulations referred to during the hearing of the cause, and also having directed the jury to assess damages.

Bramston, A.G., Pring, Q.C., for the defendant in support of the rule.

Lilley, Q.C., Blake, Q.C., and *Paul* for the plaintiff, showed cause.

Pring, Q.C., cited *The Bankers' Case, 14 Howard's State Trials, 1 Baron de Bôdes'* case, 3 H. L. C. 449; '8 Q. B. 208; 10 Jur 773; 13 Q.B. 380; 14 Jur. 970; *Viscount Canterbury v. Attorney-General,* 1 Ph. 306; 12 L. J. (Ch.) 281; 7 Jur. 224; *Tobin v. Queen,* 16 C. B. (N. S.) 310; 33 L.J. (C.P.) 199; *Feather v. Queen,* 35 L.J. (Q.B.), 200, 6 B. & S. 257, 2 L. T. 114; *Churchward v. Queen,* L. R., 1 Q. B. 173; 14 L.T. 57; *Queen v. Hughes,* L.R. 1 P.C. 81; 35 L.J. P. C. 23; 12 Jur. (N.S.) 195; 14 L.T. 808, 14 W.R. 441; *Campbell v. Queen,* 4 S.C.R. (L) N.S.W. 142; *Robertson v. Dumaresq,* 2 Moo. P. C. (N. S.) 65.

Lilley, Q.C., Robertson v. Dumaresq (supra) shews that the promise of a Governor representing the Crown is binding on the Crown, and that, for breach of such a promise, unliquidated damages can be recovered. The Order-in-Council was such a promise binding the Crown. *Canterbury v. Attorney-General (supra)* is not a case arising out of a contract. For a mere tort the maxim that the Sovereign can do no wrong is conclusive, but that maxim does not apply to matters arising out of a contract. In none of the cases cited by the Attorney-General in support of his argument was the question of contract involved. In *Canterbury v. Attorney-General (supra)* it was held that an action would not lie against the Crown for damage to property occasioned by the negligence of a servant of the Crown; but the present is not a case arising out of personal negligence or tort, but out of a contract. In *Feather v. The Queen (supra)* it was held that the Crown could not be sued for damages for the infringement of a patent. In *Tobin v. The Queen (supra)* it was held that for a mere wrong done by the Sovereign, an action for damages would not lie. There is no authority to show that, when a breach or a loss to the subject arises out of a contract, the subject cannot have his petition of right and damages. In *Oriental Bank Corporation v. The Queen* (6 S.C.R. (L), N.S.W. 122, 273) the Crown was sued for breach of contract as common carriers, and damages were awarded against it. *Campbell v. The Queen (supra)* merely decided what a certain contract was. With regard to the alleged grounds of misdirection, a formal survey was not a condition precedent to the granting of a lease (section 13 of Order-of-Council of March, 1847, paragraph 9 of the Regulation of January 1, 1848, thereunder, *Tenders for Crown Lands Act of 1860)*. With regard to whether there was a contract or not, it being competent for the Crown to enter into a contract with regard to the lands, all the incidents with respect to a contract followed. It might be put, however, on the lower ground, of an obligation or promise on the part of the Crown ; *Ryves v. Duke of Wellington,* 9 Beav. 579 ; 15 L. J. (Ch.) 461; 10 Jur. 697. If there was a contract under which plaintiff could recover, it was competent for him to seek unliquidated damages, and for the Judge to direct the jury to assess them. With regard to the point as to the admissibility as evidence of certified extracts from the Registry Book of the Lands Department, that evidence was tendered under section 41 of *The Evidence and Discovery Act of 1867,* which provided that, whenever any book was of such a public nature as to be admissible on evidence in its production, an extract certified by the officer in charge of the original would be admissible. In this case, moreover, the book was kept by the nominal defendant; Taylor on Evidence, section 1577 ; *Mortimer v. M'Callan,* 9 L. J. Ex. 73 ; 4 Jur. 172 ; 6 M. & W. 58. The case of *Queen v. Hughes (supra)* was cited by the Attorney-General to show that the plaintiff's proper remedy was by *scire facias.* But if plaintiff had that remedy, it did not debar him from taking another open to him.

Pring, Q C., in reply. There is no cause of action shown in the record for a breach of which an action will lie against the Crown for unliquidated damages, inasmuch as, firstly, there is no contract; secondly, if there were a contract, it is not one for which unliquidated damages would lie ; thirdly, if cause of action was for a tort, and I submit it is, no action for such will lie against the Crown. The tender and acceptance being so dissimilar, there can be no contract as based on them. Yet, if there was a contract, then it is ; but, according to the Statute of Frauds, it could not legally be considered a contract. Again, no promise can be binding on the Crown, except under seal, and Burrowes' acceptance was not so made.

MACDONALD
v.
TULLY.

There is no mutuality. Was a contract established by the subsequent proceedings of the parties? Hay became possessed of a title under the Act, and a good one. Plaintiff, his transferee, acted absurdly in going out on Richards' notice. Richards' lease was then worth nothing. If the Government has been guilty of anything it is maladministration, though not intentional, in not giving plaintiff the lease; and for that they are liable to Parliament, from whom only could redress be obtained. This, therefore, is not an action on a contract. If possible, though, they could have been sued on a misfeasance. For a breach of a statutory duty, the Government are not liable either for tort or for breach of contract. If plaintiff is right in his premises, he is entitled to a lease under a statute, but not under a contract between him and the Government *qua* contract. The case of *Queen v. Hughes (supra)* gives the value of a statutory assurance under a Colonial Act, besides being an authority on the question of *scire facias*. A Sovereign's promise or contract, except under seal, is not enforcible, except by appeal to his conscience or honour. If the Crown can only be bound by a promise under its seal, no agent acting under it could enter into a contract to bind it with less solemnity. The whole tenor of the allegations in the petition and declaration show clearly that plaintiff sought a remedy for a tort. The question of damages from the Crown for tort had never been definitely settled before the decision in *Tobin v. Queen (supra)*, on which point *Feather v. Queen (supra)* is also an authority. With regard to the point as to the erroneous admission of evidence; before it could have been admitted under *The Evidence and Discovery Act* it should first be shown that the book from which the extracts were made is itself admissible. It is simply a book in which extracts were made for reference in the office, in which abstracts of leases were made, but it does not show that the leases had been duly issued.

COCKLE, C. J., delivered the judgment of the Court.

We think that there was evidence of a survey, and no misdirection on that point. The question on the direction to assess damages is incidentally determined by our judgment on other parts of the rule. A question arose as to whether the interest of Mr. Hay was transferable, but the point was waived on the argument; and, indeed, there may have been a novation of the contract. Accordingly, we assume that such interest was transferable and transferred, and that the plaintiff thereupon succeeded to all the rights of Mr. Hay. On these assumptions, the case appears to us to stand thus:—

The plaintiff had paid and the Crown had received the rent. The plaintiff had occupied and stocked the lands tendered for. He had done so under an accepted tender, the interest wherein had been transferred to him. All this he had done in pursuance of *The Tenders for Crown ·Lands Act*, 24 Vic., No. 12. Unless he had so occupied and stocked within twelve months from a certain date, he would have been liable, under the 5th section of the Act (a), to pay double rent in advance. If, within six months after paying such additional rent, he had not stocked, he might have risked a forfeiture. Now, the statute which requires the occupation and stocking gives him who occupies in pursuance of it a right to occupy. That right the plaintiff might have maintained against those who sought to disturb him in its exercise. Instead of maintaining his right, he acquiesced in the claim of right to disturb him, the loss of which he complains has, substantially, at least, arisen from this acquiescence, and he is entitled to no damages in respect thereof. But damages have been assessed on the whole declaration; consequently, were this the only point, there would have to be a proceeding analogous to a new *venire*, viz., a trial *de novo*. We add a few words on this branch of the case. Although no lease had been actually granted to the plaintiff under the 3rd section of the Act (b), he was a lessee within the meaning of the 5th section. The date and parcels of the lease are rendered certain by the 3rd section, and the rent by the 4th (c).

(a) [*24 Vic., No. 12. Sec V.*] Every lessee whose tender has at the time of the passing of this Act been accepted or whose tender shall hereafter be accepted shall within twelve months from the date of his lease occupy and stock the lands comprised in such lease to an extent equal to one-fourth of the number of sheep or equivalent number of cattle which such lands shall be deemed to be capable of carrying according to section nine of the said last-mentioned Act (*The Unoccupied Crown Lands Occupation Act of 1860*) And should such runs not be stocked as hereinbefore provided every lessee of same shall be liable to pay in advance twice the amount of rent imposed by his lease and if within six months after the payment of such additional rent such runs shall not have been stocked as hereinbefore provided the same shall be absolutely forfeited.

(b) [*24 Vic., No. 12. Sec III*]. The Governor with the advice of the Executive Council shall grant a lease of the lands comprised in any accepted tender for the term of fourteen years and the term of any such lease shall commence from the first day of January or July nearest to the acceptance of any such tender. Provided that all lessees who have occupied their runs for the first time since the first January eighteen hundred and sixty may come under the provisions of this Act.

(c) [*24 Vic., No. 12. Sec IV.*] Every lessee shall during the continuance of his lease pay a yearly rent for the same to be fixed and payable at the same rates and times and ascertainable in the same manner as provided for in *The Unoccupied Crown Lands Occupation Act of 1860*.

MACDONALD
v.
TULLY.

Cockle, C.J.
Lutwyche, J.

The more formal lease would in general be only a better authenticated statement of particulars comprised in, or apparent on the face of, the amended tenders and the acceptance thereof. The lease might be a more convenient document of title than the tenders and acceptances. But to say that in this vast territory, where communication in general involves a long interval of time, is often difficult, and sometimes dangerous or even impracticable ; where the passage of stock to its destination may occupy months ; where a countermand of such destination might have to be transmitted to some uncertain spot, in some inaccessible region ; to say that, in such a country, a person whose tender has been accepted could not safely take any steps towards occupation until the formal lease had been actually issued, would scarcely be consistent with the supposition that the object of the Act was to facilitate occupation. The interval allowed for stocking commences, not from the issuing of the formal lease, but from the January or July nearest to the acceptance of the tender. The issuing of the formal lease might, owing to pressure of business in the office or other causes, be delayed until the unexpired portion of the period prescribed for stocking, was insufficient to enable the lessee to stock in pursuance of the 5th section. It might even be delayed until the whole period had elapsed. It was, in fact, so delayed in the present instance, for it appears by the declaration that the tenders were accepted on the 17th of July, 1861, and that the plaintiff was in occupation without a formal lease, and, so far as appears, without having made a demand or request for a formal lease, until about the 13th of March, 1866, paying rent and assessment in the meanwhile. This right of the plaintiff to occupy was, in our opinion, capable of being maintained against any disturber, whether assuming to disturb in virtue of an alleged lease or otherwise. The plaintiff's case, so far as the same relates to the disturbance of his occupation, fails, because he acquiesced in the disturbance instead of defending his right. And this acquiescence appears on the record, as well as his right, then at all events existing, to occupy. Independently of his right to a trial de novo, the defendant ought to have a new trial granted. We think that the objections made to the admissibility of the certified extracts were valid. We only feel called upon to remark upon one of the answers to the objections. It was urged that the extracts, being certified by the nominal defendant, were evidence against him. It is true that the admissions of a nominal party, using the words in their ordinary sense, are evidence against him. But, used in that sense, the words " nominal defendant," mean a defendant who has an interest, and the only interest which courts of law in general recognise.   His interest may have been passed to, or may vest in, another, but not by any process or matter which such courts will notice.   A trustee or assignor may stand before the court of law as the legal owner, while the *cestui que trust* or assignee may be ignored.   For all legal purposes the nominal is the party ; the only real party, the party in interest ; and in virtue of such legal interest his admissions are evidence.   But the words " nominal defendant " in the present case have a statutory and not a colloquial meaning. Their meaning is ascertained by section 2 of 20 Vic. No. 15 (*d*) (*e*).   The nominal defendant is made such, not because he has an interest which renders him a necessary legal party to the litigation, but merely that there may be some defendant on the record, some person upon or to whom notices, for instance, may be served or given.   It would be going very far if we were to say that admissions made by him, not as a nominal defendant, but in some independent capacity, were evidence against him as nominal defendant.   We think that certified extracts, made by Mr. Tully as Chief Crown Lands Commissioner, and inadmissible on other grounds, are not rendered admissible by

(*d*) [*20 Vic., No. 15. Sec II.*]   At the time of such reference for trial as aforesaid the Governor with such advice as aforesaid shall name some person or persons to be nominal defendant in the matter of such petition the petitioner being the plaintiff therein.   Provided that nothing in this Act shall be construed to extend so as to subject any such nominal defendant to any individual responsibility in person goods chattels estate or otherwise by reason of his being such nominal defendant.

(*e*) [*20 Vic., No. 15. Sec III.*]   It shall be lawful for the Judges of the Supreme Court or any two of them to make all such general rules and orders for the regulation of the pleadings practice or proceedings in any such petition as to such Court shall seem necessary for the purpose aforesaid and all such rules orders or regulations shall be laid before both Houses of Parliament of the Colony if Parliament be then sitting then within five days after the next meeting thereof and every rule and order so made shall be of the like force and effect as if the provisions contained therein had been expressly enacted by Parliament.   Provided always that it shall be lawful for the Governor with the advice of the Executive Council in Her Majesty's name by any proclamation inserted in the *Government Gazette* at any time within three months after the making of any such rule or order or for either of the Houses of Parliament by any resolution passed at any time within three months next after such rules orders and regulations shall have been laid before Parliament to suspend the whole or any part of such rules orders or regulations and in such case the whole or such part thereof as shall be so suspended shall not be binding and obligatory.

MACDONALD
v.
TULLY.

Cockle, C.J.
Lutwyche, J.

MACDONALD
v.
TULLY.

Cockle, C.J.
Lutwyche, J.

the accident of Mr. Tully happening to be the statutory nominal defendant. This evidence being inadmissible, there must at all events be a new trial, for there was no other evidence of the refusal to grant leases to the plaintiff than the alleged grants to some one else, and the only evidence of these grants was the certified extracts. But this is a further point for our decision. The 3rd section of 24 Vic. No. 12 enacts that the Governor, with the advice of the Executive Council, shall grant a lease of the lands comprised in any accepted tender for the term of fourteen years, and that the term of every such lease shall commence from the first day of January or July nearest to the acceptance of any such tender. The effect of this 3rd section is, not to cut down the right of occupation given by, or necessarily implied in, the 5th section, but to confer an additional advantage on the lessee. The formal lease may be a more convenient document of title, and more satisfactory evidence thereof to a proposed transferee, than the accepted tenders. The possession of such a formal lease is an advantage which a lessee may be entitled to expect, but not a qualification necessary for his protection against disturbance in the occupation of lands which, relying on the right of occupation conferred upon him by the 5th section, he has stocked and paid rent for. The point is, whether the plaintiff is entitled to recover damages in respect of the refusal to grant the leases? If he is, our order can go no further than a trial *de novo* or a new trial. If he is not, the judgment must be arrested. So far as a new trial or a trial *de novo* is concerned, we did not deem it necessary to inquire whether the transactions between Mr. Hay and the plaintiff, and the recognition of the plaintiff's occupation by the office, constituted the plaintiff a lessee or occupier within section 5 of 24 Vic., No. 12 All that we thought it needful to say was that, assuming the affirmative to be the true answer, the plaintiff is not entitled to recover compensation on account of his own withdrawal from the runs without notice to, or knowledge on the part of, the Crown. So far as the arrest of judgment is concerned, we should, but for the waiver of counsel for the nominal defendant, probably have been led to inquire whether this *quasi chose in action*, the right to the advantage of a lease, was transferable. Acting on the waiver, and not losing sight of a possible novation of the contract, we assume it to have been transferable and transferred. Still, it seems to us, there are difficulties in the plaintiff's way. It is by no means clear that the 3rd section of 24 Vic., No. 12, even when read in the light of the 8th section of

22 Vic., No. 12(*f*), confers such a right as is capable of being enforced by a proceeding under 20 Vic., No. 15.   The 3rd section of 24 Vic., No. 12, confers an authority, but it would be hard to say that it does more.   The Governor is to act with advice, but advice implies an adviser exercising a discretion.   We think that that section merely authorises, and that a mere authorisation gives no right to sue under 20 Vic , No. 15.   And even if, in place of an authority, there had been a direction to a particular person, still no actual damage stated on this record is traceable to the refusal of a lease. All such damage seems to have arisen from the plaintiff's withdrawal from the runs.   For all that we can see, the damages arising from the refusal are, at the utmost, only nominal.   Thereupon the question arises, to which class of cases does the present belong ?   To that in which, from an act or omission, damage is conclusively presumed, or to that in which damage is presumed, but not conclusively, or to that in which particular or special damage must be shown?   If to the last, the judgment should be arrested.   For, even assuming that the refusal of a lease is a sufficient ground of suit when followed by particular or special damage, no such damage is alleged ; and, if we are right in holding that no damages are recoverable in respect of the residue of the declaration, the whole case fails.   We hold that particular or special damage should have been averred.   Such damage would not necessarily follow from the refusal of a lease.   For instance, a lessee might have no occasion to sue or to transfer, or a proposed transferee might be content with a transfer of a title constituted by the occupation under accepted tenders, and so on.   Unless the point were very clear we should be unwilling to hold that a plaintiff might litigate a question of nominal damages at the expense of the colony.   The foregoing remarks dispose of the whole case.   But there are other difficulties in the plaintiff's way.   We are not called upon to say whether 20 Vic , No. 15, extends to all cases in which the claim is upon a *quasi* contract, that is to say, in which it is made under circumstances such as, could the Crown be regarded as a private person, would constitute a contract between the Crown and the

MACDONALD
v.
TULLY.

Cockle, C.J.
Lutwyche, J.

(*f*) [*22 Vic., No. 12. Sec 8*].   When in any Enactment passed after the present session a power is conferred on any officer or person by the word "may " or by the words " it shall be lawful," or the words " shall and may be lawful" applied to the exercise of that power.   Such word or words shall be taken to import that the power may be exercised or not at discretion but when the word "shall " is applied to the exercise of any such power the construction shall be that the power conferred must be exercised.

MACDONALD
v.
TULLY.

Cockle, C.J.
Lutwyche, J.

claimant. But we say that, however far that Act may extend the remedies for, and facilitate the recovery of, liquidated damages, it does not confer a right to claim as for unliquidated damages against the Crown. Proceedings under that Act have a more extended operation than those upon petition of right, and suffice to meet cases to which the remedy by such petition would not extend, if they apply, for example, to cases of *quasi* contract in which the conditions essential to the successful prosecution of a writ of right are not fulfilled. The view which we take of the range of the Act 20 Vic.' No. 15, seems indeed to be the same as that taken in New South Wales by the framers of the rules made under section 3 of the Act. These rules have the force of an Act of Parliament, and are, we believe, still binding upon this Court. Rule 2 orders that the petitioner shall set forth specifically, his claim, which may be in specie to some particular thing or matter, or to compensation for its loss or deprivation. Consequently, no other sort of claim is cognizable by us It may be taken that the jury, by their finding on the first issue, have found that the plaintiff was, and is, entitled to leases. Our decision is not thereby affected. The claim is not for leases, but for damages. The finding as to the leases is only incidental as to that as to damages. We have not been asked to give a judgment that leases be granted, and we think that such a judgment could not be given. How could we adjudge that the Executive Council advise the Governor under section 3 of 24 Vic., No 12? Why should we so adjudge, when it does not appear that the plaintiff has paid rent, or been in any way recognised as a tenant, since his' withdrawal from the runs? It appears probable, if it does not actually appear on the face of the declaration, that the land from which the plaintiff, in a certain sense, voluntarily withdrew, is in possession of third persons, in whose favour he relinquished it. Certainly the contrary does not appear. We could give no judgment that would affect the interests of those absent persons. They might contend, and ought to be at liberty to show, that the lands in question are properly occupied by them, that their holdings are correctly described in their leases, and are not comprised in the accepted tenders of Mr. Hay, and that the difficulties arise from the obscure topography of the recently-explored country. They should, at least if their interests are to be affected, have been brought before the Court as parties to the litigation. So far as they are concerned all these proceedings, verdict included, are *res inter alios actæ.* The mere issue of a lease to a person not in possession by himself or his stock, and who does not appear to have paid any rent or assessment since 1866, would not cut down a title lawfully accrued to third persons, though such lease were ante-dated. Even if there were no present occupiers, and the lands were vacant or vacated, we could not order leases to be granted on a claim founded, not on 24 Vic., No. 12, but on the *laches* or withdrawal of the plaintiff. It may be a question whether, in every such case as the present, it should not be a rule that all the persons interested in the specific subject matter should be parties. Otherwise it seems not impossible that the Crown may some day be saddled with damages, in separate suits, by distinct persons, whose individual claims are mutually destructive, and who could not both have succeeded against the Crown had they been simultaneously before the Court.

We think it would be well to remark that if a lessee, in addition to his title under section 5 of 24 Vic., No. 12, wishes for a lease, then it may possibly be necessary that he should, being duly qualified in that behalf, have made demand or request therefor; and that no claim, even to nominal damages, can arise without such demand or request, and that the petition is not such a demand or request. In order to give rise to a valid claim, it may be found essential that the refusal should be something more than a mere omission, that it should be an omission to grant the lease on a demand or request capable of being complied with without sending an exploring party to find the lessee. After verdict, at all events, we shall presume refusal to mean omission after demand or request made. But such presumption may be contrary to fact, for we notice that no evidence of a demand or request was given at the trial. However, the leave to move for a non-suit not having been reserved upon this ground, we do not further enter upon it. It may, moreover, be questionable whether the grant of leases to third persons, even if proved, would have been any evidence of a refusal to grant the leases to plaintiff. The destruction or other appropriation of a specific chattel may be evidence of a refusal to deliver it up to the owner; but it might be difficult to say that the plaintiff's leases were appropriated to Richards and Co., or to Mr. Moriarty, or to Mr. Watt, or that the issuing of the latter leases improperly would have prevented the issue of others to the plaintiff.

The case of *Robertson v. Dumaresq* (2 Moo., P. C., N. S., 6; 10 L.T. 110; 13 W. R. 280) was decided upon admissions made by counsel. There were no such admissions here. On the contrary, counsel strenuously

MACDONALD
v.
TULLY.

Cockle, C.J.
Lutwyche, J.

MACDONALD
v.
TULLY.

Cockle, C.J.
Lutwyche, J.

resisted the claim on all points, save that of the assignability of Mr. Hay's interest. We are desirous so to shape our judgment as to avoid as far as may be practicable inflicting on the plaintiff the hardship of successive appeals, and to enable him, if so advised, to raise all the questions before the higher tribunal in one appeal, or one appeal and cross appeal should the latter be deemed advisable. And we have a precedent for modifying the form of our judgment so as to meet the case of a possible appeal (*Betts v. Menzies*, 1 E. and E. 990). The substance of our order is, accordingly, as follows :—Let the judgment be arrested. And, in the event of the plaintiff appealing, and of the foregoing part only of the present order being set aside, then let a trial *de novo* be had. And, in the event so much only of the present order as orders an arrest of judgment and a trial *de novo* being set aside, then let there be a new trial.

Judgment arrested accordingly.

Solicitor for the plaintiffs : *Murphy.*

Solicitor for the defendant : *Crown Solicitor.*

In Re THE BANK OF QUEENSLAND, LIMITED.

Company — Winding up — Contributories — Notice — Stay of proceedings.

[IN EQUITY.]
1870.
*25th April.
2nd May.
5th December.*

Lutwyche, J.

On a motion by certain contributories for stay of proceedings in the winding up of a Company, it appeared that several contributories had not assented to the application.

An order was consequently made, that notice should be sent by post to each of the latter, and that the application should be advertised in various newspapers.

MOTION, on the part of Arthur Hodgson, Hugh Muir, and Henry Brockett, contributories, that all proceedings in the winding-up of the above bank be stayed ; that the bank assets in the hands or under the control of James Cairns, official liquidator, be forthwith handed over to Hugh Muir, as special agent for the shareholders and contributories of the bank, and duly constituted attorney of Henry Brockett and C. F. Kemp, liquidators in England of the bank, and representatives of the English shareholders; and that the official liquidator be ordered to pass his accounts within a reasonable time, and that any of the parties may be at liberty to apply to the Court with respect to the said accounts, and to the past conduct of the official liquidator.

The matter was argued on the 25th April and now came on for judgment.

Bramston, A.G., Blake, Q.C., and *Baird,* in support of the motion.

Lilley, Q.C., Harding, and *Griffith,* for the Official Liquidator.

LUTWYCHE, J. The bank of Queensland has a nominal capital of £1,000,000, in 10,000 shares of £100 each. This application is supported by the written assent of 208 shareholders, holding 6,460 shares; while 56 shareholders, representing 1,888 shares, are non-assenting—not opposing, because no formal opposition has been offered. The Official Liquidator appeared not to oppose, but, in accordance with what he very properly conceived to be his duty, to show the Court the real facts of the case, and prevent its being misled. At the meeting of shareholders, held in London, on December 14th, 1868, certain resolutions were passed. The wishes of

H

In re THE BANK OF QUEENSLAND, Limited.

Lutwyche, J.

the 208 shareholders could be gathered from the fact that a report of those proceedings being sent to them, they assented thereto, and signed a document under which the present application was duly made, so far as they were concerned. But the real question is, whether sufficient notice of the intention to make this application has been given to the 56 non-assenting shareholders. If I could be satisfied that these non-assenting shareholders were aware that this application would be made, I should have no hesitation in acceding to it. Mr. Blake contended that there was acquiescence on their part; but, unless it was shown that they were aware that the application was to be made, the Court could not infer any such acquiescence. ¦An application of this kind has only been made in two instances. In the case of the *Worcester, Tenbury, and Ludlow Railway Company* (3 De G. and S , 189), all the shares, except 845, were represented before the Court. It was proved that these 845 shares could not be heard of, though advertisements had been repeatedly inserted in the papers calling upon the allottees to come in, and receive what was due to them. It was also sworn that there was reason to believe that these 845 shares had been lost or destroyed. Under those circumstances, the Court granted an order directing the official liquidator to pay the money in his hands over to the directors. That was no authority in support of the present application, where no less than 56 shareholders had not given assent. The other case, the *South Barrule Slate Quarry Company* (L. R. 8 Eq., 688), told against the present application. There was only one opposing shareholder there; yet the Court held he must be protected, and the option given him of retiring from the company. He elected to do so, and his vacation of his position was made part of the order. Here we must take it that it must be proved that the 56, as well as the 208 shareholders had been asked to assent to the application, and that they did not assent. Before making the order asked for, it must be proved that the 56 shareholders had full knowledge of the intention to ask for it. The order is, that this motion stand over till Monday, December 5th, 1870; that notice be sent by post to the 56 non-assenting shareholders, and be advertised in the *London Gazette*, *Times*, and *Daily Telegraph*, once a week in the months of August and September next. Of course, it will be the duty of the persons making the application to see this carried out.

Bramston, A.G.: Will the Official Liquidator remain in his present position at his present remuneration?

LUTWYCHE, J. I am not called on to make an order on that point. *In re* THE BANK OF QUEENSLAND, Limited.

On 5th December, as no appearance was made on behalf of the contributories, His Honour refused the motion with costs.

In re THE BANK OF QUEENSLAND, Limited.

Motion refused with costs.

Lutwyche, J.

Solicitors for the liquidator: *Little and Browne.*

Solicitors for contributories: *Roberts and Hart.*

CURPHEY (*qui tam*) *v.* HOFFNUNG & Co.

[IN BANCO.]
1870.
7th September.
14th, 25th Nov.
9th, & 15th Dec.

Customs Regulation Act of 1845 (9 Vic. No 15) s. s. 9, 16, 24, 25, 82, 86, 93, 108, 109, 110—Unshipment of goods—Non-report —Non-entry—Forfeiture—Fraud—Practice of Custom House— Qui tam action—Judgment in rem—Challenge of a juror for cause—Discharge of jury from returning a verdict on immaterial issues — Arrest of judgment —Passengers' Luggage defined — Evidence of Custom.

H. & Co. forwarded certain dutiable goods to Brisbane, by a steamer, with their traveller S. On arrival in the Bay the goods were removed to a smaller boat, with cases and portmanteaux, alleged to contain dutiable goods also. S. claimed the latter as his personal luggage. No report or entry was made and part of the goods were landed at a wharf, without the presence of an officer of the Customs. No duty was paid.

An information in the nature of a *qui tam* action was brought for forfeiture of goods, by a duly authorised Customs officer.

COCKLE, C.J., *held* there was an unshipment prohibited by the Act and declared the goods forfeited.

The challenge for cause of a juror, who had given a bond for defendant's costs, was allowed.

Held by COCKLE, C.J. and LUTWYCHE J., on an motion for arrest of judgment, that either non-entry or non-report was sufficient to create a forfeiture within the meaning of Sec. 9 of 9 Vic. No. 15.

Held further, that if the unshipment be prohibited, it becomes illegal *ex vi termini*, and it is unnecessary to prove fraud, and the jury may not take into consideration the irregular practices of the Custom House officials, to modify the plain meaning of the Act.

A Judge may discharge a jury from returning a verdict on an immaterial issue, and judgment on the whole record will not be arrested, although one count be bad, if there is one good count, which will support the whole finding of the jury.

On an information in the nature of a *qui tam* action, a judgment *in rem* may be given, where the only penalty is forfeiture.

"Passengers' luggage" may be defined as such articles as are required for the health, comfort, convenience or personal ornamentation of a passenger.

INFORMATION presented by Thomas Curphey, an Officer of Her Majesty's Customs, against certain goods.

Lilley, Q C., for the Crown, moved that the information be read and proclaimed.

The information was read, and a proclamation made by the Registrar requesting all persons claiming the goods to attend, when they would be heard.

Pring, Q.C., accordingly appeared to claim the goods on behalf of S. Hoffnung & Co., jewellers and merchants, of Sydney.

Lilley, *Q.C.*, referred to s. 117 of the Customs Act, 9 Vic. No. 15 (Pring 140), and moved that a writ of appraisement issue to value the goods in the hands of the officer (Curphey), returnable on the 15th September.

The COURT ordered the writ to issue, directed to the Sheriff.

On the 15th September, the information was again proclaimed.

Pring, *Q.C.*, tendered on behalf of Hoffnung & Co., his claim and appearance, and asked to be permitted to enter it (s. 117).

An affidavit of Mr. Murphy was read. A bond, with two sureties, was handed to the Registrar (s. 118).

The COURT granted leave, allowed the appearance to be entered, and ordered the writ to be served within eight days, and the rest of the proceedings to be had as nearly as may be, in the same manner as actions at law.

14th November.

COCKLE, C.J.

The case was tried before Cockle, C.J., and a Special Jury of twelve.

The goods seized were valued at £2,052 18s. 6d.

Bramston, *A.G.*, *Lilley*, *Q.C.*, and *Griffith* for the plaintiff.

Pring, *Q.C.*, and *Blake Q.C.*, for the defendant.

J. C. Heussler, a juror, was challenged by the plaintiff for cause in that he had a pecuniary interest in the case, having given a bond for the payment of the defendants' costs (the defendant being resident beyond the colony), in the event of the verdict going against them.

Pring, *Q.C.*, demurred to the challenge as being insufficient in law. The bond was given as security for the payment of costs, which might be incurred by the plaintiff up to the time of defendants entering an appearance and a claim, and on defendant doing so, the costs in question became costs in the cause. The bond itself said "costs liable to be paid in respect to said appearance and claim." It was, in fact, a bond given to secure the payment of costs which might arise through a fictitious claim being made and abandoned, and, as soon as defendant entered his claim, it became of no value.

COCKLE, C. J., overruled the demurrer, and allowed the challenge.

The trial lasted from the 14th—25th November.

The information, which contained ten counts, was to the following effect:—(1) Thomas Curphey, officer of Her Majesty's Customs, at Brisbane, who was directed by the Collector of Customs to prefer the information came there in his own proper person, and as well as

CURPHEY *(qui tam) v.* HOFFNUNG & Co.

CURPHEY *(qui tam) v.* HOFFNUNG & Co. for the Queen as for himself, gave the Court to be informed, that after October 3rd, 1866, and before September, 1870, the said Curphey, officer of Her Majesty's Customs, at Brisbane, did seize and arrest, to the use of Her Majesty as forfeited, a large quantity of goods, that is to say—(here follows the description of the goods)—for that, within the time aforesaid, one Frederick Solomon, at Brisbane, did unload the said goods, being goods liable to duty on importation, from a ship arriving at the port from Sydney, the goods not having been reported to the Custom House, at Brisbane, contrary to the form of the Statutes in such case made and provided, whereby and by force of such Statutes, the goods were and became forfeited ; (2) that no entry inwards of such goods had been made ; (3) that the said goods were unshipped without the presence or authority of any officer of Her Majesty's Customs ;   (4) that they were landed without the presence or authority of any officer of Her Majesty's Customs ; (5) that besides the said goods, four portmanteaux and eight cases had been seized, in which the first mentioned goods and other goods were contained, and that Solomon imported the first mentioned goods and concealed them in the portmanteaux and cases with the second mentioned goods, subject to a lower rate of duty than the first mentioned, with intent to defraud the revenue ; (6) that Solomon imported the first mentioned goods and concealed them in the boxes with goods not subject to any duty, with similar intent ; (7) that the said first-mentioned goods were imported and concealed with others subject to a lower rate of duty, with similar intent ; (8) that they were imported and concealed with others not subject to any duty, with similar intent ; (9) that the duties not having been paid or secured, Solomon unshipped the first-mentioned goods, making use of the boxes in the removal and shipment thereof ; (10) that the said goods were unshipped and the boxes made use of in the removal and unshipment thereof.   The said Curphey, therefore, prayed the consideration of the Court in the premises, and that the whole of the goods and the boxes be and remain forfeited, and that all persons claiming the said goods might appear in Court to answer concerning the same.

From the evidence it appeared that certain dutiable goods were forwarded by Hoffnung and Co., on the s. s. *City of Brisbane* from Sydney, with their traveller, Solomon, to Brisbane.   On arrival in Moreton Bay, the goods were removed to a smaller vessel, the *Nowra*, with certain cases and portmanteaux.   No report or entry was made, and part of the goods were landed at a wharf in Brisbane, not belonging to the A.S.N. Company, without the presence of an officer of Her Majesty's Customs.   No duty was paid, or security given by Solomon, and no bill of sight given.   The goods were seized, and the plaintiff was authorised to lay an information for forfeiture.

Evidence was tendered, purporting to establish a practice by the Customs authorities, of allowing goods to be removed from intercolonial steamers and stored at the Company's wharf, and it was claimed that commercial travellers were allowed to land as passengers' luggage goods liable to duty, before entry and payment of duty.

COCKLE, C.J., directed the jury that the removal of the goods from the *City of Brisbane* to the *Nowra* was an unshipment within the meaning of the Act.   If, therefore, there was no report of the ship, the verdict on the first count would be for the plaintiff, and the evidence tended to show that there was no such report ; if there was no entry inwards, in respect to which the evidence was pretty clear, a similar verdict would be entered on the second count.   The third count was, that the goods were unshipped without the presence or authority of a Customs House officer, and it appeared from the evidence, that there was no Customs officer on board the *Nowra*, when the goods were removed from the *City of Brisbane* in the Bay. In regard to the ninth and tenth counts, there was an unshipment, and the evidence produced by the defendants proved that there was no payment of duty, and the duty had not been secured as required by the Act.   The fourth count was, that the goods were landed without the presence or authority of a Customs officer, and, in considering this, it would be necessary to review the evidence of the landing of the goods from the *Nowra*.   The verdict should apply only to such goods as had been landed, when the Customs officer arrived on the wharf.   The evidence as to which of the packages had been landed was conflicting, and if there was any doubt, the defendants would be entitled to the benefit of it.   The fifth and seventh counts were withdrawn, and the verdict for these would, therefore, be for the defendants.   The sixth and eighth counts referred to concealment of the goods, with intent to defraud the revenue.   If the goods were concealed, fraud was implied, and the onus of disproving any intention to defraud rested on the defendants.   The jury would, therefore, have to weigh the evidence carefully, before arriving at a conclusion on this point.   It was necessary that a verdict should be entered on each count.

CURPHEY (*qui tam*) *v.*
HOFFNUNG & Co.

Cockle, C. J.

Pring, Q.C., took several objections to His Honour's direction. These are fully set out on the application for a new trial (*infra*).

The Jury returned a verdict for the plaintiff on the 1st, 2nd, 3rd, 9th and 10th counts; and for the defendants on the 4th, 5th, and 7th. On the 6th and 8th they were unable to agree.

The jury were discharged and judgment for forfeiture entered for the plaintiff.

COCKLE, C.J.
LUTWYCHE J.

Pring, Q.C., on December 9th, moved for a rule *nisi* for a new trial, or arrest of judgment, on the ground of misdirection (1) with regard to the first count (*a*) that, considering the practice of allowing dutiable goods to be brought up by intercolonial steamers to be transhipped from such steamers into river steamers, His Honour should have told the jury that in the absence of any evidence of fraud at the time of landing at the Queen's wharf, or subsequent fraud, so as to render the original unloading illegal *ab initio*, there was no illegal unloading; (*b*) that he should have told them, that the removal of goods from the *City of Brisbane* to the *Nowra*, was not, under the circumstances, an unloading from a ship in the true construction of s. 9, of the *Act*, (¹) and that that section only applies to the unloading

(¹) 9 Vic., No. 15, s. 9. And whereas it is expedient that the officers of Customs should have full cognizance of all ships coming into any port in the said Colony or approaching the coasts thereof and of all goods on board or which may have been on board such ships and also of all goods unladen from any ship in any port or place in the said Colony Be it therefore enacted That no goods shall be unladen from any ship arriving from parts beyond the seas at any port or place in the said Colony nor shall bulk be broken after arrival of such ship within four leagues of the coasts thereof respectively before due report of such ship and due entry of such goods shall have been made and warrant granted in manner hereinafter directed and that no goods shall be so unladen except at such times and places and in such manner and by such persons and under the care of such officers as is and are hereinafter directed and that all goods liable to duty on importation not duly reported or which being so liable shall be unladen contrary hereto shall be forfeited and if bulk be broken contrary hereto the master of such ship shall forfeit a sum not exceeding one hundred pounds nor less than ten pounds.

9 Vic., No. 15, s. 16: And be it enacted That the person entering any goods shall deliver to the Collector or other proper officer a bill of the entry thereof fairly written in words at length expressing the name of the importer and of the ship and of the master of the ship in which the goods are imported and of the place whence they were brought and of the place within the port where the goods are to be unladen and the particulars of the quantity and quality of the goods and the packages containing the same and the marks and numbers on the packages and two or more duplicates as the case may require of such bill in which all sums and numbers may be expressed in figures and the particulars contained in such bills shall be written and arranged in such form and manner and the number of such duplicates shall be such as the Collector or other principal officer or other proper person shall require and such person shall at the same time pay down all the duties due upon the goods and the Collector or other proper officer shall thereupon grant his warrant for the unlading of such goods.

of cargo, and does not apply to intercolonial steamers; (c) that they
should have been asked to consider the evidence with reference to trade
and custom, and that, if they believed the evidence, the section could
not be taken to apply to intercolonial steamers and intercolonial trade;
(d) that they should have been directed, that non-report and non-
entry were both necessary to create a forfeiture; (e) that the
unloading should be a removal with intention to evade the Customs
duty and for the purposes of fraud.   Substantially, the same objections were entered in respect of the second count.   (2) With regard
to the third and fourth counts, (a) the jury should have been told to
consider the evidence with respect to practice and custom, and
say, whether a practice of this nature did not take acts of this nature
out of the true construction of section 28 of the Act (¹); (b) that the
unshipment and landing charged in the counts, must be found by
them to mean an unlawful and fraudulent unshipment and landing.
(3) In respect to the sixth and eighth counts, (a) that they should
have been told, that the portmanteaux were not packages within the
true construction of s. 86 of the *Act* (²); (b) that the contents of the
portmanteaux were not dutiable goods as contemplated by the section.
(4) In respect to the 9th and 10th counts, (a) that he should have
told the jury, that the unshipment mentioned in s. 93(³), must amount

(¹) Ib. s. 28. And be it enacted That no goods whatever shall be unshipped
from any ship arriving from parts beyond the seas or landed or put on shore except
on days not being Sundays or holidays and in the day-time nor shall any goods
be so unshipped or landed unless in the presence or with the authority of the
proper officer of the Customs and such goods shall be landed at some wharf quay
or place appointed for the landing of goods by sufferance and that no goods after
being put into any boat or craft to be landed shall be removed into any other
boat or craft previously to their being duly landed without the permission or
authority of the proper officer of the Customs.

(²) Ib. s. 86. And be it enacted That if any goods or merchandise imported into
the said Colony which shall be subject to the payment of duty shall be concealed in
the same packages with other goods or merchandise subject to any lower rate of
duty or not subject to duty with intent to defraud the Revenue of Customs all
such goods contained in the same packages shall be seized by any officer of
Customs and forfeited together with the packages containing the same Provided
always that the proof that such goods or merchandise were not so concealed with
intent to defraud the said Revenue shall lie upon the owner of or importer
thereof.

(³) Ib s. 93. And be it enacted That if any goods liable to the payment of
duties shall be unshipped from any ship vessel or boat in the said colony customs
or other duties not being first paid or secured or if any prohibited goods whatsoever shall be imported into any part of the said colony or if any goods whatsoever shall have been warehoused or otherwise secured in the said colony either
for home consumption or exportation shall be clandestinely or illegally removed
from or out of any warehouse or place of security that then and in such case all
such goods as aforesaid shall be forfeited together with all horses and other
animals and all carriages and other things made use of in the removal of such
goods.

CURPHEY (*qui*
tam) *v.*
HOFFNUNG & Co.

to a fraudulent removal of the goods, so as to render the unshipment illegal ; (e) that the unshipment contemplated by the *Act*, must be an illegal unshipment, and if the removal of the goods had been with the sanction of the Customs authorities, either express or implied, such removal would not be a legal unshipment ; (c) that if Solomon removed the goods from the *City of Brisbane* with a *bonâ fide* intention to pay the duty when he got to Brisbane, it was not an illegal unshipment.

Another ground for a new trial was, that the learned Chief Justice improperly discharged the Jury from giving a verdict on particular counts, without the consent of the parties, or unless such counts were immaterial.   *Tinkler v. Rowland*, 4 A. & E. 868 ; *Empson v. Fairfax* (8 A. & E. 296). In *Powell v. Sonnett*, 3 Bing 381 ; 11 Moore 330, consent was presumed. In *R. v. Johnson* (5 A. & E. 488 ; 6 N. & M. 870), the count had become material. All the other counts, except the sixth and eighth, referred to dutiable goods, and these referred to both dutiable and non-dutiable, and were the only counts alleging fraud. Therefore, though the goods might have been forfeited on the finding of the jury, the portmanteaux would not, and in this respect they were material. The question of costs had an important bearing on this part of the case. The sixth and eighth counts were framed under s. 86 of the *Act*, and alleged an intent to defraud, which was, in fact, the gravamen of the charge, and the *Act* imposed on the defendants the necessity of disproving fraud. Witnesses had been brought from Sydney at great expense, and the fact, that there was no verdict on those counts, precluded the possibility of getting costs.

On the general question of misdirection, His Honour was right on the literal construction of the clauses, but practice and custom of the authorities should have been taken into consideration. Where a practice sanctioned by the authorities led to a breach of the law it should have been put to the jury, that if the unshipping, or landing, was *bonâ fide*, and with the authority of the Custom's officer, either express or implied, that fact would not, so far, take it out of the literal interpretation of the *Act* so as not to create forfeiture, unless there was evidence of subsequent fraud, which would render the

landing illegal *ab initio*. Under s. 24 of the *Act*, (⁵) goods could be CURPHEY (*qui*
landed under a bill of sight, and, although there was no bill of sight *tam) v.*
here, if the evidence could be relied on, a bill of sight was merely a HOFFNUNG & Co.
permission to land, and unless there was subsequent fraud, the
landing by permission, implied by practice and custom, would not be
illegal in the true construction of the *Act*. For instance, a man
might be charged with unlawfully wounding, but he would be at
liberty to prove, that it was the result of an accident ; and so in this
case, the defendants ought to be allowed to have the advantage of his
bonâ fide action (*A. G. v. Hurel*, 11 M. & W. 585, 12 L. J. Ex. 4!3).
An innocent man, though literally wrong, should not be punished.

S. 9 did not apply to intercolonial steamers or to passengers'
luggage, but to cargo in the ship's manifest. How could the master
report a passenger's luggage ? He simply reported the cargo, and the
consignees passed the entries. Solomon was neither consignee nor
consignor, but he would have to pass entries under another clause of
the *Act*. S. 9 was prohibitory and directory in the first part, and
penal as to dutiable goods. There must be a fraudulent removal of
goods to make a transaction illegal, and if they were landed with the
authority of the Customs, there would be no illegality. *R. v. Badger*,
25 L. J. (M.C.) 81 ; *Hammill* on *Customs*, p. 209. The goods were
landed at the wharf. There was no forfeiture under s. 28, under
which the third and fourth counts were framed   With regard to

(⁵)Ib. s. 24. And be it enacted That if the importer of any goods or his known
agent shall make and subscribe a declaration before the Collector or other proper
officer that he cannot for want of full information make perfect entry thereof it
shall be lawful for the Collector or other proper officer to receive an entry by
bill of sight for the packages or parcels of such goods by the best description
which can be given and to grant a warrant thereupon in order that the same may
be landed and secured to the satisfaction of the officers of Customs and at the
expense of the importer and may be seen and examined by such importer in the
presence of the proper officer and within three days after the goods shall have
been so landed the importer shall make a prefect entry thereof and shall either
pay down all duties due thereon or duly warehouse the same and in default of
such entry within such three days such goods shall be taken to the Queen's
warehouse and if the importer shall not within one month after such landing
make perfect entry of such goods and pay the duties due thereon together with
charges of removal and warehouse rent such goods shall be sold for the payment
thereof and the overplus (if any) shall be paid to the proprietor of the goods or
other person duly authorized to receive the same.

Ib. sec. 25. And be it enacted That where any package or parcel shall have
been landed by bill of sight and any goods or other things liable to duty on
importation shall be found in such package or parcel concealed in any way or
packed with intent to deceive the officers of Her Majesty's Customs as well all
such goods and other things as the package or parcel in which they are found
and all other things contained in such package or parcel shall be forfeited.

CURPHEY (qui tam v. HOFFNUNG & Co. counts nine and ten, "unshipment" is defined in s. 82, (⁶) and the practice amounted to a warrant. As to arrest of judgment, (1) the form of procedure is misconceived and erroneous; (2) the informer is not entitled in law to the judgment prayed in the information; (3) it is not competent for the Court to enter up such a judgment; (4) if entered, it would be contrary to law; (5) and the prayer was inconsistent and bad in law. The action was brought as a *qui tam* action, in order to get a standing in Court, but it sought a judgment *in rem*. A *qui tam* action must always be for a money penalty, and could not lie, unless debt would lie. The plaintiff's right to come into Court must be a money consideration, for which he might sue as a debt (*3 Blackstone*, 536). The whole proceedings had been on an action *in rem*, and yet there was nothing in the Statute to enable the plaintiff to bring an action in that form (s s. 106, 108, 109, (⁷) 110) (⁸). A common informer could not sue *in rem* (*2 Hawkins*,

(⁶)Ib. s. 82. And be it enacted That all spirits tobacco and other goods liable to duty which shall be found in the act of removal or be removed without a legal warrant for the same shall be deemed to be goods respectively liable to and unshipped without payment of duty unless the party in whose possession the same shall be found or seized shall prove to the contrary.

(⁷) Ib. s. 109. And be it enacted That all forfeitures and penalties recovered under this or any other Act relating to the Customs shall be paid into the hands of the Collector of Her Majesty's Customs at the port or place where or nearest to where the same shall have been recovered and shall be divided paid and applied (after deducting the charges of prosecution and other contingent expenses) as follows that is to say one moiety to the Colonial Treasurer for the purpose of the General Revenue of the said Colony and the other moiety to the seizing officer or to the person or persons who shall sue or shall have sued for such penalty.

(⁸) Ib. s. 110. And be it enacted That all ships vessels boats and goods which shall have been or shall be hereafter seized as forfeited under any law relating to the Customs and which shall have been or shall hereafter be ordered to be prosecuted by the Collector or other proper officer of the Customs shall be deemed and be taken to be condemned and may be sold in the manner directed by law in respect to ships vessels boats and goods seized and condemned for breach of any law relating to the Customs unless the person from whom such ships vessels boats and goods shall have been seized or the owner of them or some person authorized by him or acting on his behalf shall within one calendar month from the day of seizing the same give notice in writing to the Collector or other chief officer of the Customs at the nearest port that he claims the ship vessel boat or goods or intends to claim them and as soon as the party claiming shall have entered into the security required by the law for prosecuting such claim the vessel or boat seized shall if required be delivered up to the claimant on his entering into bond in double the value thereof with two or more sufficient sureties to be approved of by the Collector or other proper officer of Customs at the port where or nearest to where the seizure was made with condition that in the event of the said vessel or boat being condemned the single penalty of the bond shall be forthwith paid to the aforesaid Collector or other proper officer of Customs.

P. C. 356; *Kennet qui tam v. Lloyd, Bunbury* 59). The plea to a qui tam action would be *nil debet*, and, therefore, the action should be for a money demand. The penalty in a *qui tam* action was against the actual offender, and not against the owner, which should be brought *in rem*. Judgment should be arrested on the counts under s. 28, and the rule granted.

CURPHEY (*qui tam*) *v.* HOFFNUNG & Co.

Cockle, C. J.
Lutwyche, J.

C. A. V.

16th December.

LUTWYCHE, J., delivered the judgment of the Court.

In this case, which was tried before the Chief Justice at the last sittings, Mr. Pring moved on the 9th instant for a rule *nisi* for a new trial, or for an arrest of judgment The grounds on which the learned counsel rested his application for a new trial, were, first, that the Chief Justice improperly discharged the jury from returning any verdict on the sixth and eighth counts of the information; and, secondly, misdirection. As to the discharge of the jury *Powell v. Sonnet*, 1 Dow. (N.S.) 56; 3 Bing 381; 11 Moore 330, and *Rex v. Johnson* (5 Ad. & El., 488), are decisive authorities to show, that when a jury has found their verdict on all the material issues joined, the remaining issues being immaterial, the jury may be discharged by the Judge who tries the cause, from returning any verdict on such immaterial issues, without the consent of the parties. The only question, therefore, which the Court has to consider in disposing of this part of the case is, whether the issues raised on the sixth and eighth counts were material after the finding of the jury on the other issues, or not? The jury found a verdict for the plaintiff on the first, second, third, ninth and tenth counts of the information; and for the defendants on the fourth, fifth, and seventh counts. On the sixth and eighth counts, they were unable to agree. But, if they had agreed, and had found for the defendants on those counts, such a finding would not have precluded the plaintiff from recovering, as a forfeiture, the whole of the goods seized, nor would it have deprived him of the general costs of the cause. The ninth and tenth counts, which were found in his favour, covered all the goods seized (portmanteaux and cases included), and which the information prayed might be, and remain forfeited. After such a finding, and the forfeiture subsequent thereon, it became quite immaterial to ascertain, for the purpose of entering up judgment on the whole record, whether a portion of the goods seized were liable to forfeiture, because they had been concealed in portmanteaux and cases, with an intent to defraud the revenue. And, it may be

CURPHEY (qui
(tam v.
HOFFNUNG & Co.

Cockle, C.J.
Lutwyche, J.

observed, that even if the sixth and eighth counts had included some
goods not covered by any of the other counts in the information on
which the finding of the jury was for the plaintiff, the Court would
not, under the circumstances disclosed in this case, have granted a
rule *nisi* for a new trial generally, but would have confined the
operation of the rule to the sixth and eighth counts, in pursuance of
the authority conferred by the *Supreme Court Act of 1867* (31 Vic.
No. 23, s. 62).   At the best, the defendants would have gained a
dubious advantage by this concession.   But the issues raised on the
sixth and eighth counts having turned out to be immaterial, it appears
to the Court that the jury were properly discharged from giving a
verdict upon them, and that no new trial can be granted in order to
give defendants a chance of getting their costs upon those issues,
costs being merely incidental to a verdict.   The grounds of misdirection were substantially, that the Chief Justice omitted to tell the
jury that in the absence of any evidence of fraud, and on taking into
consideration the practice of the Custom House authorities, they
ought to find that the unloading and unshipment of the goods seized,
were not illegal, if they believed they were so unloaded und unshipped,
with the sanction, expressed or implied, of the Custom House
department.   These objections to the direction of the Chief Justice
assume, that there was evidence of a practice among the Custom
House authorities, having the force of a custom, to allow commercial
travellers to land as passengers' luggage goods liable to duties, before
entry of the goods and the payment of duties upon them.   But a
close examination of the evidence does not reveal the existence of
any such practice, nor does it disclose any fact leading to an inference
of its existence.   There is evidence, that the stores of the A.S.N.
Company at their wharf, were placed by the Custom House authorities
on the same footing as the holds of the Company's steamers, but none
to show, that commercial travellers were ever permitted to land
dutiable goods, even samples, upon the plea that they were passengers'
luggage.   By "passengers' luggage" is meant such articles as are
required for the health, comfort, convenience, or personal ornamentation of a passenger ; the term, certainly, would not include the
contents of a whole jeweller's shop.   But even if it had been proved,
that the alleged practice had prevailed through the negligence or
connivance of subordinate officers of the Customs, the Chief Justice
would not have been justified in telling the jury, that they might take
that evidence into their consideration for the purpose of modifying

and controlling the plain meaning of the language of the Act of
Parliament.   A custom, to be of any value, must be a reasonable
custom, and it would be most unreasonable to hold, that the loose
and irregular practice of a Government department furnishes a
sufficient excuse for the infringement of that very law, which it is
the duty of the officers of the department to enforce in all its
strictness.   And further, it is to be observed, that Solomon, the
commercial traveller of the defendants, appears not to have taken any
steps to obtain the sanction, express or implied, of the Custom House
authorities for the removal of the goods.   They were transhipped by
him from the A.S.N. Company's steamer to the *Nowra*, which neither
belonged to the Company, nor was chartered by them for the occasion,
and they were landed not at the Company's wharf, where a Custom
House officer is always stationed, but at the Queen's wharf, which is
not the station of a Custom House officer, and where, in point of
fact, no Custom House officer was present until after part of the
goods were landed and deposited on a dray for removal.   He did not
even take the precaution, which, under the circumstances, would seem
the most natural to follow, of making an entry inwards by bill of
sight, under the provisions of s. 24 of 9 Vic. No 15.   There may
have been nothing fraudulent in the conduct of Mr. Solomon.   He
may have been animated by the most excellent motives.   But fraud
was not a question which should have been left to the consideration of
the jury.   The offences charged by the first, second, ninth and tenth
counts of the information are not *mala in se*, they are simply *mala
prohibita*.   If the acts prohibited to be done are committed, the
prescribed penalty follows, whatever may have been the intention of
the person committing them.   The Chief Justice told the jury, they
were to say aye or no, whether the goods were unladen before
report, whether they were unladen before entry inwards, and whether
they were unshipped before payment of, or security given for duties,
and, in the opinion of this Court, that direction was right ; any other
would have been manifestly wrong.   And this view is in accordance
with s. 86 of *The Customs Act*, which throws upon the owner or
importer the disproof of fraud.

    There was another objection to the direction of the Chief Justice
on the first and second counts, but it was not much pressed, and only
requires a passing notice.   It was contended, that he should have
told the jury that s. 9 of the *Act*, on which those two counts were
formed, did not apply to intercolonial steamers.   It is sufficient to

CURPHEY (*qui
    tam*) *v.*
HOFFNUNG & Co.

Cockle, C. J.
Lutwyche, J.

say, that the language of the section is general, and applies to ships of all kinds, and it may be observed—although the observation may not be of much importance—that steamers from South Australia, Tasmania, and New Zealand would not generally come within four leagues of the coast, until near their destined port. The suggested exemption would only apply to steamers from New South Wales and Victoria. There will be no rule, therefore, for a new trial.

It remains for the Court to determine, whether sufficient grounds have been shown for an arrest of judgment. The grounds formally assigned for the motion were : (1) That the form of procedure was misconceived and is erroneous ; (2) that the informer is not entitled in law to such judgment as is prayed in the information ; (3) that it is not competent for the Court to enter up such a judgment ; (4) that, if entered, it would be contrary to law ; (5) that the prayer was inconsistent and bad in law. These grounds, however, so far as they related to the whole of the information, were, by the argument, resolved into one, viz., that the information, which was a *qui tam* information, sought a judgment *in rem*, and that a *qui tam* information must always be for a money penalty, and could not lie unless an action for debt would also lie. The Court was referred to 2 *Hawkins* P. C. 356 *et seq.* ; *Com. Digest Action* upon Statute (E) 1.-2. ; and 3 *Blackstone* 536, as authorities for that proposition. But we do not see, that it is made out. All that can be collected is, that when a money penalty is imposed by Statute, and half of it is given to anyone who will sue for it, the informer ought, as a general rule, to sue for the Queen as well as for himself.

On the other hand, there are cases in Bunbury's Reports (see particularly *Idle qui tam v. Vanbeck*, p. 231, which approaches very closely the case before the Court), where a *qui tam* information had been brought for a judgment *in rem*—the thing forfeited. Under s.s. 9 and 93 of *The Customs Regulation Act* no pecuniary penalty is inflicted ; the penalty for a contravention of the provisions of those sections, is a forfeiture of the goods. S. 108 enacts, that all forfeitures incurred by the *Act* may be sued for by information in the name of some officer in Her Majesty's Customs, and s. 109 provides that all forfeitures recorded, shall be paid into the hands of the Collector of Customs and shall be divided (after deducting charges, &c.) as follows:—viz., one moiety to the Colonial Treasurer, and the other moiety to the person who shall sue for such penalty. The plaintiff appears on the face of the record to be an officer of Customs, directed by the Collector of Customs, to prefer the information for the forfeiture of the goods seized, and that being so, he has a sufficient interest to support a *qui tam* information, which can only seek a judgment *in rem*, when the only penalty imposed is forfeiture. A consideration of s. 110 and of form A of the Schedule would be almost enough, even before verdict, to justify the form given to this information, and, besides, the case of *Idle qui tam v. Vanbeck*, Bunbury p. 231, and *Kennet qui tam v. Lloyd*, *ib* p. 59, is an instance in which, though the form was a *qui tam* action, the substantial judgment prayed was *in rem*.

The defendants also seek to arrest the judgment on the grounds that neither the first nor the second counts of the information separately contain an averment of the non-report and non-entry, and that in the ninth and tenth counts there is no averment of an illegal unshipment. We will examine each of these objections in their order. As to the first, we are of opinion, that upon the true construction of s. 9 of the *Act*, either non-report or non-entry is sufficient to create a forfeiture. But even if it were otherwise, the objection could only have been taken by demurrer. After verdict and finding of the jury, that there was no report and no entry, the Court will not allow the judgment to be arrested.

With regard to the second objection, we think it is unnecessary to introduce the word "illegal." In the first place, if the unshipment be prohibited, it becomes illegal *ex vi termini*; and, secondly, it is sufficient, after verdict, if the counts of the information follow, as they do, the words of the sections of the *Act* upon which they are framed. Even in criminal cases after verdict, an indictment is by express enactment sufficient to warrant the punishment prescribed by a Statute, if it describe the offence in the words of the Statute (See 29 Vic. No. 13, s. 39).

We are further asked to arrest the judgment, because the third count contains an averment that the goods were forfeited, although s. 28, upon which that count is framed, does not impose a forfeiture. We do not feel called upon to say whether the count is bad or not. If, as is now clear law, a Judge at *nisi prius* may discharge a jury from giving a verdict upon an immaterial issue of fact, the Court in Banco may as well be at liberty to refrain from expressing an opinion upon an immaterial issue of law. But, assuming the count to be bad, that would afford no ground for arresting the judgment. No precedent can be found—and this observation will apply to the

CURPHEY (*qui tam) v.*
HOFFNUNG & Co.

Cockle, C. J.
Lutwyche, J.

I

CURPHEY (*qui tam*) *v.* HOFFNUNG & Co.
———
Cockle, C.J.
Lutwyche, J.

objections raised to the validity of the first and second, of the ninth and tenth counts—for an arrest of judgment on the whole record, because one count is bad, if there be one good count which will support the whole finding of the jury. Even on error brought in the Exchequer Chamber, it has been held, that a bad count may be treated as inoperative (*Gregory v. the Queen*, 15 Q. B 957).

And if we were so to modify the rule, as to arrest the judgment on the third count only, the defendants would only save the costs of the pleadings, which would hardly pay the costs of the rule. And besides, the plaintiff is still at liberty to enter a *nolle prosequi* to the third count, and might do so, even after entering up judgment on the whole record, when the *nolle prosequi* would become equivalent to a *retraxit.* (*Bowden v. Horne*, 7 Bing, 716.).

Upon the whole, therefore, we are of opinion, that the rule must be refused.

Bramston, A. G., moved for judgment that the goods be declared and remain forfeited..

The motion was granted.

Judgment for Plaintiff.

Solicitor for defendants : *Murphy.*

LAWRENCE v. POOLE.

Capias ad Respondendum.—Money lodged in lieu of bail by third party—Non-fulfilment of condition—Application for return of money—Form of application.

[IN CHAMBERS.]
1871.
18th, 25th Jan.
13th Feb.

Lutwyche, J.

A defendant was arrested on December 31st, 1870, under a writ of *ca re,* and on the same day T offered to put in bail for the appearance of the defendant in the action ; but the office being closed at the time, he paid into the hands of the arresting officer the sum of £46 1s., on the understanding that the money was to be repaid to him if bail was put in. On January 5th, 1871, defendant was adjudicated insolvent. No bail was ever put in.

Held, on an application by T for payment of the money out to him that the form of the application was misconceived ; and as the condition on which the money was lodged had not been fulfilled, the money was bound.

APPLICATION for an order for payment of money out of court.

The facts sufficiently appear in the judgment of the learned Judge.

Bramston, A.G., for the plaintiff : the money having been lodged in Court in lieu of bail, and such bail not having been perfected the money became the property of the plaintiff, and the application must be dismissed. *Reynolds v. Wedd*, 4 Bing, N.C. 694 ; *Edelsten v. Adams*, 8 Taunt 557 ; *Cooke v. Bell*, 11 W. R., 732 ; 8 L. T. 431.

Porter, for the applicant : the cases cited do not apply ; in the present case bail could not be perfected, because the money was lodged with the Sheriff after office hours on Saturday. The following Monday and Tuesday were holidays, and on the next day defendant was made insolvent ; the money must be returned.

C.A.V.

13th February.

LUTWYCHE, J. An application was made to me in Chambers on Wednesday, 25th January last, for an order directing the payment, out of Court, of a sum of £46 1s. to the applicant, Richard Thomas, being the amount of debt and costs paid by Thomas, out of his own pocket, in lieu of bail, to the Sheriff, on behalf of the defendant. Cause was shown in the first instance, by the Attorney-General, who contended that the plaintiff was the only person entitled to the money. The only question, however, which I have now to deal with is whether the defendant is entitled to it.

The defendant Poole was arrested on the 31st December, 1870, under a writ of *ca re*, and on the same day the applicant offered to put in bail for the appearance of the defendant in the action, but the office being closed at the time of this offer, he was induced to pay into the hands of the arresting officer the sum of £46 1s.´ in lieu of the bail, upon the understanding that the money would be returned to him if bail was put in. The office was closed on Monday and Tuesday, the 2nd and 3rd January, 1871, and on Thursday, 5th January, the defendant was adjudged insolvent. No subsequent steps were taken, either by the insolvent or the applicant, to put in bail above, and upon this state of facts I am called on to decide whether the applicant has a right to have the £46 1s. returned to him ?

In the first place it is to be observed that the form of the application is misconceived. A reference to the report of *Edelsten v. Adams*, 8 Taunt 557, will show that the application, if valid on other grounds, should have been made by the defendant, and not as erroneously stated in the text of *Chitty's Archbold*, p. 803 (edn., 1866), by a third person who has deposited the money. But, secondly, assuming it to have been made by the defendant, it could not have been entertained. The money was lodged in lieu of bail, and the condition on which it was lodged not having been fulfilled within the time required by the statute, the money remains at the disposal of the Court, and cannot be taken out by the defendant. (See per Littledale J. in *Ferrall v. Alexander*, 1 Dowl 137). If the applicant had put in bail within the time required by the practice of the Court, and had surrendered his principal, he might have been relieved, but as he failed to do so his money is bound.

Application dismissed without costs.

Solicitor for applicant: *Doyle.*
Solicitors for plaintiff: *Macpherson & Lyons.*

BULLEN v. TULLY.

District Courts Act (31 Vic. No. 30), s. 83 *—*Non-transferable land order—Regulation—Ultra vires—Rejection of evidence— Immigration Act of 1864 (28 Vic., No. 17), s. 7—Crown Lands Alienation Act of 1868 (31 Vic. No. 46). s.s. 46, 53, 97, 124, Schedules C. and E.—Non-suit—Agent—Power of Attorney— Action brought by agent without instructions.*

[In Banco].
1871.
18th March.

Cockle, C. J.
Lutwyche, J.

A regulation alleged to have been made pursuant to authority conferred by *The Crown Lands Alienation Act of 1868*, whereby it was notified that non-transferable land orders would not be received by the Land Agents or the Treasury in liquidation of the first year's rental of land selected by lease or of purchase money of land, unless they were presented by the person in whose favour they were drawn, was held *ultra vires*, and to have been rightly rejected in evidence.

Where an action is brought by an agent under a power of attorney, and, without instructions, the Judge is not bound to non-suit.

Special Case by way of appeal, stated by the Judge of the Metropolitan District Court.

Bramston, A.G. and *McDevitt*, for the appellant.

Lilley, Q.C., Blake, Q.C., and *Griffith*, for respondent.

The action was brought by the plaintiff, Henry Bullen, against W. A. Tully, nominal defendant under *The Claims against the Government Act*, and the plaint set forth that after the passing of *The Immigration Act of 1864*, the plaintiff was the lawful holder of two £30 non-transferable land orders issued under the provisions of that Act, and he was the person named therein as being authorised to purchase land by means of such orders. On the 12th December, 1867, he deposited them with the Government, who advanced £6 on each, and on the 12th April, 1870, he redeemed them, by payment of the amount due thereon. On the 22nd of March, 1870, he made a declaration of two years' residence in the colony. He subsequently left the colony, having previously appointed John Wallace Barnett his agent to make use of the land orders in the purchase of land. Afterwards a piece of land, portion 67, in the parish of Cannning, containing 80 acres, having been offered for sale by auction, and not bid for, was open for selection under *The Crown Lands Alienation Act of 1868*, as

*See 55 Vic., No. 3, s. 132.

agricultural land at the upset price of 15s. per acre, and this was applied for in the form prescribed by the Act on behalf of the plaintiff by his agent, who at the time of making the application delivered the land orders to the land agent at Brisbane in payment of the land, which amounted to £60, and he also paid £5 17s. deed and survey fees. He also, by his agent, made application, accompanied by the declaration of residence, for the deed of grant of the said land to be issued to him. The Government refused to receive the application unless it was presented by the plaintiff in person, or to issue the deed of grant, or to allow the plaintiff to use the land orders unless they were produced and delivered by the plaintiff in person. Damages were claimed for the loss of the cash paid, and the use and benefit of the land orders. At the trial it was proved that the plaintiff, before leaving for England, appointed Mr J. W. Barnett, by power of attorney, under seal, as his agent, to act as alleged in the plaint. The application for the land was made on the 15th September, and was regular and in conformity with the Act and regulations made thereunder, but it was not signed by the plaintiff in person, but by Mr. Barnett as his agent. The other allegations in the plaint were also proved or admitted. On the 22nd September, 1870, Mr. Barnett received a letter from the land agent's office stating that the application had been submitted to the Minister for Lands, who declined to receive it, on the ground that it was in contravention of the regulation published in the *Government Gazette* of the 3rd December, 1868. With this letter was returned the application, the power of attorney, and the land orders, but not the £5 17s. Mr. Barnett returned the documents to the land agent's office, and was informed by letter that he could have them upon application, but he did not apply, and the documents and money were in the hands of the Government when the action was commenced. The application would have been granted if plaintiff had presented his land orders in person.

In cross-examination Mr. Barnett stated that he had no authority to bring the action except the power of attorney, and Mr. Murphy, plaintiff's solicitor, stated that he received instructions from Mr. Barnett under the power of attorney, and he signed the petition as agent for the plaintiff. At the close of the plaintiff's case counsel for the defence moved for a non-suit on the ground that the action had been commenced and continued without the authority of the plaintiff. The Judge declined to direct a non-suit, holding that if the attorney on the record were acting without authority that was a

matter for an application to the Court in the exercise of its jurisdiction over its officers, but was not in issue at the trial of the cause.
The defendant's case was then proceeded with, and his counsel
tendered as evidence the notice of the 3rd December, 1868, which
was as follows :—

BULLEN v.
TULLY.

" Department of Public Lands,
" Brisbane, December 3, 1868.

" NOTICE.—Non-transferable Land Orders.—His Excellency the
Governor, with the advice of the Executive Council, directs it to be
notified that non-transferable land orders will not be received by the
land agents or the Treasury in liquidation of the first year's rental
of land selected by lease or of the purchase money of land otherwise
acquired under the provisions of *The Crown Lands Alienation Act of
1868* in those cases where payments as aforesaid can be made with
land orders, unless they are presented by the person in whose favour
the non-transferable land orders are drawn.   The land agents
throughout the colony are particularly required to satisfy themselves
as to the identity of the individuals tendering non-transferable land
orders in order to see that the above requirement is fulfilled.

" By His Excellency's command,
" A. MACALISTER."

This notice was objected to on the ground that it was irrelevant
unless it operated as a regulation under some statutory power; that
it did not purport to be a regulation, and that, if it were, the Government had exceeded their powers in issuing it.   The Judge rejected
the evidence, deciding that when the original holder of a non-transferable land order wished to exercise the right of making such an
order available as payment for land purchased from the Government,
the Government had no authority to impose on such holder the
obligation of a personal attendance at the land office for the purpose
of tendering a land order ; that the notice had the effect of restraining
the right given to holders of non-transferable land orders under
section 7 of *The Immigration Act of 1864* ; and that no power was
given by *The Crown Lands Alienation Act of 1868*, or other Act, to
make regulations affecting *The Immigration Act of 1864*. No other
evidence was offered by the defendant, and a verdict was given for
the plaintiff for £65.   The defendants gave notice of appeal, and the
parties disagreeing to the terms of the special case, the present case
was stated in accordance with *The District Courts Act* and rules.
The questions submitted by the Judge of the District Court were—

BULLEN *v.*
TULLY.

(1.) Was I correct in holding that the objection taken as to the absence of authority of the attorney on the record to bring the action formed no ground for a nonsuit? (2.) Was the proposed evidence of the notice in the *Gazette* of the 3rd December, 1868, properly rejected?

Bramston, A.G. The application made by Barnett in the name of the plaintiff was refused by the Government on the ground that they required the personal attendance of the plaintiff, in accordance with the regulation of the 3rd December, 1861, and on the refusal Mr. Barnett proceeded to bring the action, and instructed Mr. Murphy to sign the petition as attorney for the plaintiff. The questions now to be decided are—(1) whether the power of attorney authorised Barnett to sue in the name of the plaintiff, because, if it did not, it would not authorise Mr. Murphy to take instructions from Barnett to enter upon the proceedings; and if there was no authority to bring the action, was that a point on which the defendant was entitled to take advantage on the trial, and get a non-suit? (2.) If he was not entitled to take that course, was the defendant justified in refusing to recognise Mr. Barnett as Mr. Bullen, as the Regulation required holders of non-transferable land orders to present them in person? On the first point there was no authority to bring the action, and the defendant was therefore entitled to take advantage of the point on the trial as ground for a non-suit. Although the power of attorney gave power to defend actions, it gave no power to bring them, and it would appear that such power was intentionally omitted. If it was intended to import such a power, it surely would have been stated. The point was therefore rightly raised. It would be so in the Supreme Court, and was still more so in the District Court. The 83rd section of the *District Courts Act* (a) provides that "the Judge shall have power to non-suit the plaintiff in every case in which satisfactory proof shall not be given entitling him to the judgment of the Court." The plaintiff must satisfy the Judge that he is entitled to judgment of the Court, or he is bound to be non-

(a) [31 Vic. No. 30 s. 83]. Every judgment of any District Court except as herein provided shall be final and conclusive between the parties but the Judge shall have power to non-suit the plaintiff in every case in which satisfactory proof shall not be given entitling him to the judgment of the Court and shall also in every case whatever have the power if he think fit to order a new trial to be had upon such terms as he shall think reasonable and in the meantime to stay the proceedings.

suited.   Of course, the first thing for a plaintiff to do is to show his existence, and here there was no plaintiff.   It could not be Mr. Bullen, because he was ignorant of the proceedings, and could not be Mr. Barnett, because he had no power to sue in Bullen's name.

COCKLE, C.J.   Can a non-suit be granted in a case in which a verdict for the defendant could not be entered if the case went on ? If he is not the attorney of the plaintiff, how can you non-suit him and visit him with costs?   You say, "You have no authority for these proceedings, and therefore we will make you pay the costs of the whole of them."

Bramston, A.G.   I refer to *Mudry v. Newman*, 1 C., M. & R., 402; *Ancona v. Marks*, 31 L. J. (Ex) 163.

COCKLE, C.J.   Assuming that the plaintiff knows nothing about the proceedings, is he not to have the advantages of a verdict ?

Bramston, A.G.   Certainly not, if another man brings the action. He could not have the chances of a verdict in his favour while he would be in a position to repudiate the whole of the proceeding if the verdict was adverse.   The defendant could not plead judgment in this case on an action brought against him by the real plaintiff   Payment of the verdict in this case would be no answer to an action brought by the real plaintiff.   In fact there was no plaintiff here.

LUTWYCHE, C.J.   There is a plaintiff on the record, and the person there named is shown to have a claim against the defendant. If he has a claim, how can he be non-suited ?

COCKLE, C.J.   Proof of the authority of an attorney is not a condition precedent to having a case.

Bramston, A.G.   If the plaintiff was not before the Court, another man had no right to use his name.   There is not the same power to stop proceedings in the District Court as in the Supreme Court, and the facts in this case were not disclosed until the trial, and there being no authority to bring the action, the defendant was entitled to a non-suit.   Proof of the inability to bring the action was proof of the absence of the liability of the defendant, because he was not responsible to Mr. Barnett.

COCKLE, C.J.   That did not prove absence of liability.   It might be that the defendant was liable, but that the plaintiff had not given authority to sue.

LUTWYCHE, J.   The District Court Judge says, in substance, that the plaintiff has proved his case.

Bramston, A.G. If Bullen has not given authority, the defendant will be liable to be sued a second time.

COCKLE, C.J. If there could have been a non-suit, are we bound to order a non-suit?

Bramston, A.G. No; you will order a new trial. If there could have been a non-suit, we are entitled to be placed in the same position we were in before the trial.

LUTWYCHE, J. I refer you to the case *Bayley v. Buckland*, 1 Ex. 1. According to that case, a person whose name was used without authority would have his remedy against the attorney. In this case, if plaintiff had been non-suited, he would have had his remedy against Mr. Murphy.

COCKLE, C.J. The question appeares to me to be, Was' the learned Judge below bound to non-suit?

Bramston, A.G. It is whether the objection was a good ground for a non-suit. The next question is whether the Regulation of the 3rd December was properly rejected. It ought to have been admitted on two grounds. It was a Regulation under *The Crown Lands Alienation Act of 1868*, and, if not, it was notice to the world that the Government would refuse to receive land orders in payment for land except presented by the holders in person. It was admissible as explaining the letter of 22nd September, 1870, which formed part of the plaintiff's case. The 124th section of the Act (*b*) gives power to the Governor-in-Council to make, alter, or rescind all necessary regulations for the due carrying out of the provisions of the Act, and this was a regulation under that section. Some point might be raised upon the word "Notice," but I submit that whether the instrument is headed

(*b*) [31 Vic., No. 46, s. 124]. It shall be lawful for the Governor from time to time to make and alter or rescind all necessary regulations for the due carrying out of the provisions of this Act and for the care protection and management of all public parks and reserves and for the preservation of good order and decency therein and all such regulations shall be proclaimed and be posted in some conspicuous place in every such park or reserve and every person who shall knowingly and wilfully offend against any such regulation shall on conviction before a justice forfeit and pay a penalty not exceeding five pounds for each such offence in addition to any other penalty he may receive for the same action under any other law and every person who shall knowingly and wilfully offend against any such regulation and after being warned by any bailiff of Crown lands park keeper or police constable shall not desist from so offending may be thereupon apprehended by such bailiff park keeper or constable and taken before some justice of the peace and shall be liable on conviction to forfeit and pay a penalty not exceeding ten pounds.

"Notice" or "Regulation," will not affect its validity.   It will
not cease to be a regulation because it is headed "Notice," and by
looking at its terms it is evident what it is intended to be.
It operates in respect to lands acquired under the present
Act, and therefore it is a regulation which appeared to the
Governor-in-Council necessary to carry out the provisions of the Act.
The 46th section of the Act provides (c) that "any person (except
as hereinafter excepted) may on any office day, during office hours,
tender to the Commissioner or Land Agent for the district an application in the form contained in schedule E. of this Act for selection of
land within any area proclaimed as open for selection as aforesaid,
accompanied by a deposit in cash or land orders equal to the first
instalment on the land to be selected." The 53rd section of the Act (d)
requires a person making application for a conditional purchase to
make a solemn declaration to the effect contained in schedule E.,
which is that he applies for such land on his own behalf, and for
his own use, and not as agent or trustee for any other person whatsoever; and also that he has not entered into any agreement to sell,
demise, or mortgage the said land.   These were provisions for the
acquisition of land for personal occupation, and it was advisable in the
case of non-transferable orders being used, that the holder should
attend in person and make the declaration.   Conditional purchasers
have ten years to pay for the land, and persons holding non-transferable land orders may pay the first year's rent with such orders,
and it is only carrying the condition one step further to require

(c) [31 Vic., No. 46, s. 46]. The mode and terms of selection shall be as
follows——Any person (except as hereinafter excepted) may on any office day
during office hours tender to the Commissioner or land agent for the district
an application in the form contained in Schedule E of this Act for selection of
land within any area proclaimed as open for selection as aforesaid accompanied
by a deposit in cash or land orders equal to the first instalment payable on
the land to be selected at the price of——
    Fifteen Shillings per acre payable in ten annual instalments of one
    Shilling and six pence per acre for agricultural land Ten shillings per acre
    payable in ten annual instalments of one Shilling per acre for first-class
    pastoral land Five Shillings per acre payable in ten annual instalments of
    Six pence per acre for second-class pastoral land.
Together with the survey fees payable respectively in each case.
    (d) [31 Vic., No., 46. s. 53]. On making application for any land under the
foregoing clauses of this Act a conditional purchaser shall be required to
make a solemn declaration to the effect contained in Schedule E.   Provided
always that this shall not apply to Conditional Purchasers or Selections of
land made by a pastoral tenant to secure his homestead or improvements on
the reserved half of his original run or to secure his improvements on the leased
half as provided by this Act.

BULLEN *v.*
TULLY.

BULLEN v.
TULLY.

presentation in person. The notification in question must, therefore, be taken to be a regulation under the Act, and having the force of the law, and should have been admitted on the trial. The next question is—Was it an answer to the plaintiff's case? and I submit that it is.

LUTWYCHE, C.J. As I read the case, it was an application to purchase land under the 97th section of the Act (*e*), not to lease it under the 46th.

Bramston, A G. : It is a regulation under the Act, and ought to have been admitted, but still it might have been no answer to the plaintiff's case. Its admissibility is one thing, and its value another. I contend, however, that it was an answer to the plaintiff's case.

CCCKLE, C.J. : If it could have no possible effect on the verdict, it ought in strictness to have been admitted, but its rejection would not be a ground for a new trial.

LUTWYCHE, J. : Suppose the application was to lease land before survey, what authority has the Government, under the 124th section of the Act, to say that non-transferable orders should be presented by the applicant in person? What is to prevent him from making application in form E., and sending it by post? Why should the Government compel a man to travel from one end of the colony to the other—say from the Gulf of Carpentaria to Brisbane—to present his land order?

Bramston, A.G. : Because land orders are possessed by persons who are not the owners, and who use them as their own. In fact, they neutralise the provisions of the Act, and this regulation was made to meet such cases. Can a letter in post be a tender?

LUTWYCHE, J. I should say so. I see nothing which requires the attendance of an applicant in person.

Bramston, A.G. : Admitting that a tender through the post would be good, we still hold that it should be made by the applicant himself, and not by another party. The regulation was made to prevent abuses. A land order is an authority under the 7th section of *The*

(*e*) [31 Vic., No. 46, s. 97]. Any person desiring to purchase country lots by selection after the same shall have been offered at auction and not sold shall apply to the land agent in the form in the Schedule C to this Act and shall at the same time pay into the hands of the land agent the full price of the land together with the deed and survey fees and such applicant shall thereupon be deemed to be the purchaser of such lot.

Immigration Act of 1864 (*f*)for the purchase of land by selection or by auction. They are issued by the Government for certain considerations, and the Government have a right to insist on the owner identifying himself. The object is that the Government may be satisfied that the holder is the person to whom they are indebted. The regulation does not restrict the availability of the land order; it merely requires that the person to whom it is issued shall be the purchaser under it.

COCKLE, C.J.: You insist upon one species of identification?

Bramston, A.G.: Yes, because nothing is easier than for a holder to dispose of his order and leave the colony, and if the Government have not the power to require the identification of the person in order to prove that the transaction is *bona fide*, the land revenue and the public interest will suffer materially, and where public and private interests clash the interest of the public must prevail. A land order is a personal privilege to a particular person, and it is a privilege which it is easy to throw away or to work wrongfully, and the interests of the State should be preserved.

COCKLE, C.J. May not a merchant send his clerk to receive payment of a non-negotiable bill of exchange?

Bramston, A.G.: It would not be paid unless the party was known. A cheque payable to a certain person would not be paid to any one else without his direct authority.

LUTWYCHE, J.: As I read the case this is not an application to lease land but to purchase land under the 97th section of the Act, and Schedule C, which says nothing about not being the agent or any other person or about occupation. It simply says, "I——— am desirous of purchasing the portion of Crown lands hereinunder described, which is now open to selection without competition, having been previously offered for sale and not bid for, and I hereby tender the sum of——as the price thereof including the fee on the deed."

Bramston, A.G.: The regulation was an act which the Government had a right to do as a protection of the public interest. The land orders gave a personal right to the owner only.

COCKLE, C.J.: A personal right may be exercised by an agent.

Bramston, A.G.: No doubt, but where personal right comes in conflict with public interest, the former must give way.

(*f*) [28 Vic., No. 17, s. 7]. The said non-transferable land order shall be available to its full nominal value for the purchase of any country or suburban lands which may be offered for sale by auction or which may be open to selection in any part of the Colony.

BULLEN *v.*
TULLY.

COCKLE, C.J.: Where is the evidence that they do conflict?

Bramston, A.G.: The Government was clearly of that opinion, and accordingly made a regulation to meet the case.

LUTWYCHE, J.: After all, that is no real security. We have heard of such things as personation.

Bramston, A.G.: No doubt it is frequently practised.

COCKLE, C.J.: Supposing the regulation is admissible as evidence, what is it evidence of ?

Bramston, A.G.: I contend it is admissible as a regulation under the Act, and has the force of law, and that we are entitled to have the second question answered in our favour.

Lilley, Q.C. It cannot be made a ground of non-suit that the attorney is not authorised.

COCKLE, C.J.: We are satisfied as to that.

Lilley, Q.C. The so-called regulation is not a regulation, but simply a notice. It does not profess to be a regulation, and it is not evidence under *The Evidence and Discovery Act* It is merely an advertisement, and can have no effect whatever, because in looking into the case a striking fact would appear. How can an advertisement published on the 3rd December, 1868, contravene a contract made in 1867, when Bullen got the land orders ? There is no pretence made of *mala fides* in the case. The Government issued the notice and took the hazard in respect to a man who was a *bona fide* agent acting on behalf of his principal. They issued land orders, which were equivalent to cash for the purchase of land, to the plaintiff in 1867, and in 1868 they issued a notice which said he must present the order in person. Can such an order be insisted upon ? I maintain it cannot. As an advertisement the notice is not admissible, and even if it was a proclamation, if it had no bearing on the case, the Judge was not compelled to admit it, and it would not be ground for a new trial. *The Immigration Act of 1864* gives no power to make regulations, but the terms on which land orders are issued are explicitly set out. The land orders in this case were issued to the plaintiff, and were held by Barnett for him, and so far from any fraud being possible *The Immigration Act* required that the title to the land should be issued in the name of the holder, which in this case would be Bullen. The plaintiff has performed the only condition required by the Act—that of two years' residence in the colony ; but the Government now endeavour to add to this land order a condition not imposed by statute. If there was a general

power to make regulations, the Government could not make regulations requiring personal attendance. They could not take away from
a man his Common Law right to do by an agent what he could do
by himself. There is no power in the Act of 1864 to make regulations, but it is sought to make a notice under the Act of 1868 apply
to the Act of 1864. A regulation professing to be made under the
Act of 1868 clearly does not apply to things done under the Act of
1864. There is nothing in the Act to say that a person should
present his order in person, and there should be some such provision
in the Act if the regulation is to have any effect. The Government
can only deal with the waste lands of the colony by statute; and
they can only make regulations consistent with the provisions of the
Act. The plaintiff did not apply under the 46th section of the Act,
but for an absolute purchase under the 97th section. There is
nothing in the Act to prevent an agent doing anything that could be
done by the principal. The Government cannot deprive a man of
his Common Law privilege when there is no authority in the Act
to do so. Such a power would have a most pernicious effect in regard
to land transactions, and personal attendance would preclude some
persons from using their land orders where they might desire. The
regulation does not affect the purchase of land, but the cash availability
of the land order, which *The Immigration Act of 1864* declares to be
perfect, and there is therefore no power to make it.

COCKLE, C.J. : It does not purport to have been made under the
provisions of the Act. It merely refers to the Act as being
descriptive

Bramston, A.G., replied.

COCKLE, C.J. This was a case the facts of which are sufficiently
known to all of us, and upon it two points have been referred to us
for our decision. With regard to the first question, had it been
" Was I bound to non-suit ?" I would unhesitatingly answer " No,"
and I may still make that answer. It may, however, be well to notice
S. 83 of *The District Courts Act of 1867*, which gives power to the Judge
to non-suit the plaintiff in every case in which satisfactory proof is
not given entitling him to the judgment of the Court. But we think
that section makes no difference, as it would appear to relate to a
Judge deciding in favour of the defendant if there was no evidence to
go to the jury. That appears to be a much more reasonable view of
the section, than to say it was intended to give a Judge power to non-
suit because there was not sufficient proof of the authority. We

BULLEN *v.*
TULLY.

Cockle, C. J.

BULLEN *v.*
TULLY.

Cockle, C.J.

think such an objection might be a ground for a motion to stay proceedings, but it is certainly not a ground for a non-suit. With regard to the second question, I suppose as this case is framed we can only look at the reasons given for the rejection, as no judgment was given on the ground that the regulation was not a regulation. Something was said about interpretation, and I understood the learned Attorney-General to say the regulation did not necessarily entail personal attendance, and if so, no harm has resulted from its rejection.

Bramston, A.G. I did not go quite as far as that. I said a person might make an application by letter under his hand.

COCKLE, C.J. At all events that question was raised, and it was contended in the Court below that that was the principal grievance complained of, because nothing else required personal attendance. We may take notice also of this, although the evidence was utterly useless, the Judge might have admitted it, but if he rejects it, and it is seen by the Court of Appeal to be useless, they would not interfere, and the verdict must stand. Although this question is not expressly raised, I hardly like to say positively that it is excluded from our consideration. Unquestionably it would require a considerable straining of interpretation of language to hold that this was a regulation. It is good practice that when anything is done in the name and behalf of the State, reasonable notice should be given that it is done as an act of public authority. It should purport to be done in pursuance of authority, but here there is nothing. The heading of the notice, or regulation, or whatever it may be, is "Non-transferable Land Orders." That might lead or mislead one to think, unless instructed by a lawyer, that it was intended to be a regulation made in pursuance of *The Act of 1864*, but on reading it through there is a distinct mention of *The Crown Lands Act of 1868*. So there may be a struggle between the two Acts for this regulation. The heading is of *the Act of 1864*, but the latter part is of *the Act of 1868*. I think without a more definite expression of opinion from the Legislature, we should not be justified in saying that such a regulation applied to *the Act of 1868*, and still less so *the Act of 1864*, because it would then be a decided alteration of the whole contract made betwen the colony and the owner of land orders given in 1867. It does not affect the purchase of the land, but the cash availability of the land order. I have every wish to execute loyally the regulation of the Government, but in this case I do not think it would be safe, and I agree in the opinion of the learned Judge below.

LUTWYCHE, J. I think the judge below was quite right on both points on which he gave his decision. With regard to the notice or regulation of December, 1868, I consider it is *ultra vires*. It was not made in pursuance of *the Act of 1868*, but in contravention of it, and it imposed on the holder of a non-transferable land order an obligation which would be onerous and burdensome to him, and which, if created at all, should have been created by an express Act of the Legislature, and not by a notification issuing from the Governor-in-Council. I also think, looking at s.s. 46 and 97 of the Act, and schedules C. and E., that it may reasonably be inferred that personal attendance was not necessary, and the owner of non-transferable land orders might apply and act by an agent. In one place he makes a personal declaration that he applies to lease land before survey on his own behalf; whereas in Schedule C. under the 97th section he purchases land, and no such declaration is required. A single form is given to be filled up by him, or by any one else authorised by him. As to the other point with reference to the authority of the attorney, I think with the Chief Justice that it is no ground for a non-suit.

Appeal dismissed with costs.

Solicitor for Appellant: *The Crown Solicitor.*

Solicitor for Respondent: *Murphy.*

MORRISON *v.* ROBERTS & HART.

1871.
28th April.
Sheppard,
D.C.J.

*Real Property Act of 1861 (25 Vic., No. 14), S. 46—Trial of action—
Evidence—Production of instrument by Registrar-General*

Section 46 of 25 Vic. No. 14 does not refer to judicial proceedings.

The Registrar-General was held bound to produce an application to bring
land under the Act, which he had stated was in his possession.

TRIAL of an action in the District Court brought by the plaintiff,
John W. Morrison, to recover a sum of £200 for money payable by
the defendants, Daniel Foley Roberts and Graham Lloyd Hart, to the
plaintiff, for money had and received by the defendants for the use
of the plaintiff, and for money found to be due by the defendants to
the plaintiff on accounts stated between them, and the plaintiff
abandoned the excess of his demand above £200, and claimed that
amount.

Griffith, for the plaintiff.

Lilley, Q.C., for the defendants.

The action arose out of certain transactions with respect to the
purchase of certain property at Bowen Bridge, Brisbane.   Henry
Scott, Registrar-General, was called to prove that he had an application in his custody, signed by one Meyer on February 16th, to bring
land under *The Real Property Act of 1861*.   Witness believed that
he had the document in his possession, but before producing it
wished to know whether he had any right to do so under 46th section
of *The Real Property Act*, which provided that, " So soon as any land
shall have been brought under the provisions of this Act, no transferee or mortgagee shall be entitled to the production of any deed or
other instrument surrendered by the proprietor or any memorandum
of transfer or other instrument dated prior to the exisiting certificate
of title of such land unless such instrument be recorded in the
register book and upon the existing certificate of title as an encumbrance lien or interest affecting the said land.   Provided that nothing
herein contained shall interfere with any order that may be made by
a Judge of the Supreme Court for the production of any such deed
or instrument."

SHEPPARD, D.C.J., held that the clause did not refer to judicial
proceedings, and that the instrument should be produced.

Solicitor for Plaintiff : *Bunton*.

Solicitors for Defendants : *Roberts & Hart*.

R. v. CASTLES & GRIFFITHS.

Criminal Law — Information — Joinder of several felonies in different counts against two prisoners in one information— Larceny Act of 1865 (29 Vic., No. 6), s.s. 10, 11.

[IN BANCO.]
1871.
31st May.

Cockle, C.J.
Lutwyche, J.

In an information against two prisoners a count for feloniously stealing a cow had been joined with counts for feloniously killing a cow, with intent to steal the carcase and hide, and one prisoner was found guilty on the second count, but not guilty on the first and third, and the other prisoner was found guilty on the first, but not guilty on the second and third.

The conviction was affirmed, the right being reserved for the prisoners to sue out a writ of error.

An application should have been made to quash the information.

CROWN case reserved by the Judge of the Metropolitan District Court.

James Castles and Spencer Griffiths were tried on 22nd May at Warwick on an information containing three counts (1) that on the 13th May last they did feloniously steal, take, and drive away one cow, the property of Frank Buttner; (2) that they did feloniously kill the cow with intent to steal the carcase; (3) that they did feloniously kill the cow with intent to steal the hide. The prisoners pleaded not guilty, and were defended by their attorney. There was ample evidence to go to the jury against the prisoner Griffiths on the first, second, and third counts, and also against Castles on the second and third counts; the judge ruling there was no evidence against him on the first. It appeared from the evidence that the cow in question was in possession of the bailee of the owner on 11th May, and it was found in the stockyard of the prisoner early in the morning of 13th; and the evidence adduced by the prisoner as to how it came into his possession was found by the jury to be false. About sunrise on the morning of the 13th the prisoners killed the cow, and before skinning and cutting up the carcase they were interrupted by the police. No objection was taken by the prisoners' attorney that they were charged in the first count with one felony, and in the second and third with another felony; nor was any application made that the Crown Prosecutor should elect to proceed on one or other of the counts. The jury first brought in a verdict of not guilty against Castles on

R. v. CASTLES
& GRIFFITHS.
———
Cockle, C.J.
Lutwyche, J.

the first count, and guilty on the first and third, and guilty against Griffiths on all counts. The judge then explained to the jury that there was no necessity to convict the prisoners on more than one count, and a verdict was then returned against Castles of " guilty " on the second, and " not guilty " on the first and third counts ; and of " guilty " against Griffiths on the first, and " not guilty " on the second and third counts. No motion was made in arrest of judgment, and each prisoner was sentenced to three years' penal servitude. Before passing sentence, the Judge entertained some doubt, whether from the evidence adduced, the count for feloniously stealing should have been joined with those for feloniously killing with intent to steal the carcase and hide. He also entertained a doubt, whether on the information, one prisoner could be found guilty on the first count, and not guilty on the second and third, and the other could be found guilty on the second, and not guilty on the first and third counts. The prisoners were undergoing sentence, and the opinion of the Court was requested on the questions (1) whether on the information the prisoners, or either of them, ought to have been convicted, and (2) whether the record was correct.

Bramston, A.G., for the Crown, in support of the conviction it was competent to join several descriptions of offences in the same indictment, and therefore on the first point the conviction must be maintained. *R. v. Heywood*, 33 L. J. (M.C.) 133 ; *R. v. Moah*, Dears 626 ; *R. v. Trueman*, 8 C. & P. 727 ; *R. v Mitchell*, 3 Cox, C. C. 93. [LUTWYCHE, J., mentioned *R. v. Hinley*, 2 M. & R. 524; *R. v. Kingston*, 8 East 41; 9 R.R. 373; *Young v. R.*, 3 T. R. 98, 106]. On the second point the counts being joined, and the transactions which created the offence charged against each prisoner being the same, it was competent to find them guilty on different counts. *R. Butterworth*, R. & R. 520 ; *R. v. Hempstead*, R. & R. 344 ; *R. v. Pulham*, 9 C. & P., 280 ; *R. v. Hayes*, 2 M. & R. 155 ; 2 *Hawkins*, P. C. 622.

COCKLE, C.J. An application should have been made to quash the information. The conviction must be affirmed. *R. v. Hayes*, 2 M. & R. 155. We reserve the right to the prisoners to sue out a writ of error, if they think fit.

LUTWYCHE, J., concurred, and referred to *R. v. Wheeler*, 7 C. & P. 170.

Conviction affirmed.

PECHEY v. CRAWFORD.

Real Property Act of 1861 (25 Vic., No. 14), s. 91—Judgment—Writ of execution—Caveat.

[IN CHAMBERS.]
1871.
28th June.

Lutwyche, J.

The registration of a writ of execution upon a judgment against land under *The Real Property Act* cannot be entered as a caveat.

SUMMONS by E. W. Pechey calling on W. Crawford to show cause why a caveat lodged by him in the office of the Registrar-General, in respect of certain land at Drayton, should not be withdrawn. Pechey was the registered proprietor of the land in question, which he obtained by grant from the Crown.

On 17th September, 1866, he executed a mortgage of the land to the trustees of the Toowoomba Building Society, No. 2, to secure the repayment of £200 then advanced to him. This money and the interest was still due, but the mortgage had not been registered. On 3rd September, 1867, Crawford obtained a judgment against Pechey and others trading under the name and style of "The Highfields Steam Saw Mills Company" in the District Court for £72 5s. 10d., and on 11th January, 1868, Crawford entered a writ of execution upon the judgment as a caveat against the mortgaged land, and the society was merely prevented from realising the amount of their debt. The summons was brought to remove the obstruction.

Pring, Q C., in support of the summons.

Murphy showed cause.

LUTWYCHE, J., held that the registration of the judgment was not a caveat within the meaning of *The Real Property Act*, and dismissed the summons with costs.

Summons dismissed with costs.

Solicitor for applicant : *Bowker.*
Solicitor for respondent : *Murphy.*

In re PENTECOST, Ex parte MISKIN.

[IN INSOLVENCY.]
1871.
10th, 24th July,
4th August.

Lutwyche, J.

Insolvency Act of 1864 (28 Vic., No. 25), s.s. 3, 17, 74, 100—Mortgage —Fraudulent Preference—Specific Performance.

A Judge of the Insolvency Court has jurisdiction under s. 100 of the Act of 1864 to determine, in a summary way, claims relating to realty, and has power to enforce its orders on the losing claimant.

A mortgage not made in pursuance of a written agreement made at the time of contracting an antecedent debt, but given within sixty days of the adjudication of the mortgagor for an alleged antecedent debt, was held to be a fraudulent preference under s. 74 of the Act aforesaid, and the mortgagee was directed to discharge the said mortgage.

It is not necessary to the specific performance of a written agreement that it should be signed by the party seeking to enforce it, but the agreement must be certain, fair and just in all its parts.

MOTION to make absolute a rule *nisi* calling on Henry Spiro to shew cause why the Court should not determine the claim of the Official and Creditors' Assignees (W. H. Miskin and E. Goertz) to certain premises comprised in a mortgage executed on 20th March, 1871, by the insolvent in favour of Spiro ; and why he should not be ordered to discharge the same from the mortgage ; and why he should not pay the costs of these proceedings on the grounds (1) that the making of the bill of mortgage was an act of insolvency, and (2) that the mortgage was a fraudulent preference.

According to the evidence the insolvent Pentecost, who had been the owner of the Picnic Hotel and grounds near Toowoomba, mortgaged them to the Bank of New South Wales in November, 1866, to secure the repayment of £440 and the interest thereon. Some of this amount had been paid off, and on 26th January, 1869, Pentecost addressed a letter to Spiro, in which, after stating that he had just returned from Gympie, where he had vainly endeavoured to get payment of dishonoured bills amounting to £233, he continued : " I have been very unlucky ; in fact, I don't know what to be at, as Walker is continually pressing me for the payment of the bank's claim. I have been paying him £6 5s. 0d. a month up to this, but I do not know how I am to do it now, as I am out of business. I wanted Goertz to take up the mortgage before their last bill got dishonoured, but they said they could not. Well, you know, I got those goods for Wappet,

and as I did not get his money, and trade being so dull, I could not
pay for them; but the garden is looking first-rate, and, if all goes well, I will be able to clear every one off soon. Goertz's people are very kind, and say they will never press me, and they won't lose anything by that. The fact of the matter is, I want to know if you will give me a start again in the public-house. I have no money. Goertz says he will wait, as there is Kohn and Co., Ocock, and the Bank pressing me very tight, all threatening. Now, if you like to take the risk, you will be doing me a favour, and if you want security let me know, because if I am pressed by those parties, I will try and manage something for you; I don't know what, unless you like to take a second mortgage for £200 or £300 on the place I live in, for it is worth a good deal more than I have borrowed on it; but any time will do for that. I would rather Goertz would do it, but he refuses, and it would be a pity to have to lose this place now, for if I could manage to open the house I think it would pay, and I shall be able to clear off the old debts, and look after the garden too. P.S.—Consider this matter and let me know as soon as you can."

On the strength of this letter Spiro inspected the property, and believing it was a sufficient security for the sum requested, he promised to make the advance. On 1st February following he advanced Pentecost £150. He subsequently advanced further sums and goods to a considerable amount, and various sums were paid by Pentecost. On 16th March, 1871, legal proceedings were instituted by Goertz and Co. against Pentecost, and the writ of summons was sent to the Sheriff's bailiff at Toowoomba for service. The bailiff called at Pentecost's place on 20th March, and was informed that Pentecost was not at home, and he received the same reply on two subsequent occasions. At length he served the writ on Pentecost's wife on the 24th. Judgment was signed on 12th April, and execution was issued for £289 9s. 9d. on 18th April. The execution not having been satisfied, Pentecost was adjudicated insolvent on 27th April on the petition of Goertz and Co. Previously, on 20th March, under pressure from Spiro, he executed the mortgage now in question, in consideration of the debt of £300 then due by him. Spiro was not then aware of any legal action having been taken against Pentecost.

Pring, Q.C., and *Harding* moved the rule absolute.

Lilley, Q.C., for Spiro, showed cause.

The arguments appear in the judgment of the learned Judge.

C. A.V.

4th August.

In re PENTECOST,
v.
Ex parte MISKIN.
———
Lutwyche, J.

LUTWYCHE, J. A rule *nisi* was obtained by Mr Harding on the 10th July last calling upon Henry Spiro to shew cause why the Court should not determine a claim of W. H. Miskin, the official assignee, and Ernest Goertz, creditors' assignee, in the insolvent estate of Pentecost, to the hereditaments and premises contained in a Bill of Mortgage dated 20th March, 1871, and made in favour of Spiro by the insolvent, discharged from the said Bill of Mortgage, and why Spiro should not be ordered to discharge the same accordingly with costs upon the grounds (1) that the making of the said Bill of Mortgage was an act of insolvency, (2) that the said Bill of Mortgage was a fraudulent preference. Cause was shown against the rule by Mr. Lilley on the 24th July, and after hearing Mr. Pring and Mr. Harding in support of the rule, I took time to consider my decision. The application was made to the Court under the provisions of s. 100 of *The Insolvency Act of 1864*, which enacts that in case of any claim, dispute or difference between the official assignee, the creditors' assignee, and the creditors, or any such persons, to any money or property claimed as part of the estate of any insolvent, either party may apply to the Court, and it shall be lawful for the Court to determine the same, and to give such directions and make such orders relative thereto as shall to the Court seem just and expedient, and to award costs. It was contended by Mr. Lilley that this section does not give the Court jurisdiction over claims to the real property of the insolvent, but only over claims to the personal estate. But that point has already been decided by this Court. It was held *in re Sams* (10th July, 1866,) that the terms of the section were large enough to embrace real as well as personal property. There was no appeal from that decision, and it was acted upon by the Court subsequently in *The Assigned estate of Godfrey Freeman White; ex parte M. B. Goggs*, decided 5th December, 1866 (1 S. C. R. 149). It was also further argued by Mr. Lilley that even if s. 100 gave the Court power to determine claims to realty, no provision was made in it to enforce the determination of the Court on the person of the losing claimant. But by s. 3 of the *Insolvency Act* every decree or order of the Judge in Insolvency shall be as valid and effectual as if it had been made and pronounced by the Full Court, and I am satisfied that this Court possesses the means to give effect to its orders, if any person should be so ill-advised as to disobey them. Mr. Lilley also urged that even if the Court had the power to

determine and enforce the present claim, it was still a discretionary
power, and one which the Court would not exercise in a summary
manner, when the claim of the assignee rested on an alleged
fraudulent preference, which was a question which ought to be
tried by a jury.   No doubt there may be, and probably will be,
many instances in which the assistance of a jury in trying questions
of this kind would be very valuable, but where the facts are simple
and undisputed, and especially where the question of fraud or no
fraud turns principally on the construction of an instrument in
writing, it seems to me that it is the duty of the Court to determine
that question without putting the parties to the expense of a trial by
jury.   I have some doubt whether the rule can be supported on the
first ground, but it is unnecessary to decide the point, because
I am clearly of opinion that it ought to be made absolute on
the second ground, namely, that the bill of mortgage was a
fraudulent preference within the meaning of section 74 of
*The Insolvency Act.** The mortgage was executed on 20th March,
1871, and the petition for an adjudication of insolvency against
Pentecost was filed on 22nd April following.   It is clear from
the evidence that on 20th March Pentecost was unable to meet his
engagements to Goertz and Co, and it is equally clear that there was
no reasonable or sufficient consideration given for the mortgage at
the time of its execution, for the cheque for £300, which Spiro
handed to Pentecost at that time, was immediately afterwards returned
by him to Spiro.   Unless, therefore, the mortgage was made in
pursuance of an agreement in writing, made at the time of the contracting of an antecedent debt, the mortgage must be deemed to have

* [28 Vic., No. 25, s. 74].   Any conveyance or equitable mortgage made
and executed or given by any insolvent within sixty days next before filing of
the petition not being for a reasonable and sufficient consideration given or
agreed to be given at the time or in pursuance of an agreement in writing
made at the time of the contracting of an antecedent debt and produceable
under the adjudication such insolvent being at the time of making and executing
or granting the same unable to meet his engagements shall be deemed a fraudulent preference of the creditor to whom or in trust for whom or to or for the use
benefit or advantage of whom such conveyance or mortgage shall have been
made and executed or granted and shall not be available to him as against
the official assignee but such creditor shall be paid rateably with the other
creditors and the property conveyed or charged or the full value thereof
shall be recoverable by the official assignee from such creditor or from the
person who shall hold the same in trust for such creditor or from any person
to whom such creditor or such trustee shall have conveyed or mortgaged the
same if such person had at the time of such conveyance or mortgage notice of
an act of insolvency committed by the insolvent.

re PENTECOST,
v.
ex parte MISKIN.

Lutwyche, J.

.

been a fraudulent preference shown to Spiro. The agreement in writing relied on is contained in a letter written by Pentecost to Spiro, and dated 26th January, 1869; and it seems to me to amount to an offer to give Spiro a second mortgage over the premises on which he lived (the Picnic Hotel and grounds) for £200 or £300, if Spiro would "give him a start again in the public-house." I assent to the proposition laid down in *Story's Eq. Jur.*, s. 736a., and quoted by Mr. Lilley that it is not necessary to the specific performance of a written agreement that it should be signed by the party seeking to enforce it; but then, as stated by the same authority, the agreement must be certain, fair, and just in all its parts. Now, to my mind, the offer contained in this letter is extremely vague and uncertain. I cannot collect from it whether Pentecost required the larger sum of £300, or the smaller sum of £200, or whether he was to be started again by Spiro in the public-house with money or with goods or both. Nothing is said about the duration of the mortgage, or the rate of interest to be paid for the money borrowed. I think that this is not an agreement which a Court of Equity could decree should be specifically performed. And I think it clear, from other parts of the letter, that Pentecost did not intend, when he made his offer, that the second mortgage should stand as a security for the balance of a current account, which he did not even open until six months later. It appears that he was anxious to open the public-house, because he thought it would pay, and enable him to pay off his old debts; not that he contemplated the possibility of becoming still further involved. The mortgage was given for £300, of which only £200 15s. 0d. was advanced in money. I must hold, therefore, that the mortgage in question was not made in pursuance of an agreement in writing made at the time of the contracting of any antecedent debt, and the rule must be made absolute as prayed, with costs to be paid by Spiro. He will, however, under the provisions of s. 74 be now entitled to be paid rateably with the other creditors in respect of the £300 for which the mortgage was executed.

Rule absolute.

BURRELL AND ANOTHER *v.* HOPE.

1871.
10th, 15th August.
———
Paul, D.C.J.

District Courts Act (22 Vic., No. 18) s. 7*—Acts Shortening Act (16 Vic., No. 1) s 6**—Real Property Act of 1861 (25 Vic., No. 14) s. s. 40, 77, 79 —Jurisdiction—Title to Land — Equitable Mortgage—Trusts under Real Property Act.

A grant from the Crown and a nomination of trust were deposited with the defendant as a security for the indebtedness of the plaintiff to him.

Held in an action brought for the detinue of the title deeds, that the depository took sufficient interest to deprive the District Court of jurisdiction.

Deeds belong to the owner of the land, and to decide to whom the deeds belong would raise a question of title.

The deposit of a Crown grant and a nomination of trust creates an equitable mortgage.

ACTION in detinue for a Crown grant, and an instrument of nomination of trustees.

W. Burrell, A. Adsett, and R. Hamilton were appointed trustees of the land in question for the benefit of Hamilton's wife. In 1867 Hamilton, who was then storekeeper for the defendant, and was also a butcher, became indebted to the defendant, who demanded security from him. Hamilton informed the defendant that the land in question belonged to his wife, and was vested in trustees, but at defendant's request he took the documents from the Registrar-General's office, and handed them to the defendant without the consent of his wife or co-trustees. The defendant subsequently sued the plaintiff in the Supreme Court, and obtained a verdict for £81 5s. 11d. Hamilton became insolvent, and the defendant, his agent, proved in the estate for the amount of the judgment debt without mentioning anything about the security. The defendant had been applied to and refused to give up the documents. The evidence of the defendant was that finding Hamilton getting heavily into his debt he refused to supply more cattle without security. The plaintiffs never proposed to hand him over the documents in question, but said nothing whatever about the land being held in trust for Hamilton's wife. He acccordingly took the papers and continued to supply cattle. When the plaintiff left his service, about eighteen months after the deposit of the docu-

* See now 55 Vic., No. 33, s. 56.   ** See now 31 Vic., No. 6, s. 11.

BURRELL AND
ANOTHER *v.*
HOPE.
___
Paul, D.C.J.

ments, the plaintiff owed £80, for which he gave a promissory-note, and subsequently paid £20 on account. ·

Lilley, Q C., for the defendant. The Court has no jurisdiction, inasmuch as the case raises a question of title to land. Under *The Real Property Act* trustees are recognised as the legal and equitable owners of land, and have power to sell or mortgage the property. The plaintiff has some interest in the land in question, and the deposit of deeds with the defendant created an equitable mortgage with which the Court has no power to deal.

Griffith, for the plaintiffs. A question of title to land is not raised, only the right to the documents.

C. A. V.

15th August, 1871.

PAUL, D. C. J. In this action the plaintiffs sue the defendant in detinue for title deeds The defendant pleads first to the jurisdiction, and secondly that he is equitable mortgagee by deposit of the title deeds. In the year 1867 the plaintiff, Hamilton, was indebted to the defendant in the sum of £80 After some conversation between the plaintiff Hamilton and defendant, Hamilton deposited with the defendant the title deeds now sued for, to secure all money due, and for any further debt which might accrue. The deeds deposited consisted of a grant from the Crown to one Benjamin Bathurst, and a nomination, under *The Real Property Act of 1861*, by Bathurst of the plaintiff as trustee for Eiliza Hamilton, the wife of the plaintiff Hamilton. The matter for inquiry in the first instance is, whether the title to land is in question in this action. I have jurisdiction to try that question, but I can only inquire into the case so far as to satisfy myself that the claim to title set up by the defendant is a *bona fide* one, but under this head it is not competent for me to go further, and decide whether the party raising the question of title has a claim which is good in law or equity. By s. 7 of *The District Courts Act* (22 Vic., No. 18) (excluding the jurisdiction of the Court), "title to land" is the term used, and by the Act 16 Vic., No. 1, s. 6, it is enacted that the "word 'land' shall include messuages, tenements, and hereditaments, corporeal or incorporeal, of any tenure or description, and whatever may be the estate or interest therein." S. 77 of *The Real Property Act of 1861* entitles any registered proprietor of land under the provisions of .that Act to vest it in trustees by instrument of nomination. The deed of nomination now sued for is made under that section. S. 79 of the same Act declares that no entry of trusts under such deed shall be made in the register book of the Real Property Office; that the trustees are to receive the certificate of title, and deal with the same as beneficial owners, to sell, mortgage, or dispose of, and that their receipt shall be a discharge to purchasers or mortgagees. It is clear that *The Real Property Act* does not recognise trusts, and that the trustees shall have full power over the property so conveyed to them. Then, in what position do they stand? They are joint tenants of the estate or interest so held by them under s. 40 of the same Act, which enacts that " persons who may be registered as joint proprietors of an estate or interest in land under the provisions of this Act, shall be deemed to be entitled to the same as joint tenants." So Hamilton, being a joint tenant—a partial owner—he can affect his own interest by a deposit of deeds upon the same principle as a tenant for life. (*Williams v. Medlicot*, 6 Price 495). In the present case it is admitted by both sides that Hamilton deposited these deeds with the defendant as security for a sum of money. What effect has this? It gives the creditor in whose hands they are placed an interest in the land to which they relate, *Russel v. Russel* (White & Tudor's L. C., Vol. I, 441). Such a deposit is held to imply an obligation to execute a legal conveyance whenever it should be required. Lord Eldon, in giving judgment in *Hiern v. Mill* (13 Ves., 122) said, "So much is the equitable title from the possession of deeds recognized even at law, that, if a man, having made the deposit previously, makes a title accordingly, only two minutes before he absconds, it is a legal title, and cannot be impeached; for though the legal act was done in contemplation of bankruptcy, it is protected by the previous equitable title; being only effect given to a title, created not in contemplation of bankruptcy, and, except in form, complete by the deposit." On the other hand, supposing Hamilton to be merely a trustee, and that he deposited the deeds in breach of trust, the depository would then take an equitable interest in the land although such interest must yield to the prior equity of the *cestui-que trust*, and I cannot say that the defendant does not possess that interest until a Court of Equity deprives him of it, which it has not yet done, *Maningford v. Toleman* (1 Coll 670). On these authorities I consider the depository takes sufficient interest in the land to take it out of the jurisdiction of this Court, and if I say what interest, I would be deciding a question of title to land. Deeds no doubt belong to the owner of the land, and

BURRELL AND
ANOTHER *v.*
HOPE.

Paul, D.C.J.

in deciding to whom the deeds belong, I should be deciding to whom the land belongs, and here again crops up the question of title to land. Therefore I decide that I have no jurisdiction, and decline to entertain the case.

Solicitor for plaintiffs : *Bunton.*

Solicitors for defendant : *Little & Browne.*

LILLEY v. PARKINSON AND OTHERS.

Practice—Action for Libel—Change of Venue.

[In Chambers.]
1871.
23rd August.
——
Cockle, C.J.

Change of venue of an action for libel will not be ordered from Brisbane to a circuit town, where the newspaper containing the libel was printed, when the plaintiff alleges that the principal ground of complaint is in respect of the publication in Brisbane.

SUMMONS by the defendants Parkinson, Sloman, and Kidner, proprietors of the *Queensland Times,* calling on the plaintiff, Charles Lilley, to show cause why the venue in the case should not be changed to the Circuit Court at Ipswich, and why the declaration should not be amended and allowed accordingly, and all further proceedings under the venue of " Queensland " be stayed.

The action was brought for libel. The ground of the present application was, that the cause of action, if any, arose in Ipswich, and not elsewhere. Affidavits to that effect made by George Hellicar and George Crawford were filed.

The affidavit of the plaintiff in reply was to the effect that his principal ground of complaint was in respect of the publication in Brisbane of the libel set forth in the declaration, although he believed that the said libel had been published by the defendants in many other parts of the colony besides Ipswich and Brisbane.

Mein in support of summons.

Griffith, for the plaintiff, to oppose, was not called on.

COCKLE, C.J. If any portion of the cause of action arose in Brisbane the plaintiff is entitled to have the case tried there. The allegation in the declaration is that the defendants printed and published, or caused to be printed and published, in a certain newspaper within the colony the libel complained of, and this is rendered more definite by the plaintiff's affidavit that "the principal ground of complaint was in respect of the publication in Brisbane." That appears to me to satisfy all that is required, and the summons must be dismissed. The summons is accordingly dismissed, with £3 3s. costs for the plaintiff.

Summons dismissed.

Solicitors for applicant: *Macalister & Mein*, agents for *J. M. Thompson.*

Solicitors for plaintiff: *Macpherson & Lyons.*

COMMERCIAL BANK OF SYDNEY *v.* HENRY.

[IN BANCO.]
1871.
21st June.
7th, 8th Sept.

Cockle, C.J.
Lutwyche, J.

Real Property Act of 1861 (25 Vic., No. 14), s.s. 98, 99—Caveat, withdrawal of.

An order was made against the defendant for the withdrawal of a caveat within one month, which period was considered ample time for a bill to be filed in Equity for an injunction against dealing with the land, costs to be allowed to the plaintiff unless an injunction be obtained on notice within one month.

MOTION to make absolute an order *nisi* granted on 21st June, calling on Patrick Henry and his wife Catherine, to show cause why a caveat lodged by the said Catherine Henry in respect of certain lands in Dalby, should not be withdrawn.

It appeared from the affidavits in support of the motion, that on 5th May, 186), Henry mortgaged to the Bank the land in question, which is situated in the town of Dalby, to secure the repayment of an advance of £110, and such further sums as he might at any future time become liable to pay upon an overdrawn account, promissory-note, bill of exchange, letter of credit, or otherwise with interest, on demand. On the 26th August, 1870, the Bank claimed payment of £137 16s. then due under the mortgage, and Henry having failed to pay the same, the Bank, on the 31st December following, sold the land in question by private contract to Patrick Landy, of Dalby, in accordance with the power contained in the mortgage. In the same month transfers were executed by the Bank in favour of Landy, and the same were lodged in the Registrar-General's office, about the 6th March. In September, 1870, Henry was adjudicated insolvent, and on the 11th February, 1871, the caveat sought to be removed was lodged in the Real Property Transfer Office, Catherine Henry claiming the estate or interest in the land as purchaser from W. H. Miskin, Official Assignee, in her husband's estate, and hence the present action.

The rule *nisi* was granted on the grounds that the plaintiffs were entitled to pursue their remedies under the mortgage, and to sell the land, and that the estate or interest claimed by Catherine Henry was not such as would prevent the registration of any memorandum of sale or other instrument executed by the Bank respecting the land.

The affidavit of Patrick Henry was to the effect that the balance due to August, 1870, was £74 16s. 8d.; and in a conversation which he had with E. P. Ashdown, manager of the Bank at Toowoomba, about that time, he (Mr. Ashdown) agreed to deliver up all deeds and documents in connection with the land on payment of that sum. He had not borrowed any further sums since that time; but a promissory-note for £50, which he had given to Landy Brothers, was discounted by the Bank, and duly retired by Landy Brothers prior to this conversation. This note was payable under his insolvency, being due about two months previous thereto, but Ashdown subsequently informed him that the note had again come into his hands, and he had charged it to his (Henry's) account. On the 11th February last his wife received £85 from Hugh Johnston, of Dalby, to pay the claim of the Bank, and, although the sum was tendered, it was refused.

Griffith, for applicant, moved the rule absolute, and cited s.s. 57, 59, 98, 99, 103, 113 of 25 Vic., No. 14.

Blake, *Q.C.*, for the caveator: The Bank could not charge the promissory-note against Henry under the mortgage, because the moment Landy Brothers paid it, Henry was no longer indebted to the Bank, but to Landy Brothers. Apart from this sum there was tender of the balance due, and all rights of the mortgagee over the property then ceased. If the caveat was withdrawn the transfer could be registered, and as the property would then pass, all the rights of the defendant would be swept away, and the Court should therefore retain the caveat until the right of the parties to the property was decided.

Griffith, in reply: No estate or interest passed to Catherine Henry from the assignee; and, in addition to this, the tender of the money referred to was made after the sale to Landy.

COCKLE, C.J.: The caveat must be taken off within a month, which will allow ample time for a bill to be filed in equity for an injunction; costs to be allowed, unless an injunction is obtained on notice within the month.

Solicitors for applicant: *Macpherson & Lyons*.
Solicitors for caveator: *Macalister & Wilson*.

COMMERCIAL
BANK OF
SYDNEY v.
HENRY.

Cockle, C.J.
Lutwyche, J.

In re DALLEY.

[IN BANCO.]
1871.
15 September.

Cockle, C.J.
Lutwyche, J.

Barrister—Admission of—Barrister of New South Wales admitted there prior to Separation—Residence.

A barrister who has been admitted by the Supreme Court of New South Wales before the separation of Queensland from that colony, is entitled to be admitted as a barrister of the Supreme Court of Queensland, and is entitled to sign the roll of barristers.

MOTION that the name of William Bede Dalley, Esq., may be added to the roll of barristers of this Court, and that he may be at liberty to sign the roll.

It appeared that Mr. Dalley was, in the year 1856, admitted as a barrister of the Supreme Court of New South Wales, and he had ever since continued to practise in that Court, and at the time of Separation he was entitled to practise at Moreton Bay. He was desirous of appearing and practising in the Supreme Court of Queensland before the commencement of Michaelmas term.

Griffith, for Dalley: The motion will raise the question whether a gentleman who was entitled to practise as a barrister in the Supreme Court of New South Wales at the time of Separation is entitled to practise in this colony. Mr. Dalley's name does not appear on the roll at present, and if he appeared in Court under such circumstances, there is nothing to show that he is entitled to practise.

LUTWYCHE, J. Mr. John Hubert Plunkett, formerly Attorney-General of New South Wales, applied in 1861 to have his name placed on the roll, on the ground that he was a barrister of the Supreme Court of New South Wales before Separation, and his claim was allowed. That, however, was when I was sole Judge of the Court in this colony, and I was of opinion that the Act of Separation was not intended to operate injuriously against the *status* of any man. The Orders-in-Council were very careful to guard existing rights. Mr. Plunkett never signed the roll, but was admitted on the 30th April, 1861. Mr. Burdekin, whose name appears on the roll, applied in person, and he also was admitted.

Griffith. The real question is whether Separation took away the rights which previously existed.

Cockle, C.J. That has been settled by the judgment of Mr. *In re* DALLEY.
Justice Lutwyche.

Cockle, C J.
Lutwyche, J.: I do not know how that may be affected by rules   Lutwyche, J.
passed since.

Lilley, Q.C. (on being invited by the Court to express an opinion):
I have great delicacy in speaking on the matter, because I am aware
that Mr. Dalley is coming to Queensland on a special retainer in a
case in which I am the plaintiff, and that gentleman will appear on
the other side. From my knowledge of Mr. Dalley I have no doubt
he will do honour to the Bar if allowed to practise here. In Mr.
Plunkett's case it was held, on the interpretation of the Orders-in-
Council, preserving their existing rights, that members of the Bar of
New South Wales at that time were entitled to practise here. But
some alterations have been made since, and one of the rules is that a
gentleman on applying for admission, or for leave to sign the roll,
shall swear that he is about to reside and practise in the colony. It
is only on the invitation of the Court that I offer these observations,
and I desire to expressly state that I have no wish to preclude Mr.
Dalley from giving his services to any person who may employ him
against me. I think, however, that as I am the only leading member
of the Bar in Court, I am justified in drawing attention to the rule.

Griffith. The rule does not apply to the present case.

LUTWYCHE, J. Mr. Dalley is *de jure* a barrister of this Court.
He only wants to go through the formality of signing the roll in order
that the Court may take cognisance of the fact.

Lilley. I wish it to be distinctly understood that I do not object,
but the case may be made the ground for other special retainers.

COCKLE, C.J. The Court called upon Mr. Lilley merely as
amicus curiae. It should be distinctly understood that this case will
not extend to any barrister of New South Wales admitted since
Separation.

Order accordingly.

Solicitors for applicant : *Macalister and Mein.*

SHELTON v. RAFF.

[In Banco.]
1871.
11th December.

Cockle, C. J.
Lutwyche, J.

Curator of Intestate Estates Act of 1867 (31 Vic., No. 10), s. 10—*
Partnership—Death and intestacy of one partner—Wrongful
seizure of goods by Curator.

To an action for breaking into a store, seizing and disposing of certain goods
brought by a surviving partner, against the defendant, who had been appointed
after the passing of *The Curator of Intestate Estates Act of 1867*, to administer
the estate pursuant to an order of the Court, the defendant pleaded the order
of the Court, and that the acts complained of were done by him *bona fide* in
the discharge of his duties, and not otherwise.

Held that the plea was good.

Cross Demurrers.

James Shelton sued Alexander Raff, Curator of Intestate Estates,
and the declaration set out that the defendant broke and entered a
store and dwelling-house of the plaintiff at Clermont, and remained
therein; that he kept the store closed, and stopped the business
thereof; that he prevented persons purchasing goods therein for a
long time, and also took plaintiff's goods, chattels, and moneys. The
second count charged similar conduct at Copperfield. The third
count charged that the defendant took, carried away, injured, and
disposed of plaintiff's goods. The damages were laid at £1000. To
this the defendant pleaded as a fourth plea, that after the passing of
The Curator of Intestate Estates Act of 1867, the defendant was duly
appointed thereunder, and he was subsequently appointed by order
of one of the Judges to collect, manage, and administer the personal
estate of M. C. Bergin, then lately deceased. In pursuance of the
said order he proceeded to manage and administer the estate, and in
the course of such management and administration he did various
things *bona fide* in the supposed and intended performance of his
duties as such Curator; and the acts complained of were so done by
him in the *bona fide* discharge of his duty, and not otherwise. To
this the plaintiff demurred that the plea was not good in substance,
and issue was joined accordingly. The plaintiff pleaded, by way of
replication to the said plea, that before the committing of the acts
complained of in the declaration, he was carrying on business in part-

* Repealed; see now 41 Vic., No. 24, s. 10.

SHELTON v.
RAFF.
———
Cockle, C.J.,
Lutwyche, J.

nership with Bergin, and whilst the partnership continued Bergin died intestate, and there were then certain goods, the property of the partnership, in premises at Clermont and Copperfield, and the defendant wrongfully and in the pretended performance of his duty, in the absence of plaintiff, broke into the said premises, and carried away and disposed of the said goods. To this the defendant demurred that the replication was bad in substance, in so much as the facts set forth did not show any liability on the part of the defendant to an action of trespass, or on the case under the circumstances disclosed in the fourth plea, and that the facts were not sufficient in law to deprive the defendant of the benefits of the defence contained in the said plea.

Blake, Q.C., and *Hely* for the plaintiff.

Griffith, for the defendant, referred to s. 10 of *The Curator of Intestate Estates Act* ; *Pratt v. Pratt*, 2 Exch. 413 ; 17 L.J. Ex. 299; *Taylor v. Cole*, 1 Smith, L. C. 126 (5th Edition) ; 3 T.R. 292; *Freeman v. Jeffries*, L. R. 4 Ex. 189; *Makin v. Watkinson*, L. R. 6 Ex. 25. The defendant must be made a trespasser *ab initio* or the plaintiff must new assign.

Blake, Q.C. The defendant was not justified in closing the store and stopping the business. Bullen & Leake (2nd Edn.), 358 ; Story on Partnership, s.s. 328, 344 ; Lindley, 429 ; *ex parte Williams*, 11 Ves. 3, 6 ; *Crawshay v. Maule*, 1 Swanst, 495, 507 ; *Thomson v. Waithman*, 3 Drew 628 ; 26 L.J., Ch., 134 ; 2 Jur. N.S. 1080; *Martin v. Crompe*, 1 Ld. Raym, 340.

COCKLE, C.J., delivered the judgment of the Court, holding the fourth plea good, and gave judgment for defendant on the whole record.

Judgment for the defendant.

Solicitor for plaintiff : *Wilson.*
Solicitors for defendant : *Macalister and Mein.*

R. v. LEVY.

[IN BANCO.]
1871.
8th, 19th Dec.

Cockle, C.J.
Lutwyche, J.

*Larceny as a bailee—Bailment—Valuable Security—Promissory note
—Passing of property—Larceny Act of 1865 (29 Vic., No 6) s. 3.*

L was convicted of larceny as a bailee of a promissory-note under the following circumstances : L called at K's store and asked for an order for goods, and K gave him an order for goods to the value of £54 10s. ; L then asked K for a promissory-note, as he was going to Brisbane that evening ; he said he put in the goods much cheaper than before, and he wanted the note. K said, " If I give you this promissory-note will you forward the goods at once ?" L replied " I will." K then said, " Should you not do so I request you to forward the promissory-note at once." L said " Yes :" then took out of a book a blank form of promissory-note, and wrote on it and handed it to K to sign. K signed it and gave it to L ; the note was not stamped when handed to K, and there was no evidence to show at what time it was stamped. K swore that L's name was in the note when he signed it ; the goods were never forwarded by L, and subsequently the note was passed at L's request to his credit by B, to whom prisoner had been previously indebted. K wrote to L for the return of the note, and received one somewhat similar from L.

Held, that there was no reasonable evidence to go to the jury in support of the information, that there was no property in K of the promissory-note, and that there was no bailment.

CROWN case reserved by Lutwyche, J.

The prisoner, Lawrence Levy, was tried before Mr. Justice Lutwyche on 5th December on a charge of larceny as a bailee, and the information alleged that he being the bailee of a certain valuable security—namely, a promissory-note for £54 10s., and one piece of paper, the property of D. T. Keogh, of Ipswich, unlawfully and fraudulently converted it to his own use. The second count charged him with larceny of the said note. It appeared from the evidence that the prisoner, on the 28th June, called at Keogh's store, and asked him for an order for goods. Keogh gave him an order accordingly for goods to the value of £54 10s., and prisoner then asked him for a promissory-note, as he was going to Brisbane by the coach that evening. He said he had put in the goods much cheaper than before, and that he wanted the note. Keogh said he would do so, and the following conversation then took place: Keogh said "If I give you this promissory-note, will you forward the goods at once ?" Prisoner replied, "I will." Keogh then said, " Should you not do so I request you to forward the promissory-note at once." The prisoner said

"Yes," and then took out of a book a blank form of promissory-note, and wrote on it and handed it to Keogh to sign. Keogh signed it and gave it to the prisoner. The note was not stamped when handed to Keogh by the prisoner, and there was no evidence to show at what time it was stamped. Keogh when asked if the name "Laurence Levy" was put in the note by the prisoner when he was in his (Keogh's) shop, said he could almost swear it was in the note when he signed it, and on re-examination said he had not the slightest doubt about it. The goods for which the promissory-note was given were never forwarded by prisoner, and on the 3rd July the note was passed at his request to his credit by Mr. E. Barnett, to whom the prisoner had been previously indebted. On the 17th August Keogh wrote to prisoner to send him the note or the goods, and on the 18th the prisoner wrote to Keogh in reply, stating that he had done as requested. Enclosed in the prisoner's letter was a piece of paper, purporting to be a cancelled promissory-note, similar in all respects to that signed by Keogh, except that it was unstamped, that the date when due was wanting, that part where the signature should have been was torn off, and that it bore only one endorsement, which was cancelled. The promissory-note signed by Keogh was dishonoured when it arrived at maturity. At the close of the case counsel for prisoner submitted that there was no case to go to the jury, and urged that there was no evidence. (1) of a bailment by Keogh to prisoner; (2) of the note being available security within the meaning of the Act, 29 Vic., No. 6, s. 3; (3) of Keogh's property in the promissory-note; (4) of the existence of any piece of paper as such after Keogh had signed the promissory-note; (5) of the completeness of the instrument as a promissory-note when it left the hands of Keogh; and (6) of the value of the piece of paper charged to have been stolen by the prisoner as a bailee. The case was left to the jury, who found the prisoner guilty of larceny as a bailee, and he was sentenced to imprisonment with hard labour for twelve months in Brisbane Gaol. The question reserved was—was there any evidence to go to the jury in support of the conviction upon the information laid against the prisoner? If the Court should be of the opinion that there was such evidence, then the conviction was to stand affirmed; but if there was not such evidence, then the conviction was to be avoided, and the proper entry made on the record accordingly.

Blake, Q.C., and *Hely*, for the prisoner: There is no evidence of bailment; the whole transaction does not constitute that which the

law calls a bailment. Whether there was fraud or not on the part of
the prisoner is not the question, but whether there was larceny as a
bailee. To constitute a bailment there must be a delivery of something of value to a bailee, either to be kept or to have that value
increased by something to be done by the bailee, and, at a specified
time, afterwards to re-deliver the thing in its original state, or with
some improvement on the thing into which it had been converted to
the bailor (*Coggs v. Bernard*, 1 Smith's L. C., 177), and to constitute
a bailment of the fifth kind, there must be a delivery to carry or otherwise manage for a reward to be paid to the bailee. Nothing of any value
passed from Keogh to the prisoner. This is not a case where the bill was
delivered for discount, it was delivered for payment. It was not a bailment, because the thing delivered by Keogh to the prisoner was not
to be re-delivered, nor was that into which it was to be converted, to
be re-delivered; see Cockburn, C. J. (*R. v. Hassall*, L & C.,
62). Here the prisoner was not bound to return the specific coins
he received. Does not the word, bailee, imply that the thing received
is to be specifically returned? A bailee must return either the
article received, or something into which it has been converted in
accordance with the terms of the bailment. What the prisoner had
was never the property of Keogh (*R. v. Phipoe*, 2 Leach, C. C. 673,
at page 679). "It is essential to larceny that the property charged to
have been stolen should be of some value; that the note in the present
case did not, on the face of it, import either a general or a special
property in the prosecutor; and that it was so far from being of any
the least value to him, that he had not even the property of the paper
on which it was written; for it appeared that both the paper and the
ink were the property of Mrs. Phipoe, and the delivery of it by her
to him could not, under the circumstances of the case, be considered
as vesting it in him." He had not to return the identical thing to
Keogh, and if it was worthless it was never a valuable security. (29
Vic., No. 6, s. 3.) It was merely Keogh's acknowledgment of indebtedness (*Rex v. Hart*, 6 C. & P., 106). The note was primarily
prepayment for goods which the prisoner was to send to Keogh, and if
he did not send the goods, he was to get the note back, and as he did
not send the goods it is a case of fraud, or at least a breach of
contract. The note was not a valuable security until it passed into
the hands of Barnett. If the prisoner had not discounted it before
it became due, it would have been worthless; because if he sued
Keogh, a total failure of consideration could be pleaded. The position

of the prisoner was more that of a trustee of the note than anything else, and certainly he was not a bailee. He entered into a collateral contract, and cases which tend to convert the ground of civil action into a criminal offence are to be followed with caution (*Rex v. Shea*, 7 Cox, C. C. 147). It was a contract to deliver, not to re-deliver. Another point is this, being a chose-in-action it is not the subject of larceny, *Reg v. Watts*, Dea. 326 ; *R. v. Morrison*, 8 Cox, C. C. 194. The conversation between the parties amounted to an agreement on the part of the prisoner to negotiate the note, and however the transaction is looked at it is impossible to make it appear as a bailment. The note or chattel was never the property of Keogh; he never had it in his possession except to write upon it; and as no property passed from Keogh to the prisoner there could be no bailment. All that could have passed was a future right to possession of the note. No property passed from Keogh; the paper was not a valuable security (*R. v. Lowrie*, L. R. 1, C. C. R. 61) ; and there was no bailment.

Bramston, A.G., for Crown.

THE COURT suggested that counsel for the Crown should confine himself to the question of property, as on that the whole case would turn.

Bramston, A.G. The note was the property of Keogh as soon as it was handed to him by the prisoner, *Evans v. Kymer* (1 B. & Ad. 528). When prisoner handed over the note he parted with all the property in the note—delivery on request is quite a sufficient consideration for transfer of the property. If it was not in his possession it never was a complete note, he never delivered. If it was never in Keogh's possession then he could not have signed it. He had a right to demand the note again, *Treuttel v. Barandon* (8 Taunt, 100); *R. v. Smith*, 21 L. J. (M. C. 111). Keogh could have refused to part with it after he had signed it, and when prisoner handed the complete instrument to Keogh, he parted with the property. The document was received by the prisoner on the express condition that it was to be returned to him; and that is sufficient to constitute a bailment. There was no necessity to show actual value, but the moment the note passed from the prisoner it became a valuable security for the amount stated. The cases quoted by the other side do not apply. Keogh could have recoverd on an action in trover, and if he had sufficient property in the document to sustain such an action, it cannot now be set up that he had no property in it. The

R. *v.* LEVY.

Cockle, C.J.
Lutwyche, J.

property was in Keogh, it continued his property, and there was a bailment. In fact the jury found that the bailment was complete, and therefore the conviction should stand affirmed.

.   *Blake*, *Q.C.*, in reply, was not heard.

THE COURT held that there was no reasonable evidence to go to the jury in support of the information. They were of the opinion that there was no property in Keogh of the promissory-note, and that there was no bailment, and the conviction could not therefore be sustained.

Conviction avoided.

Solicitors for prisoner : *Macpherson & Lyons.*

In re COURT.

Criminal Law—Felon—Escape—Re-arrest after expiration of period of sentence—Discharge on habeas corpus.

A felon sentenced to five years' imprisonment escaped shortly afterwards, and after the expiration of the period of sentence was re-arrested, and committed .to custody on a warrant of a magistrate.

Held on a return to a writ of *habeas corpus* that he was illegally in custody, but might be prosecuted for escaping. The prisoner was discharged.

[IN BANCO.]
1871.
8th November.
8th, 12th, 22nd December.
——
Cockle, C.J.
Lutwyche, J.

RULE *nisi* calling on the Sheriff to shew cause why a writ of *habeas corpus* should not issue, commanding him to have the prisoner, Charles Court, brought before the Court. The prisoner was sentenced on 14th September, 1865, to two concurrent sentences of five years' imprisonment with hard labour, for horse stealing. He escaped from St. Helena on 16th August, 1866, and was again lodged in custody on 4th August, 1871, under a warrant of a magistrate, after the expiration of his term of imprisonment.

Bramston, A. G., for the Sheriff. A man cannot take advantage of his own wrong, the prisoner should not therefore be allowed to escape punishment of the felony of which he was convicted because he has evaded it. He should not be punished for the offence of escaping which is only a misdemeanour, instead of the felony. The rule should be discharged. 1 Russell, 581, 586; citing 2 *Hawkins*, P. C., c. 19, s. 12; *Wilkinson's Editn. (1866) of Plunkett*, p. 281.

Blake, Q.C., and *Griffith*, for the prisoner. The term of sentence has expired. The sentence commenced from the date of conviction. *Coke*, 52 a. Pt. 3, Vol. III, 145. The proper course would be to indict the prisoner for escaping, and all the legal questions could then be decided. When the sentence commenced to run it was similar to the running of the Statute of Limitations, which could not be stopped, and at the expiration of the period from the date of the conviction the sentence expired, and could not be prolonged. The only means by which a cumulative punishment can be carried is by an indictment for an escape. *Bacon's* Abridgt, 133; 2 *Hawkins*, P. C., c. 18, s. 5; 4 Vic., No. 10 (1 *Pring*, 588); *Easton's* case, 12 Ad. & Ell. 645.

Griffith followed. The prisoner is now detained because he

In re COURT.   has escaped.   A man's liability to punishment can only be ascertained
Cockle, C. J.   by a record.   *Groome v. Forrester*, 5 M. & S. 316.
Lutwyche, J.   C.A.V.

22nd December, 1871.

THE COURT referred to 3 Wm. IV., No. 3, s. 20; 4 Vic., No. 10,
s. 1; 18 Vic, No. 7, s. 2; 11 & 12 Vic., c. 42, s. 23; Form T. 1,
(*Pring*, 582, 588, 590, 779, 793); *Easton's* Case (*ante*), and ordered
the rule to be made absolute, the writ returnable at a later hour of
the same day.

The prisoner was then produced, and the return and writ read.

Griffith moved for the discharge of the prisoner.

Bramston, A.G., did not claim to detain him as on a warrant of
commitment, two sessions of *oyer* and *terminer* having passed, but
claimed to detain him as of his original custody.

PER CURIAM.   The prisoner cannot be detained upon the
ground that he escaped before the expiration of his sentence, and
which has since expired.   He might be prosecuted for escaping if
such a course is considered necessary.

Prisoner discharged.

Solicitor for prisoner : *Bunton.*

PITT v. BEATTIE.

Municipal Institutions Act of 1864* *(28 Vic., No. 21), s. s. 50, 51,*
100—Alderman — Disqualification of — Contract — Lease—Con-
tinuing disqualification—Quo Warranto.

[In Banco].
1871.
8th, 14th, 15th
December.

———

Cockle, C.J.
Lutwyche, J.

B, an alderman, was re-elected to a Municipal Council, but previous to his
re-election he had entered into an agreement with the council to lease a wharf,
and acted as an alderman. A ratepayer, as relator, sought a *quo warranto.*

Held that the agreement was a contract within the meaning of s. 50 of *The
Municipal Institutions Act of 1864* ; that the relator was entitled to ask for the
rule ; and the disqualification continued *de die in diem.*

The rule was made absolute, no information to be filed, if B resigned within
a week.

R. v. Francis, 18 Q. B. 526 ; *R. v. Holt*, 2 Chit. 366 ; *R. v. Yorke*, 2 Q. B.
847 followed. *Ex parte Hawksley*, 8 S. C. R. (L.) N. S. W. 342 distinguished.

Rule *nisi* calling on Francis Beattie to show cause why an
information in the nature of a *quo warranto* should not be exhibited
against him, to show by what authority he claimed to be an alderman
of the City of Brisbane. The rule was granted on the affidavits of
James Pitt ; Francis Murray, Mayor of Brisbane ; and W. H. G.
Marshall, clerk in the Town Clerk's Office. The affidavit of Pitt was
to the effect that he was a ratepayer of the municipality, entitled to
vote at municipal elections, and had been informed and believed that
Francis Beattie, one of the aldermen, was now engaged and interested
in a contract with the Council of the municipality otherwise than as
a proprietor or shareholder of any joint stock company contracting
with the said council, inasmuch as he was interested in an agreement
or contract for a lease to him by the Council of a certain wharf and
lands at Petrie's Bight. Pitt had given instructions to his attorney
to institute these proceedings. The other affidavits set out that
Beattie had been an alderman for four years. He was re-elected on
14th February, 1871. The transaction referred to took place in
December, 1870.

Lilley, Q.C. and *Griffith* in support of the rule.

Blake, Q.C., and *Cansdell* showed cause.

Preliminary objections were raised to the proceeding. (1) That
the rule was wrongly entitled : " In the matter of the application of
*But see now 42 Vic., No. 8, s. 35 (P. & W. 1338).

PITT *v.* BEATTIE. James Pitt, for leave to exhibit an information in the nature of *quo warranto* against Francis Beattie claiming to be an alderman of the City of Brisbane." There was no such matter before the Court, and the rule should have been entitled "In the Supreme Court of Queensland." *Cole* on *Quo Warranto*; *Rex v. Cole*, 6 T. R. 640. (2) The rule did not state the ground of objection. *Cole*, 186. (3) The information must be made by the Master of the Crown Office, and there was no such officer in the colony. *Rex v. Darley*, 12 Cl. & F. 520. (4) The rule *nisi* must be drawn up by the Master of the Crown Office. *Interdict Act of 1867* (31 Vic., No. 11), s. 58.

Lilley, Q.C., contra, referred to (1) *Hargreaves v. Hayes*, 5 Ell. & Bl., 272; *Baird*, 133; *Goode's Crown Office Practice*, 646. (3) There was no proper officer here, 28 Vic., No. 21, s. 100; *Plunkett*, 316; *Rex v. Barzey*, 4 M. & S., 253.

The necessary amendments in the documents were allowed on payments of costs to be taxed summarily, and the case proceeded.

From the joint and several affidavits of David Stewart and James Dunbar, it appeared from information given them by Pitt, with whom they had been acquainted for many months, they believed he was in low and indigent circumstances. He was objectionable as a relator. The application was not made on his behalf, or at his expense, but he was acting in collusion with other parties, and at the expense of the Municipal Council. The matter raised was substantially the same as was adjudicated upon at the Police Court on the information of the Town Clerk, which was dismissed with costs. The attorneys of the relator were the same as those of the Council. The defendant believed at the time and still believed that a lease or agreement for a lease was not a contract within the meaning of the Act.

Blake, Q C. It was decided in *R. v. Yorke* (2 Q. B. 847) that a lease came within the meaning of contract. The corresponding English Act was immediately passed excepting leases. Beattie has not got a lease. No steps were taken by the Corporation as they acquiesced. *R v. Trevenen* (2 B. & Ald., 479). The Court should only grant the rule on security for costs being given by Pitt, *R. v. Wakelin* (1 B. & A., 50). The rule was not brought in time (s. 100). The contract was antecedent to the last election. Proceedings should have been taken within three months from his election. *Ex parte Hawksley* (8 S.C.R.(L.) N.S.W. 342). The contract was not a continuing one (s. 51). *R. v. Francis* (18 Q. B. 526), was decided under different

circumstances.   Payment was to be made for work done, and the Pitt v. Beattie.
contract was a continuing one in its essence.   Pitt's affidavit in reply Cockle, C.J.
set out he was the holder of property, and had money in the Savings Lutwyche, J.
Bank, and was proceeding at his own expense and risk.

Cansdell followed.   This is a matter for the discretion of the
Court.   No fraud is imputed to the defendant.   If the Court were
against him, the defendant should be allowed to disclaim without
payment of costs, *R. v. Holt* (2 Chit., 366).   In *Hawksley's* case the
defendant was an uncertificated insolvent.

Lilley, Q.C. If the defendant disclaims we will not ask for costs.

Cockle, C.J.   The rule must be made absolute.   We have fairly
weighed the arguments made use of.   It may be noticed that while
we adopt the English view of the interpretation of the Act, that case
was not before the learned Judges of New South Wales when they
decided *Hawksley's* case (8 S. C. R. (L.), N. S. W.,   342).   That
case was decided under another section of the Act.   We entirely
concur in *R. v. Francis* (18 Q. B., 526), that it was a continuing
disqualification *de die in diem*.   The question whether the agreement
was a contract is settled beyond dispute in *R. v. Yorke* (2 Q. B. 847).
There is no ground to exercise a discretion.   The rule must be
made absolute, or perhaps it might be discharged on the defendant
disclaiming.

Lilley, Q.C.   It would be more satisfactory to have the record
of the Court.

Lutwyche, J.   I concur in the opinion of the Chief Justice, and
in the opinion expressed at the Bar, that a record should exist of the
decision of the Court, so that it might be known that proceedings of
this kind on the part of the Muncipal Council are not to be persisted
in.   I am of opinion, taking the affidavits on the whole, that the
intending relator is a competent person for that object, and I can
easily understand why a person in his position as a ratepayer should
feel interested in municipal affairs, and take up at his own risk and
expense a prosecution of this kind.   It is very desirable that public
spirit of that kind should exist; I do not say it is desirable that
public spirit should degenerate into party spirit, but so far as I can
see from the facts the intending relator, Pitt, has placed himself in
such a position that he is entitled to ask the Court to make the rule *nisi*
absolute.   At the same time I am glad to see from the authorities
that we can with propriety allow Mr. Beattie yet to resign. Strictly,
he cannot be said to disclaim, because he has already accepted the

PITT v. BEATTIE.

Cockle, C.J.
Lutwyche, J.

office, entered upon it, and acted as an alderman since his election. So that, independent of form, perhaps the word disclaimer ought not properly to be used. In the case cited *R. v. Holt* (2 *Chit.*, 366), the defendant was a young man, he never accepted the office to which he had been elected, and never acted in the capacity he was elected to fill. In *Francis'* case it is clear that Mr. Francis had acted as a councillor and there is a note in the case stating that a disclaimer was entered on the 18th June following. [*Lilley, Q.C.* That was after the information had been filed.] I understand, that if Mr. Beattie resigns within a week, no information will be filed, and no disclaimer will be necessary. That being the case the decision of the Court will be that the rule be made absolute, no information to be filed if Mr. Beattie resigns his office within a week.

Rule absolute.

Solicitors for relator: *Macpherson & Lyons.*
Solicitor for respondent: *Macnish.*

REGINA v. PENN.

Criminal Law—Evidence—Deposition of absent witness—Evidence and Discovery Act of 1867 (31 Vic., No. 13), s. 67.*

[IN BANCO.]
1871.
18th December.

Cockle, C.J.
Lutwyche, J.

The depositions taken before justices of a medical witness, who was absent from the trial of a prisoner on account of having to go to Sydney for the benefit of his health, was held admissible as evidence.

R. v. Wicker (18 Jur., 252) followed.

CROWN case reserved.

This was a special case reserved from the last sittings of the Supreme Court at Maryborough, when the prisoner was sentenced to twenty years' penal servitude for shooting James Cleary. The point reserved was whether under the provisions of *The Evidence and Discovery Act of 1867* the depositions of one of the witnesses, Dr. Brown, should be admitted as evidence; Brown, who was suffering from consumption, having previously left for Sydney for the benefit of his health.

Bramston, A.G., for the Crown. The question is whether a witness, who leaves town for the benefit of his health, is too ill to be able to travel; if Dr. Brown had resided anywhere else the deposition must have been received. Section 67 of the Act provides for cases where the " witness shall be so ill as not to be able to travel," which means, so ill as not to be able reasonably to attend. *Archbold*, Edn., 1867, p. 230 ; *R. v. Riley* (3 C. & K., 116) ; *R. v. Cockburn* Dears, & B., 203, 26 L. J. (M.C.), 139 ; *Roscoe*, 7th Edn., 66 ; *R. v. Wicker*, 18 Jur., 252 ; *Taylor*, p. 406.

No one appeared on behalf of the prisoner.

COCKLE, C. J. I am of the opinion that the conviction should be affirmed.

LUTWYCHE, J. I am of the same opinion on the authority of *R. v Wicker*.

Conviction affirmed.

*Compare *Justices Act* (50 Vic., No. 17), s. 111.

R. *v.* COATH.

[IN BANCO].
1871.
18th December.

Cockle, C.J.
Lutwyche, J.

Criminal Law—Kidnapping—Slavery.

The ship *Jason*, from Queensland, visited certain islands in the South Seas, inhabitants from which came out to trade, and were forcibly seized, detained, and brought to Maryborough, where they were set free.

Held (affirming LUTWYCHE, J.) that as the islanders had been detained and brought to Queensland in a British ship against their wills, the offence of kidnapping had taken place, and the Court had jurisdiction to try the persons charged.

The history of slavery reviewed.

CROWN case reserved by LUTWYCHE, J., on the trial of the prisoner at the last criminal sittings of the Supreme Court at Brisbane.

The prisoner was charged in the first count of the indictment with the abduction and kidnapping of certain South Sea Islanders in the month of January, 1871; the second count charged him with an assault upon the said islanders; the third with abduction and kidnapping of nine other islanders in February, 1871; and the fourth with an assault upon the same islanders. He was found guilty on the third count, and not guilty on the other counts, and was sentenced to five years' imprisonment in Brisbane Gaol, and to pay a penalty of £50, and to remain imprisoned until such fine be paid. In summing up the Judge directed the jury that if they were satisfied that at the time of the commission of the alleged offence charged in the third count, the *Jason* was a British ship, and was sailing on the sea, she was sailing on the high seas, and that the offence was triable here. He also directed that if they were satisfied that the nine islanders, or any of them, were brought on board or detained there against their will, and carried away to another place, the charge of kidnapping would be proved. Mr. Lilley, the defendant's counsel, objected to the direction on both of these points, and the following questions were accordingly reserved for the decision of the Court: (1) "Was I right in directing the jury that if the *Jason* was a British ship, and on the sea, she was sailing on the high seas, and that the subject matter of the inquiry was within the jurisdiction of the Court?" (2) "Was I right in directing the jury that if they were satisfied that the nine islanders, or any of them, were brought on board the *Jason*, or detained there against their will, and carried away to another place, the charge of kidnapping would be made out?"

Lilley, Q.C., and *Blake, Q.C.*, for the prisoner.

Bramston, A.G., for the Crown.

Lilley, Q.C. I ask that the case as stated be amended by stating that the islanders when they were put on board the *Jason* were treated in the same way as the other islanders who were on board, and that they were landed free at Maryborough.

THE COURT. We refuse to allow the amendment, but consent to the case being argued as if the facts referred to were set out in the case.

Bramston, A.G., mentioned *R. v. Anderson*, L. R. 1, C.C.R., 161.

Lilley, Q C. I do not think that the point raised by the first question is tenable, and I will therefore address myself to the second point. The question might be shortly stated thus: "Did the case disclose any offence known to the English law?" I contend it does not, even admitting the facts to have been proved. The question substantially is: "What is the offence of kidnapping as known to the English law?" Can it be committed on a savage or barbarous people captured and brought within the protection of British law, and landed free at Maryborough? (Stephens' Comm., 4th Edn., 163) There is no precedent of any kind for this conviction. The offence of kidnapping only arises where persons are taken from under the protection of the law of England, where the Sovereign is deprived of a subject, or where there is a concealment of a person in any part of the British dominions, so as to deprive the person of the protection of the laws (*R. v. Lord Grey*, 2 Shower, 218; I. Russell, 962). Under the Roman law it was no offence to steal or capture barbarous people, and the offence only existed where a freeman, his wife, or child, was seized or held as a slave. It is no offence to go to islands inhabited by a savage and barbarous people, and to bring these people within the protection of the English law. The only qualification which exists in *The Slave Acts* is that such persons should not be captured or seized for the purpose of being used as slaves. This might be morally wrong, and I am not going to defend such transactions; but the question is whether there is an offence against the law. Until *The Slave Acts* inferior races could be enslaved. Slavery is not piracy by the law of nations, but on the contrary it is lawful, and is only made piracy by the municipal laws of England. The piracy created by *The Slave Acts* is the carrying away of these men for the

R. v. COATH. purpose of using them as slaves. The carrying away itself does not
constitute the offence, and there is no case in the books to show that
the seizure of barbarians and bringing them under the protection of
the law is an offence against the law. The case of *Turbett v. Dassigney*,
2 Shower, 221, was a pure case of kidnapping, because the person was
taken from under the protection of the law.   The moment these
islanders touched the deck of an English vessel they were free, and
had a right to *habeas corpus*. They were landed at Maryborough and
were allowed to land free: but it was possible that if they had been
landed at Fiji, which was not in the British dominions, the offence of
kidnapping would have occurred; because they would then be removed
from the protection of the law which they were entitled to by virtue
of being on board an English vessel. It is contrary to fact to state
that slavery was unknown to England, and the case of "*The Slave
Grace*," 2 Hagg, 94, showed that residence in England did not make
a slave absolutely free; for, on returning to the place from whence
they came, they again became slaves. There is clearly no kidnapping
in this case, although there might have been false imprisonment for a
short time, for which it was competent for the prisoner to have been
punished. I therefore submit the direction was wrong, and the conviction must be set aside. (The following authorities were also cited:
Dred Scott v Sanford, Howard's 19 U. S. R., 393; *Somerset's Case*,
20 S. T., 1–82; *The Penal Code of New York*, 93, Austin, Vol. II.,
242; *Santos v. Illidge* 8 C. B. (N.S.), 861; *Reg v. Serva*, 1 Den.,
C. C. 104; *The Daphne*, 10 S. C. R. (L.), N. S. W., 37; 5 Geo. IV.,
C. 113).

    Bramston, A.G.   The direction of the learned Judge was
perfectly correct. There is no doubt the islanders were taken on
board against their will, and conveyed to Maryborough against their
will. It has been argued that this does not constitute kidnapping,
because it is not possible to kidnap a person of a savage race if he is
brought within the protection of the law; but the effect of that
argument is that a man is brought within the protection of the law,
and still that protection is refused by preventing him from punishing
the man who has infringed his personal liberty. Throughout the
whole of the argument of the other side there is a fallacy which
undermines the whole. The learned counsel has confused the effect
of the law with the law itself. The illegality of man-stealing is not
in the removal of a man from England, but in the violation of that
personal liberty which the law of England recognises in every man

(*Stephens* Comm., 140; *Roscoe*, 4th Edn., 508). If the right of the personal liberty of these men was once touched, it cannot matter whether they were brought to Queensland or elsewhere; so long as it was against their will, it was kidnapping. With regard to depriving the Sovereign of a subject, and taking a person from the protection of the law, in these cases we have a condition which necessarily attests to the illegal acts done, but it does not show why the act is illegal. It can never be held to be the law of England that the protection of the law is meted in proportion to the civilisation of a people. The savage has as much right to protection under this law as the most highly educated. The rights of these people to the protection of the law attached as soon as they came on board the *Jason*; they were then entitled to the *habeas corpus*, and their right to demand the punishment of those who had seized them also accrued. These people can scarcely be called free, because they are unable to return from whence they came, and they can get no redress. They are entitled to enjoy the manners and customs and laws of their own country, and their forcible removal was kidnapping. The Court should remember that it was not the offence committed against these people alone that it has to consider. It has also to consider the serious injury done to the whole of the public by this outrage of the law. It is the public peace that has been injured, and the public has a right to demand punishment even in a greater degree than the persons directly injured. In *Lord Grey's* case (*supra*) it was the relations of the lady whom he concealed, and the public who demanded that he should be punished, and not the lady herself. I therefore maintain that the conviction must be maintained.

Lilley, Q.C., replied.

Cockle, C.J. Although I cannot say I was convinced, I was very much impressed, by the very learned argument which Mr. Lilley advanced, and which he, I crave leave to say, pressed properly on the Court, because the Court is never more in danger of going wrong than when it is disposed to be likely to decide upon emotional grounds; and this is a case which ought to be decided solely on legal grounds. However bad the law may be, the Court best does its duty by rigidly enforcing it, and thus enabling its abuses to be perceived, and leaving it to the Legislature to correct such abuses, and therefore as far as I am concerned, I do not think any emotional ground weighs with me at all in dealing with this matter; but I do give considerable scope to the argument from public policy which has been adverted to on behalf of the Crown. We have no right, certainly in the exercise of an arbitrary discretion, to say that this is a misdemeanour which the law does not say is a misdemeanour. We should be careful not to do that; but we may fairly say, and not for any rhetorical reason at all, what would be the consequences of disturbing this conviction, and of saying that the facts which constitute the evidence on which the conviction was founded do not constitute a misdemeanour? We may fairly and temperately look at these consequences. It would appear that men—whether savage or civilised perhaps we are hardly able to say, for there are degrees of civilisation as well as of everything else, but at any rate civilised enough to traffic, to come in the way of the ship with the intention of trading, as was evidenced by their holding up a pig—these men are, after a display of force, thrust into a boat, and so induced to go on board ship, and I cannot help thinking that some disregard for the lives of these men was shown, for one poor fellow jumped overboard and swam as he no doubt thought for his life He was brought back in an exhausted state, and if he had not been taken on board it is quite possible he might have been drowned before reaching land. Therefore taking all the circumstances, we say here is a display of something like treachery, a seizing of persons who came to trade, and a disregard shown to life by attending rather to the capture of those who were going on board than to the poor fellow who ventured on a long swim for his life. Then there is the example shown by these savages—one, an old man, weeping perhaps for the thoughts of those whom he had on shore, and who were weeping for him, and not only that, but after he and the others were thrust down the hold, their yams and pigs were appropriated, and their canoe used for fire-wood. I do not use this for any rhetorical effect. It is obvious that any Court would, if it could, avoid it; but we must consider whether one subject of Her Majesty is at liberty to fit out a vessel to sail amongst these apparently savage and guideless islanders, and seize them and appropriate their property as appears to have been done in this case. It is the more necessary that we should fix our attention on this, because it should be noticed that with the improved manners and greater knowledge of succeeding ages, the maxims of previous ages are deviated from. We see with regard to the English law of evidence, in the case of *Omichund v. Barker* (Willes 538, 1 Atk. 21) in which for the first time, it was recognised that difference of religion made no difference so far as giving testimony was concerned—when the great authority of Lord Coke was cited to show that the evidence of a Jew ought not

to be admitted, Chief Justice Willes said that the reasons given, R. v. COATH.
though coming from a great man, were not such as he would follow, Cockle, C.J.
and he reversed, or rather did not act on the decision of Lord Coke,
but took the more correct view—the view recognised by succeeding
ages—that such narrow reasons did not suffice to guide the law of
evidence.   Therefore we may take it for granted that with the
increasing culture and humanity, and toleration of ages, some of the
old maxims should be moderated. Though it is a difficult question to say
what the law may have been, and whether there is any authority to
show that the common law would have regarded this as anything but
a grave outrage, we know that a great many deeds of violence were
perpetrated in America—take, for instance, in Spanish America,
where such deeds were done, not with the sanction of the Spanish
Government, but against their remonstrances, and such forces as
the then King could bring to bear were found insufficient to remedy
the abuses.   We have no means of knowing how far this institution
of slavery was the result of law or perpetuation by custom of what
was originally a cruel abuse.   There is no doubt, let it arise how it
will, that colonial slavery does appear to have been recognised in the
English Courts ; but it must be remembered that these Courts did not
make the law, but that they were recognising a law made in some
other places; and I confess that when it comes to the question of
deciding upon the rights of a man to his liberty, we are called upon
to narrowly scrutinise the old doctrines.   Can it be said that because
the Courts recognised slavery in the British dominions that they
would recognise any sort of slavery ; that they would allow an un-
fortunate Frenchman to be seized by any person who chose to call
him his slave ; and if such a person asked the Court to recognise him
as his slave, there is little doubt that the Court would refuse. I believe
that any Court which is called upon to restrain the liberty of a man
on the ground of being a slave would fully examine the law and the
circumstances to ascertain how far the ground was good.   Even
among the sterner and wealthier nations of antiquity they would go
past the grounds on which a man was alleged to be a slave if any such
question did arise, and it would have to be shown how far such slavery
arose ; and, as far as I am aware, it would be the result of capture in
war, or for some crime a man might be adjudged to slavery, or for
debt ; or again, in some of those parts of the world parental authority
might empower a father to make his son a slave, or there might be a
contract by which a man might become a slave, or a custom—such, as

I hope, sprung up in the colonies in spite of the Common Law of
England.   There may be so many origins to restraining the liberty
of human beings, but to which of these sources could the right of
anyone be traced to sail out of the port of this colony, and act as
these persons have done to these people of the Southern Ocean ? The
state of the law might have escaped notice at home ; but it ought not
to escape notice here.   In England these matters were comparatively
unimportant. The persons whose rights were torn away were for the most
part from the coast of Africa, a long line of trade across portions of the
ocean through which no man went except engaged in the nefarious and
cruel traffic.   Ordinary persons at home were not likely to be depend-
ing on barbarous treaties or the like; but here it is a very different
question.   This trade is carried on across the highway through which
much of the commerce of these parts passes, and along which, as time
rolls on, probably more of it will pass, and in which are islands inhabited
by tribes, or nations—or call them what you will—of the very class of
persons brought under our notice in this case; and if once amongst
these nations an opinion should get abroad that our law proceeded
upon principles so inhuman that their rights could be violated with
impunity by any man who may choose to sally forth to outrage them,
I say that the safety of commerce itself and the blessings it maintains
—the safety of our fellow-subjects and fellow-colonists—would be
endangered ; and I think that in saying this I am only drawing an
inference that the Common Law itself would draw.   It is not on any
narrow or technical principle that I base my opinion that this conviction should be sustained.   I think that the cases decided upon the
point of slavery are valuable and important, but still in this particular
case I cannot help thinking that there is a strong bias, not, I hope,
affecting the Court consciously, but we must remember that different
views may be entertained, and we must expect to find different views
prevailing there. Taking a general view of the case, we cannot do otherwise than affirm the conviction.   I had some doubts as to the meaning
of kidnapping, but Mr. Justice Lutwyche threw out an observation
which removed the difficulty. Of course, we decide the case simply
as it comes before us, and therefore the conviction must stand.

LUTWYCHE, J.   I adhere to my ruling at the trial, and I think
the direction I gave the jury was right.   I told them that if they
were satisfied that these nine islanders, or any of them, had been
taken on board and carried away to another place against their will,
the charge of kidnapping had been made out. One form of kidnapping

is stealing and carrying away a man—not any British subject, not any civilised man, but any human being—man, woman, or child, and if so, the Common Law of England will undoubtedly apply to the offence of which the defendant has been found guilty, as kidnapping. It has been said that there are no instances of a case of this kind having been brought before the English Courts, and the cases referred to are principally cases of abduction, which is a taking or carrying away, sometimes with, and sometimes against, the will of the party, and in these cases the concealment of the person was the main ingredient of the charge. But I think that although no instance has been cited, and perhaps none can be found, in which a charge of this kind has been made before the English Courts, yet that does not affect the Common Law, which says to the subjects of England you shall not, at your peril of fine and imprisonment, take, steal, or carry away any human being. And yet men are found to sail forth from a port of this colony, and seize and carry away certain persons found on the high seas—they are called islanders, and whether they are civilised or not matters not. They have a right to liberty, which is inherent in all human beings, although at times that inherent right has been taken away by force. But we have nothing to do with that; we must assume that at the time these men were taken they were freemen, and that being so it is an offence on the high seas by persons subject to the jurisdiction of the British Courts. It is an offence against the public—a serious offence against the public in this case—for, as has been pointed out, the consequence of our holding that this was not such an offence as contemplated by the Common Law, would be a lasting prejudice to the position of England, and the welfare of the colonies which form her empire. If we were to hold that men sailing from these ports were able to make these excursions, and treat persons whom they find on the high seas in the same way as these islanders, we would have a league of nations formed against Great Britain and her dependencies; and it would be impossible, if we were to maintain such a principle, to uphold the position which Great Britain at this time happily occupies. I will not say I regret, because I think justice has been done; but I may say that I should not have been surprised if the heavier charges which would have been attended by graver consequences, had been brought against the defendant in this case. There can be no doubt upon the facts set out, that robbery and depredation on the high seas were committed, and robbery and depredation amount to piracy. The defendant may, therefore, think himself fortunate

R. v. Coath.

Lutwyche, J.

that he was tried on the lighter charge, and sentenced to only five years' imprisonment and a fine of £50, instead of being tried for the graver offence, for which he might have been sentenced to penal sevitude for life. I have nothing further to add. I have only to repeat that the direction was right, and I think the conviction ought to be affirmed.

Conviction affirmed.

Solicitor for defendant: *R. K. Macnish.*

Re BELLAS, *Ex parte* HUNTER.

Costs—Taxation—Ex parte order rescinded—Costs Act of 1867 (31 Vic., No. 20), s.s. 24, 25—6 & 7 Vic., c. 73, s. 37.

An order for taxation under s. 25 of the *Costs Act of 1867* should not be made *ex parte*.

[IN CHAMBERS.]
1871.
9th October.
12th December.
1872.
14th February.

Cockle, C. J.

SUMMONS to rescind an order.

Thomas Bellas acted as attorney for a syndicate, of which Hunter subsequently became a member. Bellas died, having appointed T. S. Hall and H. W. Risien his executors, to whom probate was granted. The assets proving insufficient, an assignment of the estate was made to W. Jäger and Walter Reid as trustees for the creditors of Bellas. Reid renounced, and Risien was appointed in his stead. A bill of costs, the greater part of which was for work done before Hunter became a member, was delivered to Hunter, who obtained an order for taxation on the 9th October, 1871, under s. 25 of the *Costs Act of 1867* upon the affidavit of W. K. D'Arcy. On 12th December a summons was heard to rescind the above order.

Griffith, in support, argued that the order ought not to have been made *ex parte*. The order was served on 16th October. The summons was taken out on 13th November. Hunter's affidavit was sworn on 20th October. *Chitty*, 119; *Lush*, 301; *Ryalls v. Regina*, 17 L. J. (M.C.) 92.

Lilley, Q.C.: Contra.

C.A.V.

. 14th February, 1872.

COCKLE, C.J.: I think my order of the 9th October, 1871, must be rescinded. It was made *ex parte*. Such an order is not included in the list, of those which may be so made, given in *Lush's Practice* (1865, p. 949). The references to a summons at p.p. 301, 302 of that work do not apply to the present case directly, nor indeed do the instructions in *Archbold*, (1862, p. 120). But, in the language of 6 & 7 Vic., c. 73, s. 37, with reference to taxation applied for by a client and by an attorney, there is sufficient likeness to lead to the conclusion that, if it be the proper practice to proceed by

Re BELLAS,
Ex parte
HUNTER.
———
Cockle, C.J.

summons in one case, it is so in the other. Moreover, it is possible that the words " shall restrain " used in the former case, and " may restrain " used in the latter, a distinctive phraseology preserved in s.s. 24 and 25 of our *Costs Act*, may favour the conclusion. For a larger discretion seems to be left to the Judge in the latter case, which he might be better able to exercise if he heard both sides. Again in *Chitty's Forms* (1866, p. 29, Form 40), there is a form of summons for taxation by the attorney. The foregoing appear to be reasons for holding that the proper course of proceeding is by summons. I know of no countervailing reason. It is true that s. 24 of our *Costs Act* varies from the 6 & 7 Vic., c. 73, s. 37, but it is upon s. 25 of our Act the question mainly turns. The summons to rescind does at first sight appear to have been rather late (13th November, 1871), but I do not know that beyond serving the order of 9th October, 1871, any step in the latter order has been taken.

Order rescinded.

JÄGER *v.* GANNON, *Re* BELLAS.

Costs Act of 1867 (31 Vic., No. 20), s.s. 26, 29—Taxation—6 & 7   [In Chambers.]
Vic., c. 73, s. 43—Application by defendant to enter judgment—   1871.
31 Vic., No. 17, s. 19.   12th December.
                                                                            1872.
                                                                        12th February.

Where the taxing officer has found that a balance is due to an attorney on a   *Cockle, C.J.*
bill of costs, a judgment will not be ordered to be entered up under s. 29 of the
Costs Act of 1867, on the application of a defendant.

SUMMONS under s. 29 of the *Costs Act of 1867* for an order that
judgment be entered up for the defendant.

Thomas Bellas acted as attorney for George Gannon, and sent
him a signed bill of costs for work done by him as such attorney.
Bellas died before the costs were paid, and probate of his will was
granted to T. S. Hall and H. W. Risien. The assets proving insufficient,
an assignment of the estate was made to W. D. Jäger and Walter Reid
as trustees for the creditors of Bellas. Reid renounced, and Risien
was appointed in his stead. Jäger and Risien instituted proceedings
against Gannon for the recovery of such costs when Gannon obtained
an order for taxation on the 18th August, 1871, under s. 25 of the
Costs Act of 1867, upon the affidavit of Henry Colborn Beeston.

Griffith for the defendant, in support of the summons.

Lilley, Q.C., for the plaintiff: The proper course was to make
the order a rule of Court. The section only applies when the order
is in favour of the plaintiff. 31 Vic., No. 17, s. 19; *Lush*, p.p. 308–11.

C.A.V.

12th February, 1872.

COCKLE, C.J.: I am not aware of any case in which a judgment
has been ordered to be entered up on the application of a defendant
under 6 & 7 Vic, c. 73, s. 43, to which s. 29 of our *Costs Act*
corresponds. In *Hair's* case (7 M. & G., 510) the application was
on behalf of the attorney, so in *Lowless' Case* (6 C.B. 123); *Vallance's
Case* (7 M. & G. 511), does not touch the present because the application, though made on behalf of the attorneys, seems to have been
for an order to found a judgment under 1 & 2 Vic., c., 110, s. 18,
to which s. 19 of our *Practice Act* (31 Vic., No. 17) corresponds.

Griffiths v. Hughes (16 M. & W. 809), in which it was decided that
no writ need be issued, seemed to me at first to favour the notion
that the client might apply to me for an order for judgment, if the
result was in his favour.   But a doubt is thrown out in *Archbold*
(1862, p. 132).   In the absence of authority, I am not anxious to
make the first order of the kind.   There may be a distinction between
the cases in which the taxing officer finds that nothing is due on the
bill itself, or that the balance thereon is against the attorney, and
the cases in which the balance is against the client on the bill itself,
although in his favour on the whole taxation.   Again the latter might
be analogous to the cases in which a plaintiff succeeds on a material
issue, but by some, albeit improbable, accident the costs of the
issues found for the defendant on the same cause of action or on the
same part of the same cause of action exceed the plaintiff's costs.
But, recurring to the present case, it would seem to be the safer and
more unquestionable practice to apply according to the course of the
Court.   It is unnecessary to decide the point, because the materials
are wanting for any decision in this case.   The taxing officer has
found that a balance is due to the attorney on the bill itself.   His
Honour Mr. Justice Lutwyche ordered the costs of this action also
to be taxed.   That has not been done, consequently I can make
no order.

No order.

ELWOOD *v.* THOMPSON.

Insolvency Act of 1864 (28 Vic. No. 25), s. 177—Deed of Composition [IN INSOLVENCY.]
—Action—Time for pleading in District Court—Judgment—
Warrant of Execution—Restraining order.

1872.
21st & 23rd
February.

Lutwyche, J.

On 5th October a deed of composition was duly executed by the defendant with a majority of his creditors, and registered on the following day. The notice of filing was published in the *Gazette*, on 7th October. On 10th October, the plaintiff, who had not signed the deed of composition, obtained a judgment against the defendant in the District Court. A warrant of execution was issued on 10th January without leave of the Court.

Held, on an application to restrain the plaintiff, that the defendant had not had reasonable time to plead and prove the deed of composition, and that the rule should be made absolute.

MOTION to make absolute a rule *nisi*, granted by COCKLE, C.J., on 24th January, to set aside an execution or to restrain the plaintiff, John Elwood, from proceeding thereon against the defendant, John Charlton Thompson.

Griffith moved the order absolute.

S.S. 172, 174, 175, 177 of 28 Vic., No. 25, and *Stone v. Jellicoe*, 3 H. & C. 263; 34 L.J., Ex. 11; 10 Jur., N.S. 976 were cited on the application for the order *nisi*.

On 5th October a deed of composition was made between Thompson and his creditors, and was executed by a majority in number representing three-fourths in value of those whose debts amounted to £10 and upwards. It was duly registered in the Supreme Court on the following day, and the requirements of s. 173 of the *Insolvency Act* were complied with. Notice of the filing and registration of the deed was published in the *Government Gazette* of 7th October. On 10th October a judgment was obtained against him in the District Court at Maryborough by Elwood, who did not sign the deed of composition, for £51 5s. 5d., and execution was issued on 10th January for £52 14s. 9d. Mr. W. Barnes, Thompson's attorney, tendered to Elwood's attorney the sum of £12 16s. 4d., being the amount due therein under the deed of composition, but he refused to accept the same, and did not afterwards apply for it. When the case was before the district Court, counsel for the defendant set up the certificate of registration of the deed of composition as a defence, but the Judge rejected it on the ground that it did not bear the stamp of

ELWOOD v.
THOMPSON.
  ⸱ ——
Lutwyche, J.

the Supreme Court, and gave a verdict for the plaintiff.   The certificate was not then pleaded.

The ground upon which the rule was granted was that the leave
of the Court was not obtained before issuing the warrant of execution
as required by s. 177 of *The Insolvency Act.*

Lilley, Q C, for the plaintiff, showed cause. The Court has no
power to restrain a judgment of the District Court.   [LUTWYCHE, J.:
I have no doubt that I have the power to restrain a judgment of the
Supreme Court, and *a fortiori* a judgment of the District Court.]
The property of the defendant did not come within s. 177, and therefore it was unnecessary to obtain the leave of the Court before issuing
execution.   The registration of the deed of composition was no protection as against the execution.   Judgments have been recovered
even upon debts which existed before the registration of the deed.
Rossi v. Bailey, L.R. 3 Q.B. 621 ;   *Allen v. Carter*, L.R. 5 C.P. 414 ;
Godwin v. Stone, L.R. 4 Ex. 331.   In this case the deed was not
pleaded, but set up as a defence, and, having failed judgment, was
given and could not now be questioned.   When the defendant had an
opportunity of pleading the deed he did not do so, and could not
afterwards be entitled to the benefit of it.

Griffith: In *Rossi v. Bailey*, the defendant did some injustice to
the plaintiff.   He allowed him to go on with the action, pleaded other
pleas, put him to expense, and after judgment set up a deed, which
he might have done in the first instance.   (*Allen v. Carter (Supra.*);
Braun v. Weller, L.R. 2 Ex. 183.)   The defendant had not a
reasonable opportunity of pleading the deed.   Nothing could be done
before the notice appeared in the *Gazette* on 7th October ; five days'
notice of the plea was required by the District Court Rules, and it
was, therefore, almost impossible that the deed could be pleaded
before 10th October, on which day the case was heard.   The only day
on which it could be pleaded was Monday, the 9th, and that could not
be said to be a reasonable time, especially as it would be useless for
the defendant to plead it, unless he was prepared with the necessary
witnesses to prove it.

C.A.V.   23rd February.

LUTWYCHE, J. : I am of opinion that the defendant had not had
reasonable time to plead and prove the deed, and the rule must, therefore, be made absolute.   There will be no order as to costs.

Rule absolute.

OELKERS v. MERRY.*

*Real Property Act of 1861 (25 Vic., No. 14), s.s. 44, 60, 88, 123, 126
—Ejectment—Land not under the Act—Mortgage—Two certificates of title issued in respect of the same land.*

[IN BANCO.]
1872.
6th, 13th March.

Cockle, C. J.
Lutwyche, J.

R. purchased a block of land in T., and registered his title and obtained a
certificate of title; in 1870 M. purchased from the A.M.P. Society a corner
piece of this land with buildings thereon. R., after purchasing the land, mortgaged the whole of it to M'L., who subsequently died, leaving a will by which
he appointed the plaintiff O. his executor. Default was made in payment of
principal and interest. M. obtained a certificate of title from the Registrar; he
never asked the A.M.P. Society for a certificate, or for any title at all, as he
brought it under the *Real Property Act*; two certificates were, therefore, in
existence for the portion of land in dispute; O. brought an action of ejectment
against M., claiming as mortgagee under a prior certificate of title issued to R.
Held, that the plaintiff as executor was entitled to bring ejectment, default having
been made in principal and interest.

On the further question whether the defendant was protected against the
action under the proviso, s. 126. the Court *held* that if a purchaser *bona fide*
for valuable consideration, as M. was found by the jury to have been, purchased
from a registered proprietor he would be protected under s. 126 against the
action, but the title of the A.M.P. Society to this piece of land not having been
brought under the Act, and they not having obtained a certificate of title, M.
was not protected by the proviso.

The words "except in the case hereinbefore provided of a mortgagee or
encumbrancee against a mortgagor or encumbrancer" in s. 123 are to be treated
as surplusage.

RULE *nisi* to enter a nonsuit or a verdict for the defendant, or
for a new trial. The case was one of ejectment, in which the claimant,
John Oelkers, sought to eject the defendant from certain lands at
the junction of Herries and Ruthven Streets, Toowoomba. The trial
took place before His Honour the Chief Justice at Toowoomba, and
by direction of His Honour a verdict was returned for the claimant.
Leave was, however, granted to apply for a new trial, and execution
was stayed until after the first four days of term. The facts appear
in the judgment of the learned Judge.

Lilley, Q.C., for the defendant: I may state at the outset
that I am anxious to avoid anything like unnecessary, and perhaps
large, expense, and, therefore, unless the Court is strongly
impressed with the defendant's case—unless there is a reasonable
prospect of it being ultimately argued with success—I would prefer
that the rule should not be granted. The defendant is driven to the
present proceeding, because there are other parties against whom he
will have to proceed, and it is necessary to exhaust every means

* See *Bailey v. Cribb and Others*, 2 Q.L.J. 42.

M

before taking that step. At the trial the jury found that the defendant was a *bona fide* purchaser for value without notice, and this will be an important fact in the course of the argument. The land in question, of which the defendant holds a certificate of title, is also included in and covered by a prior certificate of title, which has been issued to G. M. Reed, who mortgaged it to James M'Lelland, whose executor is the plaintiff, and he sued as such executor, and also as the registered proprietor. All the transactions on each side were under the *Real Property Act of 1861.* Two certificates of title were issued under the hand of the Registrar-General, and both of them are, I suppose, indefeasible. That is the joke, the grim jest of the Act.

LUTWYCHE, J.: I suppose the case will be the subject of an action against the Assurance Fund.

No, it will not. That is the worst of it. We will find that the Assurance Fund is a delusion and a snare. The plaintiff might have a claim against the Fund, but the defendant has none, and the case is, therefore, a very serious one for him.

COCKLE, C.J.: I suppose the Act is clear that there cannot be two indefeasible titles.

The question is, which of them is indefeasible? Does the prior certificate override the subsequent one, both being under the hand of the Registrar-General? The plaintiff rested his case on the certificate under the executorship, and the defendant relied on the conveyance from the Australian Mutual Provident Society and the certificate of title. Plaintiff's case is based on s. 44, and the defendant relies on it also to some extent. This is the supposed indefeasible section, but it will be found that it is not a bit better than the old conveyance. It is not a Parliamentary title such as the public were led to believe they got under the Act, and it is a delusion to suppose that it is indefeasible. The next section bearing on the case is 56, and at this point the plaintiff's title begins to move in the person of the testator. This section describes how lands under the Act are mortgaged or encumbered, and s. 57 gives a remedy by power of sale in the event of the mortgagor or encumbrancer being in default. S. 60 provides that every bill of mortgage or encumbrance shall not operate or take effect as a transfer of the land, estate, or interest, and that in the case of default the mortgagee or encumbrancee might enter and take possession, or bring an action for ejectment, or foreclose the right of redemption. This section gives the mortgagee no interest in the land.

COCKLE, C.J.: He has no interest in the land, yet he may bring ejectment.

He may sell the land although he has no interest in it. That is the most extraordinary part of it. There is nothing to show what interest he has in the land when he recovers it, whether he holds it in fee simple or subject only to the power of sale under s. 57.

COCKLE, C.J.: When a mortgagee obtains possession under s. 60, he is still only mortgagee in possession.

That is all: and in order to give a fee simple, he must sell or foreclose, and then of course his certificate would be subsequent to defendant's. Reed's certificate was undoubtedly prior to ours and contained the same land. There was also no doubt a long continuing default in the payment of principal and interest; and then M'Lelland died, and the plaintiff had to establish his title, and for that purpose he put in the certificate of transmission and of the mortgage, and under s. 88 he is deemed to be the registered proprietor. The date of defendant's certificate of title is prior to this transmission which was the commencement of the plaintiff's title. At this point the question arises whether the plaintiff has any title, as executor, to bring the action? The defendant got the probate put in evidence at the trial, and he contended that there was no devise of realty to the executor, but that there was a positive devise of this very property to another person under the will. Joseph M'Lelland, brother of the deceased, is devisee and it was from him that Merry first heard of the difficulty about his title. Although s. 88 provides that by transmission the executor in this instance becomes the registered proprietor of the mortgage, I contend that the transmission is only *prima facie* evidence that he is to be deemed the registered proprietor. The objection under the will is that there is a positive bequest of the property to the brother, and there is also the fact that there is no charge of debts. That objection seems to be cut down to some extent by the concluding proviso of s. 89. This section provides that the heir-at-law or devisee may apply to the Court to order the Registrar-General to issue a certificate of title to him, and the concluding proviso is as follows :—" Provided always that the person registered consequent upon such order or any executor or administrator when registered in respect of any mortgage, encumbrance or lease shall hold such land estate or interest in trust for the persons and purposes to which it is applicable by law but for the purposes of any dealings with such land estate or interest under the provisions of this Act he shall be deemed the absolute proprietor thereof." This proviso covers both s.s. 88 and 89, and it is a horrible muddle throughout. It was not noticed at the trial, but I have since noticed it. It is a clumsy and most dangerous mode of constructing a statute of this kind. The grounds upon which the rule was asked were—first, that the verdict was against evidence; second, misdirection of the jury; third, that there was no title in the plaintiff; and fourth, that the action would not lie at all as against the defendant. The defendant's case was founded principally on sections 41, 42, 123, 124, 125, 126, and 127. Upon s. 123 alone, I maintain that the defendant, being a *bona fide* purchaser for value, no action for ejectment will lie against him, whether there is any previous remedy for the previous proprietor or not. There may be such a remedy in equity. The claimant does not come under any of the exceptions named in the section. He is not a registered proprietor, claiming under a prior certificate of title. The bill of mortgage gave no estate whatever in the land. The 88th section merely provides that he shall be deemed to be the registered proprietor of the mortgage. The defendant does not come within the operations of the exceptions in the section, although he comes within certain healing portions of it. The more I examine the Act the more I am convinced that it is a mischievous Act and the sooner it is remedied the better. The 124th section provides that the Supreme Court may order any entry in the Register book obtained through fraud to be cancelled and then to be substituted, but there is not a tinge of fraud in this case. The 126th section is still more puzzling. After providing that persons defrauded may bring an action against the fraudulent proprietor, it goes on "Provided also nothing in this Act contained shall be interpreted to subject to any action of ejectment or for recovery of damages any purchaser or mortgagee *bona fide* for valuable consideration of any land under the provisions of this Act although his vendor or mortgagor may have been registered as proprietor through fraud or error or may have derived from or through a person registered as proprietor through fraud or error or may have derived from or through a person registered as proprietor through fraud or error whether by wrong description of land or of its boundaries or otherwise." This section coupled with s.s. 41 and 42 establishes this :—That the plaintiff has no right to succeed in ejectment against the defendant and also that he has a claim upon the Assurance Fund. It is clear that the defendant, if he should be ejected, would have no remedy except as against the persons who sold him the land. This section is an absolute bar to ejectment as against the defendant. It may be argued that it applies to the case of a registered vendor selling to a *bona fide* purchaser for value and the A.M.P. Society is not a registered proprietor, but the language is much larger. It was the issue of the certificate by the Registrar-General that created the difficulty. The defendant can have no remedy against the Assurance Fund, because no title has been issued subsequent to his, but the plaintiff has. Strictly speaking, the interest in the land remains in Reed who mortgaged to M'Lelland all along, and the plaintiff can enforce his claim against the Assurance Fund through him. The 127th section provides that if the person against whom an action for damages is directed to be brought should be dead or should have become insolvent, or absconded, the action should be brought against the Registrar-General as nominal defendant for the purpose of obtaining such damages and costs against the Assurance Fund. A strong reason why protection should be afforded to a *bona fide* purchaser for value is, that the party who loses the property has his remedy against the Fund, whereas the purchaser has no such remedy. If it had been contemplated that a *bona fide* purchaser for value would be liable to ejectment, the Act would surely have made some provision for such cases; and as it does not the presumption is that the last certificate of title issued should be held to be indefeasible.

LUTWYCHE J.: If you buy from a registered proprietor then, though he is registered in error, you may be protected if you are a *bona fide* purchaser for a valuable consideration, but if you get a conveyance from the vendor, and then bring the land under the Act, you do it at your peril.

Lilley: S. S. 41 and 42 show that the defendant has no claim on the Assurance Fund, and that the plaintiff may have. I refer to 25 and 25 Vic. c 53 s. 20 on the question of indefeasible title.

C.A.V.

                                        13th March.

LUTWYCHE, J.: In this case Mr. Lilley, on Wednesday last, moved for a rule calling upon the plaintiff to show cause why there should not be a non-suit, or a verdict entered for the defendant, or for a new trial upon four grounds. First, that the verdict was against evidence; secondly, that there was misdirection on the part of the learned Chief Justice, who tried the case; thirdly, there was no title in the

plaintiff; and fourthly, that ejectment would not lie against the
defendant, under the circumstances disclosed by the evidence. I
will deal with these grounds, though not exactly in the order in
which they were brought before the Court.   The facts of the case
are not in dispute, and it appeared at the trial that one George
M'Culloch Reed purchased, some years before the defendant Merry
purchased land in Toowoomba, a block of land bounded by Ruthven
and Herries streets, and registered his title to the land in the office of
the Registrar-General and obtained a certificate of title of it.   Some
years afterwards, in 1870 or thereabouts, Mr. Merry purchased from
the Australian Mutual Provident Society a corner piece of this land
with some stores thereon.   Reed, after purchasing the land, mortgaged
the whole of it to one James McLelland, who subsequently died,
leaving a will by which he appointed the plaintiff in the present case
his executor.   It appears there was default made in payment of
either principal or interest, or both, and it also appeared that the
defendant, after he had purchased this corner piece of land, obtained
a certificate of title from the Registrar-General.   Two certificates of
title, therefore, were in existence for the portion of land in dispute.
Merry, it appears, never asked the Australian Mutual Provident
Society for a certificate of title.   He never asked them for any title
at all, but he brought the land under the *Real Property Act*.   Under
these circumstances the action was brought, and the first question
that I think it is advisable to refer to is—was there any title in the
plaintiff to bring this action of ejectment?   That question will
depend for an answer upon the result of an investigation into the
various sections of the Act.   The first section on which the title of the
plaintiff depends is the 44th, which provides : " Notwithstanding the
existence, in any other person, of any estate or interest, whether derived
by grant from the Crown or otherwise, which, but for this Act, might
be held to be paramount, or to have priority, the registered proprietor
of land, or of any estate, or interest in land, shall, except in the case
of fraud, hold the same subject to such encumbrances, liens, estates, or
interest as may be notified by entry or memorial on the folium of the
register book constituted by the land grant or certificate of title of
such land, but absolutely free from all other encumbrances, liens,
estates, or interests whatsoever, except the estate or interest of a
proprietor claiming the same land under a prior certificate of title, or
under a prior grant registered under the provisions of this Act."   The
pliantiff claims as mortgagee under a prior certificate of title issued

to the mortgagor Reed.   We must, then, look to the 60th section,
and there we find that: " Every bill of mortgage and bill of encumbrance shall be construed and have effect only as a security for the
sum of money, annuity, or rent charge intended to be thereby secured,
and shall not operate or take effect as a transfer of land, estate, or
interest intended to be thereby charged with the payment of any
money, but it shall be lawful for the mortgagee or encumbrancee upon
default in payment of the money secured by such bill of mortgage or
bill of encumbrance, or any part thereof, to enter into possession of the
mortgaged or encumbered land by receiving the rents and profits
thereof, or to distrain upon the occupier or tenant of the said land,
under the power to distrain hereinafter contained.   Provided also
that it shall be lawful for any registered mortgagee or encumbrancee,
whenever any principal or interest money, annuity, or rent charge
shall have become in arrear, to bring an action of ejectment to obtain
possession of the said land, either before or after entering into the
receipt of the rents and profits thereof." As that section stands there
is no restriction upon the mortgagee from bringing an action for
ejectment against any person whatsoever, provided the principal or
interest is in arrear; but we must look also to the 123rd section,
which contains certain exceptions in which no action of ejectment is
to be brought, and see how far we can reconcile that with the general
power given by the 60th section to a registered mortgagee.   I do
not deny that there is some difficulty with respect to the language of
the 123rd section, and it seems at first sight to be inconsistent with
the provision of the 60th section, for it says: " Except in the case
hereinbefore provided of a mortgagee or encumbrancee against a mortgagor or encumbrancer, or in the case of a lessor against a lessee or
tenant, or in the case of a person deprived of any land by fraud as against
a person registered as proprietor through fraud, or against a person
deriving otherwise than as a purchaser or mortgagee *bona fide* for
value from or through a person registered as proprietor through
fraud, or in the case of a person deprived of any land by reason of a
wrong description of any land or of its boundaries, and, except in the
case of a registered proprietor claiming under a prior certificate of
title, or under a prior grant registered under the provisions of this
Act, in any case in which two grants or two certificates, or a grant
and a certificate, may be registered under this Act in respect of the
same land, no action of ejectment shall lie or be sustained against a
registered proprietor for the recovery of land under the provisions of

this Act, and, except in any of the cases aforesaid, the grant or certificate of title shall be held in every Court of Law or Equity to be an
absolute bar and estoppel to any such action against the person
named in such grant or certificate of title as seised of or entitled to
such land." I think that the words of reference contained in the
first line, "except in the case hereinbefore provided of a mortgagee or
encumbrancee against a mortgagor or encumbrancer" crept into the
section by mistake, either on the part of the draftsman, or, what is
more probable, on the part of some person when the House was in
Committee, because the words "hereinbefore provided" can only
refer to the 60th clause, and there the restriction does not exist.
The words there are general, and give authority to the registered
mortgagee to bring ejectment against any person if the principal or
interest be in arrear. I think, therefore, to make the clauses of the
statute consistent and to give due effect to the whole statute that
these words must be considered as struck out of the 123rd section.
That being so we proceed next to the 88th clause and there we find
that: "Whenever any mortgage, encumbrance, or lease shall be
transmitted, in consequence of the death of the registered proprietor
thereof, probate or an office copy of the will of the deceased proprietor
or letters of administration, in case he shall have died intestate, shall
be produced, and left with the Registrar-General for the purpose of
being recorded in the Register book, and the Registrar-General shall
enter in the Register book the date of the will and probate, or, as the
case may be, the date of the grant of the letters of administration,
and the day and hour of the production to him of such will and
probate or letters of administration, and the names of the executors or
administrators. and, whenever the same can be ascertained, the date
of the death of such proprietor, together with such other particulars
as he shall deem necessary, and, upon such entry being made, such
executors or administrators shall be deemed to be registered proprietors of such mortgage, encumbrance, or lease." Then the 89th
section provides that: "Any executor or administrator when registered
in respect of any mortgage, encumbrance, or lease shall hold such
land, estate, or interest in trust for the persons and purposes to which
it is applicable by law, but for the purposes of any dealings with such
land, estate, or interest, under the provisions of this Act, he shall be
deemed to be absolute proprietor thereof." Now it seems to me upon
a reasonable construction of these sections of the statute that the
plaintiff, as executor of the will of M'Lelland, was the absolute

registered proprietor of the mortgage, and was entitled to bring eject-   ORLKERS *v.*
ment, default having been made in the payment of principal or   MERRY.
interest. The next question is, whether the defendant—supposing   Cockle, C. J.
the plaintiff's title to maintain ejectment be good, as it seems to me   Lutwyche, J.
to be—was protected against that action, and in respect to this portion
of the case reliance was placed upon the 126th clause of the Act, the
proviso to which is as follows: "Provided also that nothing in this
Act contained shall be interpreted to subject to any action of ejectment or for recovery of damages, any purchaser or mortgagee *bona fide*
for valuable consideration of any land under the provisions of this
Act, although his vendor or mortgagor may have been registered as
proprietor through fraud or error, or may have derived from or
through a person registered as proprietor through fraud or error,
whether by wrong description of land or of its boundaries or otherwise." That argument was met by an observation made from the Bench
when the rule was moved for. If the purchaser *bona fide* for valuable
consideration, as Merry was found by the jury to have been, had
purchased from a registered proprietor, he would have been protected;
but the title of the Australian Mutual Provident Society to this piece
of land not having been brought under the *Real Property Act*, and
they not having obtained a certificate of title, he is not protected by
the terms of this proviso. That being so, I think that the direction
of the learned Chief Justice was quite right. He told the jury to
find for the plaintiff, and I do not see what other direction he could
have given. As to the verdict being against the evidence, it seems to
me that the evidence was all one way, and could only have resulted
in the finding of the jury. I, therefore, think the rule must be refused.

COCKLE, C.J.: I have little or nothing to add to what my brother
Lutwyche has said. We disposed of the question arising on the
126th section during the argument, and I then thought, and I think
now, that the decision on that is unanswerable. The plaintiff was undoubtedly a registered proprietor, and Mr. Justice Lutwyche has
shown that he also claimed under a prior certificate. It was argued
that he was not the registered proprietor of an interest in land; but
that is immaterial in the artificial proceeding provided by this Act.
The question is not whether he is a registered proprietor of an interest
in land, but whether he has a right to maintain ejectment; and this
is expressly given to him by the 60th section.

Rule refused.

Solicitors for the applicant: *Macpherson & Lyons.*

OGLE v. TOWNLEY AND ANOTHER.

[IN BANCO.]
1872.
15th March.
27th May.

Cockle, C. J.
Lutwyche, J.

*Masters and Servants Act of 1861 (25 Vic. No. 11), s. 5—Loss of
property—Imprisonment—Prohibition.*

—A rule *nisi* for prohibition to restrain proceedings on a conviction was made
absolute, although the term of imprisonment under the conviction had been
served.

RULE *nisi* calling on Wm. Townley, P.M., and Sydney Bevan
Davis to shew cause why a Prohibition should not issue restraining
further proceedings on a conviction against Wm. Ogle under s. 5 of
The Masters and Servants Act. Ogle was a servant of Mr. McDonald
of Yandah. Davis was McDonald's agent in Rockhampton, and
discharged Ogle, a bullock driver in McDonald's service. Ogle was
discharged without wages, and summoned Davis for £12 1s. 6d.
The summons was taken out 23rd January, returnable 7th February.
Davis then laid two informations against Ogle: one charging him
with having on 8th January negligently lost a chestnut mare, bullock
bells, and rope, the property of his master; and a second with having,
on the same day, negligently abandoned a team of bullocks, dray, and
gear. The informations were sworn 26th January, returnable 6th
February. Ogle was convicted on both informations, and, for the
first, was ordered to pay £6, and £1 4s. costs, or in default one
month's imprisonment, and, for the second, £9, and £1 4s. costs, or a
similar alternative. The penalties were not paid, and Ogle was confined in the Rockhampton gaol.

The rule *nisi* was granted on the 15th March, in respect of the
conviction for losing the mare, on the ground that there was no
evidence of service, or loss, or written agreement.

Griffith, for Davis, shewed cause. Ogle had served the first
month's imprisonment before the rule was granted, and the second
had expired before it was returnable, and the only question now was
in respect to costs. The rule could not be granted on the matter of
costs only.

Hely moved the rule absolute. In the second conviction the sentence was to commence at the expiration of the first. The first conviction was for losing. It was admmitted that the mare was in his custody, running on the flat. He promised to go for her next morning. If Ogle was imprisoned wrongfully, through the precipitancy of Davis, he should pay the costs.

COCKLE, C.J.: The rule is made absolute without costs, no action to be brought against the respondents.

Rule absolute.

EGAN v. TOWNLEY.

[IN BANCO.]
1872.
27th May.
___
Cockle, C.J.
Lutwyche, J.

Vagrant—15 Vic. No. 4, s. 6—Abusive language—Public Place.

Language used in a parlour of a public house by one person concerning another, who is not present, does not constitute an offence within s. 6. of *The Vagrant Act.*

RULE *nisi* calling on William Townley, P.M., Rockhampton, John Stevenson, and D. R Walsh, of Gainsford, to show cause why a Prohibition should not issue restraining further proceeding on a conviction against Patrick Egan, under s. 6 of *The Vagrant Act*, for making use of abusive language in a public place, with intent to provoke a breach of the peace. The language complained of was used by Egan in the parlour of his own public house, in the presence of a man named Ivers, who was in the employment of one Walsh, and who repeated the statements to Walsh who was not present. Walsh lived thirty-five miles away. Walsh summoned Egan who was found guilty and fined ten shillings, and £1 10s. 6d. The rule *nisi* was granted on the grounds : (1) that there was no offence disclosed ; (2) that the language was not in a public place.

Griffith, for the appellant : The *Vagrant Act* was never intended to apply to language which was used by one party to another in respect of a third party who was not present, although the person spoken to repeated it to the person spoken of. The parlour of a public house is not a public place within the meaning of the *Act.* The complainant lived thirty-five miles away. *Wilkinson's Plunkett*, 498-n. (a) ; *Case v. Storey*, L.R. 4 Ex 319 ; 38 L.J. (M.C.) 113 ; 20 L.T. 618 ; 17 W.R. 102 ; *Hirst v. Molesbury*, L.R. 6 Q.B. 130 ; 40 L.J. (M.C.) 76 ; 23 L.T. 55 ; 16 W.R. 246 ; *R. v. Dunn*, 12 Ad. & El. 599.

Hely, for Walsh, showed cause. *Sewell v. Taylor*, 7 C.B. (N.S.) 160 ; 29 L.J. (M.C.) 50 ; 6 Jur. (N.S.) 582 ; 1 L.T. 37 ; 8 W.R. 26 ; *Cole v. Coulton*, 2 E. & E. 695 ; 29 L.J. (M.C.) 125 ; 6 Jur. (N.S.) 698 ; 2 L.T. 216 ; 8 W.R. 412. Another person was present and

heard the language. Egan distinctly told Ivers to repeat his statements to Walsh. There might have been a breach of the peace.

 The COURT, without deciding whether the place was public
within the meaning of the Act, decided that the offence complained
of was not an offence under the statute, and made the rule absolute
without costs. The conviction was, therefore, quashed. The penalty
was ordered to be returned, and it was directed that no action should
be taken against the respondents.

Rule absolute.

EGAN *v.*
TOWNLEY.
——
Cockle, C.J.
Lutwyche, J.

————

[END OF VOL. II.]

[END OF VOL. II.]

INDEX.

ARTICLED CLERK—*Solicitor—Service out of the Colony.* A clerk who had served under acticles to a solicitor in Victoria came to Queensland, and after a lapse of years he became articled to a solicitor in Queensland for five years.

An application to allow the period served in Victoria to be taken into consideration was refused.

In re PORTER (Cockle, C.J., Lutwyche J.)   79

ATTACHMENT—*Common Law Process Act of 1867 (31 Vic. No. 4), s.s. 48, 67—Capias ad respondendum—Irregularity, — Seal of Commissioner.* Where a writ of *ca re* had been issued under the hand of a Commissioner, but without his seal.

Held that the omission was an irregularity only, and not sufficient ground for setting aside the writ.

MULLIGAN *v.* BURNETT (Cockle, C.J.) 29

 Capias ad Respondem—Money lodged in lieu of bail by third party—Non-fulfilment of conditions—Application for return of money—Form of application. A defendant was arrested on December 31st, 1870, under a writ of *ca re*, and on the same day T offered to put in bail for the appearance of the defendant in the action ; but the office being closed at the time, he paid into the hands of the arresting officer the sum of £46 1s., on the understanding that the money was to be repaid to him if bail was put in. On January 5th, 1871, defendant was adjudicated insolvent. No bail was ever put in.

Held, on an application by T for payment of the money out to him that the form of the application was misconceived ; and as the condition on which the money was lodged had not been fulfilled, the money was bound.

LAWRENCE *v.* POOLE (Lutwyche, J.)   131

N

    Costs Act of 1867 (31 Vic. No. 20), s.s. 26, 29—Taxation—6 & 7 Vic., c. 73, s. 43—Application by defendant to enter judgment—31 Vic., No. 17, s. 19. Where the taxing officer has found that a balance is due to an attorney on a bill of costs, a judgment will not be ordered to be entered up under s. 29 of the *Costs Act of 1867*, on the application of a defendant.

JÄGER v. GANNON, *Re* BELLAS (Cockle, C.J.)... 189

    Taxation--Ex parte order rescinded—Costs Act of 1867 (31 Vic., No. 20), s.s. 24, 25—6 & 7 Vic., c. 73, s. 37. An order for taxation under s. 25 of the *Costs Act of 1867* should not be made *ex parte.*

Re BELLAS *Ex parte* HUNTER (Cockle, C.J.) 187

CRIMINAL LAW—*Cattle Stealing Prevention Act (17 Vic., No. 3), s. 3— Detention of a horse—Absence of stealing—Limitation—Practice—Supplementing depositions by affidavits.* A prohibition was granted to restrain further proceedings on an order for the restitution of a horse, under s. 3 of 17 Vic., No. 3, no evidence having been adduced that the horse was stolen, or stolen within twelve months of the commencement of the proceedings.

Affidavits are not admissible to supplement the depositions as to what took place before justices.

Quaere, whether s. 3 of 17 Vic., No. 3 is a penal section.

GOLDSMITH v. ROCHE. (Cockle, C.J., Lutwyche, J.) .'. 55

CRIMINAL LAW—*Continued.*

Embezzlement—Larceny Act of 1865 (29 Vic., No. 6), s.s. 73, 75, 76, 96 —Person in service of the Crown. The word "fraudulently," in s. 75 of 29 Vic., No. 6, is to be applied to the word "embezzle," which precedes it in the section, as well as to the words "apply and dispose of" which follow.

Where a servant of the Crown has received from the Treasury moneys payable .to other persons, and there is no evidence that he received them by virtue of his employment, he cannot be convicted of embezzlement of those moneys under s. 75 of the *Larceny Act.*

R. *v.* WILKIE. (Cockle, C.J., Lutwyche, J.) 33

Escape—Felon—Re-arrest after expiration of period of sentence—Discharge on habeas corpus. A felon sentenced to five years' imprisonment escaped shortly afterwards, and after the expiration of the period of sentence was re-arrested, and committed to custody on a warrant of a magistrate.

Held on a return to a writ of *habeas corpus* that he was illegally in custody, but might be prosecuted for escaping. The prisoner was discharged.

In re COURT. (Cockle, C.J., Lutwyche, J.) 171

Evidence—Deposition of absent witness—Evidence and Discovery Act of 1867 (31 Vic., No. 13), s. 67. The depositions taken before justices of a medical witness, who was absent from the trial of a prisoner on account of having to go to Sydney for the benefit of his health, was held admissible as evidence.

R. *v. Wicker* (18 Jur., 252) followed.

REGINA *v.* PENN. (Cockle, C.J., Lutwyche, J.) 177

Information—Joinder of several felonies in different counts against two prisoners on one information—Larceny Act of 1865 (29 Vic., No. 6), s.s. 10, 11. In an information against two prisoners a count for feloniously stealing a cow had been joined with counts for feloniously killing a cow, with intent to steal the carcase and hide, and one prisoner was found guilty on the second count, but not guilty on the first and third, and the other prisoner was found guilty on the first, but not guilty on the second and third.

The conviction was affirmed, the right being reserved for the prisoners to sue out a writ of error.

An application should have been made to quash the information.

R. *v.* CASTLES & GRIFFITHS. (Cockle, C.J., Lutwyche, J.) 147

Kidnapping—Slavery. The ship *Jason*, from Queensland, visited certain islands in the South Seas, inhabitants from which came out to trade, and were forcibly seized, detained, and brought to Maryborough, where they were set free.

Held (affirming LUTWYCHE, J.) that as the islanders had been detained and brought to Queensland in a British ship against their wills, the offence of kidnapping had taken place, and the Court had jurisdiction to try the persons charged.

The history of slavery reviewed.

R. *v.* COATH. (Cockle, C.J., Lutwyche, J.) 178

Larceny as a bailee—Bailment—Valuable Security—Promissory note— Passing of property—Larceny Act of 1865 (29 Vic., No. 6), s. 3. L was convicted of larceny as a bailee of a promissory-note under the following circumstances: L called at K's store and asked for an order for goods, and K gave him an order for goods to the value of £54 10s.; L then asked K for a promissory-note, as he was going to Brisbane that evening; he said he

CRIMINAL LAW—*Continued.*

put in the goods much cheaper than before, and he wanted the note. K said, "If I give you this promissory-note will you forward the goods at once?" L replied "I will." K then said, "Should you not do so I request you to forward the promissory-note at once." L said "Yes:" then took out of a book a blank form of promissory-note, and wrote on it and handed it to K to sign. K signed it and gave it to L; the note was not stamped when handed to K, and there was no evidence to show at what time it was stamped. K swore that L's name was in the note when he signed it; the goods were never forwarded by L, and subsequently the note was passed at L's request to his credit by B, to whom prisoner had been previously indebted. K wrote to L for the return of the note, and received one somewhat similar from L.

Held, that there was no reasonable evidence to go to the jury in support of the information, that there was no property in K of the promissory-note, and that there was no bailment.

R. *v.* LEVY. (Cockle, C.J., Lutwyche, J.) **166**

Voluntary confession—Evidence—Offer of pardon—Caution. A. who had been arrested as an accessory before the fact to a murder was informed by the lock-up keeper that there was a reward offered and a free pardon, to any one but the murderer, to any person giving information which would lead to the apprehension of the murderer. A. said he had intended to tell the Police Inspector what he knew on his arrest, and the lock-up keeper replied that he should have done so, as it would have been better for himself. A. then, at his own request, saw the Police Inspector, and said he wished to make a statement. The inspector then took A. before a magistrate, and both the inspector and the magistrate warned A. that any statement made by him might be given in evidence against him. A. then made a statement, and when the same was about half completed the magistrate told him that the evidence was not being received as Queen's Evidence. A. completed the statement.

Held that the statement was not induced by the offer of reward or pardon, and being voluntary was rightly admitted against the prisoner.

R. *v. Rosier* (Phillips Ev., 414), approved.

R. *v. Blackburn* (6 Cox C. C., 333) distinguished.

R. *v.* ARCHIBALD. (Cockle, C.J., Lutwyche, J.) **47**

Venire de novo—Affidavit of juror—New trial refused. On an application for a writ of *venire facias de novo*, on the ground of irregularites in connection with the deliberations of the jury on a criminal trial, *held*, that an affidavit by one of the jurymen as to the actions of the jury after their retirement from the Court could not be read upon such an application.

R. *v. Murphy*, 7 N.S.W., S.C.R., 24. doubted.

R. *v.* PEARSON. (Cockle, C. J., Lutwyche, J.) **21**

CROWN—
See GOVERNMENT **99**

CROWN LANDS—*Non-transferable land order—Regulation—Ultra vires—Rejection of evidence—Immigration Act of 1864 (28 Vic., No. 17), s. 7—Crown Lands Alienation Act of 1868 (31 Vic , No. 46), s.s. 46, 53, 97, 124, Schedules C. and E.*—A regulation alleged to have been made pursuant to authority conferred by *The Crown Lands Alienation Act of 1868*, whereby it was notified

CUSTOMS—*Continued.*

luggage. No report or entry was made and part of the goods were landed at a wharf, without the presence of an officer of the Customs. No duty was paid.

An information in the nature of a *qui tam* action was brought for forfeiture of goods, by a duly authorised Customs officer.

COCKLE, C.J., *held* there was an unshipment prohibited by the Act and declared the goods forfeited.

The challenge for cause of a juror, who had given a bond for defendant's costs, was allowed.

Held by COCKLE, C.J., and LUTWYCHE J., on a motion for arrest of judgment, that either non-entry or non-report was sufficient to create a forfeiture within the meaning of Sec. 9 of 9 Vic. No. 15.

Held further, that if the unshipment be prohibited, it becomes illegal *ex vi termini*, and it is unnecessary to prove fraud, and the jury may not take into consideration the irregular practices of the Custom House officials, to modify the plain meaning of the Act.

A Judge may discharge a jury from returning a verdict on an immaterial issue, and judgment on the whole record will not be arrested, although one count be bad, if there is one good count, which will support the whole finding of the jury.

On an information in the nature of a *qui tam* action, a judgment *in rem* may be given, where the only penalty is forfeiture.

"Passengers' luggage" may be defined as such articles as are required for the health, comfort, convenience or personal ornamentation of a passenger.

DAMAGE—*Special damage—Refusal to grant lease.*—Particular or special damage arising from the refusal of the Crown to grant a lease, must be averred.

Semble—that no claim against the Crown for damages for refusal to grant a lease can be made without a demand or request therefor before petition made.

DAMAGE FEASANT—

DEBTOR AND CREDITOR—*Appropriation of payments—Banking practice.*—A creditor has a right to appropriate if the payer omit to do so, and there is no ascertained limit to the time during which the receiver may make the appropriation.

Except with regard to a banking account, the law does not interfere with the appropriation, unless in cases where third parties or their rights are affected by the transactions between the debtor and creditor, as for instance in the cases of death, bankruptcy or change of parties.

DEBTOR'S PETITION—

DEED—*Of Composition*

Interpretation of—Parol Evidence

District Courts Act of 1867 (31 Vic. No. 30), s. s. 47, 48, 49—Joinder of Causes of Action—Jurisdiction—Acquiescence. The plaintiff sued the defendant in a District Court in two actions for wages and wrongful dismissal, under one agreement. By consent, the actions were heard together, and judgment given for the plaintiff on both. On an application for a prohibition

Held, that the causes of action were separate and distinct, and the rule *nisi* must be refused.

HAWKES *v.* CORFIELD (Cockle, C. J., Lutwyche, J.) 65

District Courts Act (21 Vic. No. 18) s. 7—Acts Shortening Act (16 Vic. No. 1 s. 6—Real Property Act of 1861 (21 Vic. No. 14) s. s. 40, 77, 79—Jurisdiction—Title to Land—Equitable Mortgage—Trusts under Real Property Act. A grant from the Crown and a nomination of trust were deposited with the defendant as a security for the indebtedness of the plaintiff to him.

Held in an action brought for the detinue of the title deeds, that the depository took sufficient interest to deprive the District Court of jurisdiction.

Deeds belong to the owner of the land, and to decide to whom the deeds belong would raise a question of title.

The deposit of a Crown grant and a nomination of trust creates an equitable mortgage.

BURRELL AND ANOTHER *v.* HART (Paul, D.C.J.) 155

District Courts Act 32 Vic. No. 31, s. 33—Non-suit—Agent—Power of Attorney—Action brought by Agent without instructions. Where an action is brought by an agent under a power of attorney, and, without instructions, the Judge is not bound to non-suit.

BULLEN *v.* TULLY. (Cockle, C.J., Lutwyche, J.) 153

GOVERNMENT—*Claims on Government—Action for liquidated damages— Nominal Defendant—Admissions by. The Claims on the Government Act* (20 Vic., No. 15) does not confer a right to claim unliquidated damages against the Crown. (Contra, *Macdonald v. Tully*, 1 Q. L. J. *Sup.* 27).

"Nominal defendant" in section 2 of 20 Vic., No. 15, has a statutory and not a colloquial meaning, and accordingly where in an action against the Crown, the Chief Crown Lands Commissioner has been appointed a nominal defendant, certified extracts made by him as Chief Crown Lands Commissioner, rendered inadmissible on other grounds, are not admissible by reason of the appointment of such officer as nominal defendant.

GROSS AND WILFUL DEFAULT—

HABEAS CORPUS—

HARBOUR REGULATIONS—

HOSPITAL—*Hospitals Act of 1847 (11 Vic., No. 59) s. 4—The Medical Act of 1867 (31 Vic., No. 33). s. 10—Treasurer—Detinue—Appeal from Justices— Objection not taken in Court below—Waiver—Evidence—Land Police Act (III.), 19 Vic., No. 24, s. 10.* A person, who had been treasurer of a hospital, was, upon the complaint of the then treasurer, ordered by Justices to deliver up a book, alleged to be the property of the hospital. On appeal it was objected that there was no evidence that the then treasurer had been registered as required by s. 4 of 11, Vic., No. 59, and that the Justices had no jurisdiction under 19 Vic., No. 24, s. 10.

Held, that as the objections were not taken in the Court below, they must be taken to have been waived, and could not be heard on appeal.

S. 4 of 11 Vic., No. 59 confers no rights, but restricts proceedings.

IMPOUNDING—

Impounding Act of 1863 (27 Vic., No. 22), s. 52,—Complaint dismissed with costs—Appeal—Special case—Mandamus. Where a complaint under the *Impounding Act of 1863* is dismissed with costs, no appeal lies to the District Court under s. 52 of that Act.

On an appeal to the District Court the Judge refused to hear the appeal, being of opinion that no appeal lay to his Court. At the request of the appellant's counsel he stated a special case.

Held, by the Full Court, that the appellant had mistaken his remedy, and should have gone by mandamus.

Impounding Act of 1863 (27 Vic., No. 22), s.s. 21, 22, 25, 27, 32, 50— Duty of Poundkeeepr—Mistake of predecessor as to description of a horse —Neglect to rectify—Certiorari—Form of Order of Magistrates. A bay gelding, the property of L., was impounded by an acting poundkeeper, who entered the horse with the brands as a bay filly. It was advertised for sale as such, and sold. The mistake was discovered at the sale by the newly appointed poundkeeper, W. The necessary advertisements had been published, the entry was not corrected, nor the true description advertised.

INSOLVENCY—*Continued.*

An order of adjudication made by one Judge sitting as a Court of Insolvency may be annulled by any other Judge exercising the same jurisdiction.

A debtor's petition must contain an attestation of the signatures of the petitioners to the petition.

Unless a full, true, and correct statement of the liabilities of the insolvent be filed in accordance with the provisions of the *Insolvency Act* (28 Vic., No. 25) and the rules thereunder, the order of adjudication made on the debtor's petition is liable to be annulled.

Deed of Composition—Insolvency Act of 1864 (28 Vic., No. 25), s. 177—Action—Time for pleading in District Court—Judgment—Warrant of Execution—Restraining order. On 5th October a deed of composition was duly executed by the defendant with a majority of his creditors, and registered on the following day. The notice of filing was published in the *Gazette*, on 7th October. On 10th October, the plaintiff, who had not signed the deed of composition, obtained a judgment against the defendant in the District Court. A warrant of execution was issued on 10th January without leave of the Court.

Held, on an application to restrain the plaintiff, that the defendant had not had reasonable time to plead and prove the deed of composition, and that the rule should be made absolute.

Insolvency Act of 1864 (28 Vic., No. 25), s.s. 3, 17, 74. 100—Mortgage—Fraudulent Preference—Specific Performance. A Judge of the Insolvency Court has jurisdiction under s. 100 of the Act of 1864 to determine, in a summary way, claims relating to realty, and has power to enforce its orders on the losing claimant.

A mortgage not made in pursuance of a written agreement made at the time of contracting an antecedent debt, but given within sixty days of the adjudication of the mortgagor for an alleged antecedent debt, was held to be a fraudulent preference under s. 74 of the Act aforesaid, and the mortgagee was directed to discharge the said mortgage.

It is not necessary to the specific performance of a written agreement that it should be signed by the party seeking to enforce it, but the agreement must be certain, fair, and just in all its parts.

Personalty in Queensland—Domicil—Bankruptcy in New South Wales—Execution creditor—Assignee—Mobilia sequuntur personam. R, who was domiciled in Queensland, had his estate sequestrated in New South Wales. H. obtained a judgment against R. in Queensland, and proceeded to levy execution on R's goods at Toowoomba. The Official Assignee in New South Wales claimed the goods.

Held, that H. was entitled to the goods in priority to the Assignee.

The Courts of this colony alone can deal with the property of a bankrupt domiciled here.

Re Blithman, L. R. 2 Eq. 23, approved.

CROWN LANDS—*Continued.*

that non-transferable land orders would not be received by the Land Agents or the Treasury in liquidation of the first year's rental of land selected by lease or of purchase money of land, unless they were presented by the person in whose favour they were drawn, was held *ultra vires,* and to have been rightly rejected in evidence.

Occupation without issue of lease—Refusal to grant lease—Acquiescence —Action for damages—Special damage—Demand for lease—Parties— Joinder of—Claims on the Government—Evidence—Admissions by nominal defendant—Interpretation of Statute—"Shall"—The Tenders for Crown Lands Act (24 Vic., No. 12), s. s. 3, 4, 5, 8—Claims on Government Act (20 Vic., No. 15), s. 2—Acts Shortening Act (22 Vic., No. 12), s 8. A plaintiff who has paid rent to the Crown, and occupied and stocked Crown lands under an accepted tender under *The Tenders for Crown Lands Act* (24 Vic., No. 12) the interest wherein has been transferred to him, and is assumed to have been transferable, although no lease has been granted to him under section 3, is a lessee within the meaning of section 5, and has a right to occupy as against disturbers.

If such lessee acquiesces in the disturbance of his occupation he is not entitled to recover compensation, on account of his own withdrawal from the runs without notice to or knowledge on the part of the Crown.

Particular or special damage arising from the refusal of the Crown to grant a lease must be averred.

The Claims on the Government Act (20 Vic , No. 15) does not confer a right to claim unliquidated damage against the Crown.

"Nominal defendant" in section 2 of 20 Vic., No. 15, has a statutory and not a colloquial meaning, and accordingly where in an action against the Crown the Chief Crown Lands Commissioner has been appointed a nominal defendant, certified extracts made by him as Chief Crown Lands Commissioner, rendered inadmissible on other grounds, are not admissible by reason of the appointment of such officer as nominal defendant.

Quaere.—Whether, in an action brought by a lessee of the Crown for compensation for refusal to grant a lease of Crown lands to him, such lands having been leased subsequently to third parties, such parties should not be made parties to the action.

Semble—that no claim against the Crown for damages for refusal to grant a lease can be made without a demand or request therefor before petition made.

CUSTOMS—*Customs Regulation Act of 1845 (9 Vic., No. 15) s. s. 9, 16, 24, 25, 82, 86, 93, 108, 108, 110—Unshipment of goods—Non-report—Non-entry— Forfeiture—Fraud—Practice of Custom House—Qui tam action—Judgment in rem—Challenge of a juror for cause—Discharge of jury from returning a verdict on immaterial issues—Arrest of judgment—Passengers' Luggage defined—Evidence of Custom.* H. & Co. forwarded certain dutiable goods to Brisbane, by a steamer, with their traveller S. On arrival in the Bay the goods were removed to a smaller boat, with cases and portmanteaux, alleged to contain dutiable goods also. S. claimed the latter as his personal

REAL PROPERTY—*Caveat—Real Property Act of 1861 (25 Vic., No. 14) s. 91—Judgment—Writ of Execution.* The registration of a writ of execution upon a judgment against land under *The Real Property Act* cannot be entered as a caveat.

    Caveat—Real Property Act of 1861 (25 Vic., No. 14), ss. 98, 99—Withdrawal of. An order was made against the defendant for the withdrawal of a caveat within one month, which period was considered ample time for a bill to be filed in Equity for an injunction against dealing with the land, costs to be allowed to the plaintiff unless an injunction be obtained on notice within one month.

    Real Property Act of 1861 (25 Vic., No. 14), ss. 44, 60, 88, 123, 126—Ejectment—Land not under the Act—Mortgage- Two certificates of title issued in respect of the same land. R. purchased a block of land in T., and registered his title and obtained a certificate of title ; in 1870 M. purchased from the A.M.P. Society a corner piece of this land with buildings thereon. R., after purchasing the land, mortgaged the whole of it to M'L., who subsequently died, leaving a will by which he appointed the plaintiff O. his executor. Default was made in payment of principal and interest. M. obtained a certificate of title from the Registrar ; he never asked the A.M.P. Society for a certificate, or for any title at all, as he brought it under the *Real Property Act* ; two certificates were, therefore, in existence for the portion of land in dispute ; O. brought an action of ejectment against M., claiming as mortgagee under a prior certificate of title issued to R. *Held,* that the plaintiff as executor was entitled to bring ejectment, default having been made in principal and interest.

On the further question whether the defendant was protected against the action under the proviso, s. 126, the Court *held* that if a purchaser *bona fide* for valuable consideration, as M. was found by the jury to have been, purchased from a registered proprietor he would be protected under s. 126 against

REAL PROPERTY—*Continued.*

the action, but the title of the A.M.P. Society to this piece of land not having been brought under the Act, and they not having obtained a certificate of title, M. was not protected by the proviso.

The words "except in the case hereinbefore provided of a mortgagee or encumbrancee against a mortgagor or encumbrancer" in s. 123 are to be treated as surplusage.

Equitable Mortgage—Real Property Act, 1861 (25 Vic.No. 14), ss. 40, 77, 79—Trusts under Real Property Act. Where a Crown grant and a nomination of trust were deposited as a security for a debt, it was held that an equitable mortgage had been created.

Production of instrument by Registrar-General—Real Property Act of 1861 (25 Vic., No. 14), s. 46—Trial of action—Evidence. Section 46 of 25 Vic No. 14 does not refer to judicial proceedings.

The Registrar-General was held bound to produce an application to bring land under the Act, which he had stated was in his possession.

Illegal impounding—Pastoral Leases Act of 1863 (27 Vic., No. 17), ss. 2, 36, 58, 59—Disputed title to land—Possession—Tort-feasor—Conversion. The plaintiff and defendant were lessees from the Crown of adjoining runs, and the former placed sheep and cattle on the alleged head of his run. The defendant entered, and impounded and sold them. In an action for trespass and damages, *Cockle*, C.J., directed the jury that possession was sufficient title as against a wrong doer, and left it to the jury to say what was the head of the creek, alleged by the defendant to be the boundary of the plaintiff's run, and the jury found a verdict in the defendant's favour.

Held, on appeal that the direction was right, but that considering the nature of the property and the great difficulty in settling the boundaries there should be a new trial on the question of title to the run, the plaintiff paying the costs of the first action, and that if the plaintiff succeeded he could bring another action for wrongful conversion.

Swinnerton v. Marquis of Stafford, 3 Taunt. 91 followed.

VAGRANT—*15 Vic., No. 4, s. 6—Abusive Language—Public place.* Language used in a parlour of a public house by one person concerning another, who is not present, does not constitute an offence within s. 6. of *The Vagrant Act.*

CPSIA information can be obtained
at www.ICGtesting.com
Printed in the USA
BVHW08*1519041018
529297BV00008B/331/P